Children, Parents and Politics

Edited by

GEOFFREY SCARRE

Durham University

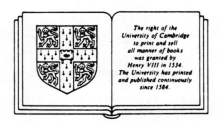

The right of the
University of Cambridge
to print and sell
all manner of books
was granted by
Henry VIII in 1534.
The University has printed
and published continuously
since 1584.

CAMBRIDGE UNIVERSITY PRESS

CAMBRIDGE

NEW YORK   NEW ROCHELLE   MELBOURNE   SYDNEY

CAMBRIDGE UNIVERSITY PRESS
Cambridge, New York, Melbourne, Madrid, Cape Town, Singapore,
São Paulo, Delhi, Dubai, Tokyo

Cambridge University Press
The Edinburgh Building, Cambridge CB2 8RU, UK

Published in the United States of America by Cambridge University Press, New York

www.cambridge.org
Information on this title: www.cambridge.org/9780521369350

First published 1989
This digitally printed version 2010

A catalogue record for this publication is available from the British Library

Library of Congress Cataloguing in Publication data
Children, parents and politics / edited by Geoffrey Scarre.
p. cm.
Includes index.
1. Children – Social conditions. 2. Children's rights.
I. Scarre, Geoffrey.
HQ767.9.C455 1989
305.2'3 – dc19   88–10146

ISBN 978-0-521-36098-2 Hardback
ISBN 978-0-521-36935-0 Paperback

Contents

Contributors

STEPHEN R. L. CLARK is Professor of Philosophy at the University of Liverpool. Among his numerous publications are *The Moral Status of Animals* (1977) and *The Nature of the Beast* (1982).

JEAN BETHKE ELSHTAIN, Professor of Political Science, Vanderbilt University, has written widely on issues concerning the family and politics. She is the author of *Public Man, Private Woman: Women in Social and Political Thought; Meditations on Modern Political Thought;* and, most recently, *Women and War*. She is editor of *The Family in Political Thought*.

JOHN HARRIS is Reader in Applied Philosophy in the Department of Education and Research Director of the Centre for Social Ethics and Policy, University of Manchester. He is the author of *Violence and Responsibility* (1980) and *The Value of Life: An Introduction to Medical Ethics* (1985).

JUDITH HUGHES teaches Philosophy and International Women's Studies at the University of Newcastle. She is co-author (with Mary Midgley) of *Women's Choices: Philosophical Problems Facing Feminism* (1983) and is currently working on a book, *The Philosopher's Child*.

LUDMILLA JORDANOVA has been Lecturer in History at the University of Essex since 1980, and is the author of *Lamarck* (1980). She is currently working on eighteenth-century concepts of the family.

HELGA KUHSE is Deputy Director of the Centre for Human Bioethics at Monash University. Her publications include *Should the Baby Live* (with Peter Singer) and *Sanctity of Life in Medicine*.

RICHARD LINDLEY is Lecturer in Philosophy at the University of Bradford and the author of *Autonomy* (1986).

GARETH B. MATTHEWS is Professor of Philosophy at the University of Massachusetts at Amherst. In addition to some fifty articles, he has written *Philosophy and the Young Child* (1980) and *Dialogues with Children* (1984).

TOM REGAN is Professor of Philosophy at North Carolina State University. Among his many books are *The Case for Animal Rights* and *Bloomsbury's Prophet: G. E. Moore and the Development of his Moral Philosophy*.

WILLIAM RUDDICK, Professor of Philosophy at New York University, has written on the philosophy of science and medical ethics and is co-editor (with Onora O'Neill) of *Having Children: Philosophical and Legal Reflections on Parenthood* (1979).

GEOFFREY SCARRE teaches Philosophy at Durham University and is a Tutor–counsellor for the Open University. He has written on philosophy and the history of ideas, and is the author of *Logic and Reality in the Philosophy of John Stuart Mill* (forthcoming).

PETER SINGER is Director of the Centre for Human Bioethics at Monash University. His books include *Animal Liberation, Practical Ethics, The Reproduction Revolution* (with Deane Wells) and *Should the Baby Live* (with Helga Kuhse).

Introduction

Hold childhood in reverence, and do not be in any hurry to judge it for good or ill.

J.-J. Rousseau[1]

The moral and political status of children has been something less than a dominant theme of Western philosophical thought. For most philosophers, children have not raised problems of any special interest or difficulty, and what little has been written about them has mostly consisted of variations on a limited and rather platitudinous range of themes: the weakness of children and their need for protection and control; their duty to love, honour and obey their parents; the obligation on parents to care for their children and to mould them according to socially determined patterns. Philosophers by and large have been content to accept without challenge whatever notions of children and their appropriate treatment they have found current.

It has been suggested that philosophers have had little to say about the family because many of them have been 'rather solitary and childless people'.[2] No doubt that is one reason why philosophy has ignored children – and ignored women too, since so many philosophers have been unmarried men. But the neglect may stem additionally from a deeper, more disturbing cause. Children have often been regarded, and not merely by philosophers, as somewhat marginal people, whose activities and experiences matter less than those of adult – and especially male adult – human beings. Though children are often found charming and amusing, their thoughts and deeds are weighed in the balance of 'grown up' standards and are found wanting. Measured by the criteria of the adult world, a child's best achievements appear flawed and imperfect, sometimes pointless and silly. No mature person likes to hear his actions described as 'childish', for that conveys the criticism not just that, as an adult, he should have done *differently*, but that he should have done *better*. It is surely significant, as Gareth B. Matthews notes in his chapter in this book, that major art galleries refuse to hang the work of children: for a painting to be produced by a child is for it to be seen as carrying an a priori guarantee of artistic worthlessness.

It is clearly true that childhood, like old age, is at a chronological margin of human life. That does not make children, or the elderly, marginal in a moral sense; they do not have a lesser worth than people we so question-beggingly refer to as being in 'the prime of life', even if their worth consists in their having different pre-eminent qualities. Children are remarkable for their lovingness, spontaneity and freshness of vision, their candour and imagination. To complain that they do not perform as well as adults at tasks more suitable for adults is to apply ludicrously inappropriate standards. Yet children in the writings of philosophers and others have usually been characterised in such adult-orientated fashion, with very negative and dismissive results. To think of children primarily as weak, ignorant, irrational, incompetent, unrestrained and uncivilised impedes working up much interest in how they are treated, and makes it easier to fall into an unquestioning, complacent acceptance of whatever social, educational and political arrangements have arisen to cope with them.

There have been encouraging signs in recent years that the situation is changing and that philosophers, both male and female, are starting to see children and childhood as a topic of major philosophical interest. The last decade in particular has seen an increasing spate of works that challenge the old images and complacencies and demonstrate the potential of philosophy to provoke a rethinking of settled ideas about children. The present volume is a symptom of this new concern. The eleven essays that follow, none of which has been previously published, are written from a variety of viewpoints and cover a number of different problems, but are informed by a common conviction of the value of subjecting our conceptual methods for handling children to critical scrutiny. It is hoped that by bringing together authors from three continents to write about children, impetus will be given to the development of the philosophy of childhood as a recognised subdivision of philosophical study.

That said, it must be added that, as several papers in this collection make abundantly plain, philosophical questions about children interlock in many ways with broader questions of moral and political philosophy. The philosophy of childhood cannot, therefore, be pursued as an entirely discrete sub-discipline; but the mutually fruitful relationship in which it stands to other parts of the philosophical field is extra reason for regarding it as both a viable and a highly profitable area for discussion.

The essays in the first section of the book explore the categories we employ for thinking about what children are. Ludmilla Jordanova brings an historical perspective to bear in arguing that a timeless, society-irrelative way of considering children is unattainable, and that children are 'constructed in particular social settings'. She uses evidence from the past to support the claim that attempts to say what is 'natural' about children face great difficulties, and emphasises that a society's view of childhood is suffused with its moral assumptions.

In a similar vein, William Ruddick, in 'When Does Childhood Begin?', is concerned with remarking the way in which 'political, metaphysical, biological and ethical factors jostle with one another' when we try to set out what we mean by 'childhood'. The task of determining the beginning of childhood (is this at conception? at quickening? at birth? or after infancy?) is made immensely more problematic because while 'childhood is a stage of growth and development, it is also a social and political status'. Ruddick sensitively traces the often conflicting influences which the various strands in our thought about childhood have on our treatment of children, and asks what the moral and political implications would be of abolishing the category of childhood altogether.

Judith Hughes, in 'Thinking about Children', sounds a warning note about some of the recent philosophical writing about children which has, in her opinion, concentrated unrealistically on the question of children's political emancipation. Such writing, she argues in a subtle criticism, often shows little understanding of the reality of childhood, of actual children's needs and desires – 'it has little to do with children and much to do with a critique of liberal democracies'. To treat a child other than as a child is a form of oppression; though *how* that means that children should be treated will vary from one society to another.

If it is true that some writers have exploited children in their desire to find a stick with which to beat liberal democracy, it is also true that the position of children in liberal democratic polities is a legitimate and important topic of concern. To what forms of authority are children of various ages rightly subjected? How much power over their offspring should parents wield, and to what extent should the state place restraints on the foundation and on the exercise of authority in families? How soon and in what manner should children be released from paternalistic constraints and be inducted into the citizen body? To what extent, if any, are the traditionally favoured theoretical devices of liberal democracy, such as the social contract, applicable to the justification of adult–child relations in a society like ours? Questions like these are the business of the chapters in Part II.

Some liberal democrats have worried that the structure of authority in families is difficult to justify, given that children do not become members of families through their free consent. In 'The Family, Democratic Politics and the Question of Authority' Jean Bethke Elshtain makes the observation, with which Judith Hughes would sympathise, that parental authority, as a form of stewardship, is a *conditio sine qua non* of parenting. But she argues that parental authority need be no source of embarrassment to liberal democrats, as the family, at its best, can be 'the locus for the emergence of socially responsible, autonomous human beings' possessed of greater individuality than if they had been produced by some more uniform, centrally controlled social process, however democratic.

There follow chapters by Richard Lindley and myself, in which the consistency of application of liberal principles by modern Western states to, respectively, teenagers and young adults is questioned on other grounds. Lindley argues that the liberal democrat should be deeply dissatisfied with our present treatment of teenage children, and favour extending to them a range of rights and responsibilities which will give them much more control over their own lives. In my own chapter, I investigate how a consistent liberalism should respond to the flux of generations within a society, and to the fact that young people arriving at the threshhold of adult life are obliged willy-nilly to accept the economic and power structures already in place as the price of being allowed access to the privileges of the adult citizen body. Lockean notions of consent seem to have little application in the real life scenario facing the young adult, who has little say over the return obtained for labour and services from the existing holders of social goods.

In a highly original essay, Stephen R. L. Clark proposes that the raising of children, with the coercive paternalist practices it involves, far from offering occasions for liberal soul-searching, actually provides a sounder model of morally ideal human relationships than any form of social contract theory. He draws both on ancient Stoic sources and on natural history to support his view that 'care for our world and our posterity [is] the centre of moral action'. Truly marginal people would be those free to bind themselves or not in a voluntary association with others; non-marginal people enjoy 'the more positive right and duty to participate in the growth and development of the tribe'. According to John Harris, in 'The Right to Found a Family', there is indeed a normal human entitlement to play a part in the growth and development of the tribe, though in certain quite limited circumstances, which he carefully attempts to delineate, there might be an obligation on some individuals *not* to form a family, and even on the public authorities to prevent their doing so.

The essays in Part III are concerned with adult attitudes to children's lives and experiences and, from quite diverse angles, pose questions about what we should value and seek to preserve in them. Gareth Matthews' essay, 'Child Art and the Place of Children in Society', urges that a closer attention to children's art not only assists us to understand more about their thought and sensibility, but also 'can help us appreciate the nature and significance of adult art, indeed, of art *ueberhaupt*'. In his opinion, hanging children's art is a step not merely towards children's liberation (in one sense of that much abused term), but towards adult liberation – the extension of our imaginative boundaries – as well.

In 'Should All Seriously Disabled Infants Live?' Helga Kuhse and Peter Singer argue that it is the kind and quality of life a child is capable of having, rather than some abstract 'right to life', that provide the proper basis for medical decision-making, and that to keep a severely handicapped infant alive or to subject him to excessively painful surgery constitutes grave abuse.

The subject of Tom Regan's chapter, which brings the collection to a close, is abuse of a different and less controversial sort. Regan begins by observing that using children for pornographic purposes, or in other ways to satisfy the sexual appetites of adults, is wrong, but then takes various standard moral theories to task for being unable to explain just why it is wrong. As an improvement on these theories he proposes a fresh account (the 'respect account' – in fact a modified Kantianism), according to which subjects-of-a-life ('biographical beings') are not to be used as mere means to satisfy the desires of other subjects-of-a-life. Apart from the intrinsic interest of its contents, Regan's essay is valuable for showing how paying closer attention to the moral status of children can put us in a better position to criticise and refine our general moral theories.

'Childhood has its place in the sequence of human life', wrote Rousseau; 'the man must be treated as a man and the child as a child'.[3] This book attempts to cast light on childhood as a distinctive and valuable phase of human life, and to clarify the moral issues surrounding child–adult relationships. If it succeeds in drawing childhood and children just a little closer to the centre-stage of philosophical discussion, it will have adequately justified its existence.

Acknowledgements

I am grateful to the many people who, by their advice and encouragement, have helped this book to come into being. I owe a special debt of thanks to Jonathan Sinclair-Wilson and Terence Moore, my editors at Cambridge University Press, for their sympathetic support over the lengthy period this book was in the making, and to Katharita Lamoza for her exemplary copy-editing.

Geoffrey Scarre
May 1988

NOTES

1 Jean-Jacques Rousseau, *Émile*, trans. Barbara Foxley (London: Everyman's Library, reprinted 1976), p. 71.
2 Onora O'Neill and William Ruddick, 'General Introduction' to *Having Children: Philosophical and Legal Reflections on Parenthood* (New York: Oxford University Press, 1979), p. 3.
3 Rousseau, *Émile*, p. 44.

Part I

What Children Are

1

Children in History: Concepts of Nature and Society

LUDMILLA JORDANOVA

Introduction

Children have recently become news. Child abuse, incest, and murder frequently occupy the headlines. Television and radio programmes are regularly devoted to these subjects. This media attention contains a drama and a voyeurism of which we should be properly sceptical. Furthermore, it may serve to confirm a sense of complacency among 'normal' parents – they are not the abusers in question. Present-day reactions to the ill-treatment of children are certainly complex enough without the additional problem of history. By this I mean that implicit historical claims are often contained in media presentations and in received opinion. Currently there is an immediate sense of crisis about the treatment of children, despite a recognition that any visible increases in child abuse may be in the reporting rather than in the occurrence itself. Readers, viewers, and listeners easily feel a sense of urgency, mixed with fear at the magnitude of contemporary ills, when they learn of damaged children. Many treatments of the subject advance a covert historical thesis which is highly morally charged. Our perceptions of contemporary issues are clearly moulded by such an unspoken historical consciousness, within which the past is often idealised and the present depicted as a decline. Of course, our implicit historical sense can go in the opposite direction morally speaking, as it does in relation to child labour. When the work of the young is considered, the past becomes barbaric and exploitative, the present enlightened by the discovery of the importance of play, which thereby becomes the antithesis of work. Because we so often construct and deploy historical myths to organise contemporary tensions, it is important to assess what kind of historical knowledge is possible about children.

We might put this same point in another way. It is common to find

I would like to thank Meg Arnot, Karl Figlio and, above all, Geoffrey Scarre for their generous help.

the dichotomy traditional/modern used in connection with current social ills, including those where children are at issue.[1] For many people, the abuse of children symbolises the negative aspects of modern life. We can easily see how widespread the identification between children and social well-being is from the prevalent use by politicians of phrases like 'our children's future', which raise questions about the present and the future in deliberately emotive terms. As a result, there is little commitment to thinking logically about children's social position, partly for the understandable reason that we are all deeply implicated, emotionally, in child welfare. Yet, until we face up to this problem, discussions of children will continue to be muddled in ways that are seldom apparent.

I want to suggest that children pose special intellectual challenges to us. This is partly because the state of being a child is temporary and hard to define. Indeed, the process of becoming an adult involves a number of fundamental shifts which, certainly from an adult perspective and probably also from a child's, are so dramatic that a gradualist language modelled on small-scale, incremental growth seems hopelessly inadequate. There are two issues, to which we shall return, which focus the problem with particular force – work and sex.

Historical writing participates in the construction of our ideas of childhood. The history of childhood has been used as a way of speaking about other social transformations, precisely because it can so easily be taken to symbolise them. Discussions about children and childhood, past or present, are suffused with moral assumptions. Furthermore, we often use such discourses as a way of speaking about other concerns. I also wish to suggest that using a language which refers to children in terms of nature, as I believe we have done for almost three centuries, is profoundly problematic. A general commitment to speaking of children in a language permeated by natural imagery (tender, pure, innocent, plantlike) and to thinking about them as asocial or presocial has certain consequences of which we should be fully aware. The term 'nature' itself is highly complex, giving rise to meanings which are not consistent with one another; indeed, this may be one reason why it plays such a central role in our social thinking. This role is particularly crucial in relation to the child. The languages of nature used about children are a major vehicle for our moral concerns.

The moral notions we use when speaking about children can usefully be explored historically. This enables us to put them in a larger perspective by exploring both continuity and change. One possible spin-off of a historical approach is that it can prevent us from taking any particular set of attitudes or behaviours as 'natural' or 'normal'. By examining the historical variety of the position of children and of ideas about childhood, and by tracing back some of the steps by which we arrived at our present situation, we can achieve a more dispassionate analysis. Studying children historically is not, however, without its difficulties. What, for example, is the proper object of inquiry? Such a question is less simple-minded than it sounds, since 'child' is not a simple descriptive category. Is age the major criterion or does this shift with class, gender, and historical period? How can a person be a child in some respects (e.g. living at home, being under parental authority) and not in others (e.g. being economically and sexually active)? We might propose that the historian study those deemed children at a specific time and place – a solution which allows for changes in concepts of the child, but not for the problem of simultaneously conflicting attributions. Furthermore, is the study of children different from the study of childhood? To this we must answer yes, since the first implies a study of groups of persons, the second that of a state of being. In the latter case, how can the historian examine such an abstraction? The only way is through those domains which consider children in general: the law, medicine, social policy, and so on. A full history of childhood has to engage with the complexity of the history of ideas.

Yet there is something inherently unsatisfactory about studying the history of childhood without any reference to specific historical personages. It offends deeply held beliefs about authenticity and historical method. Historians persist in searching for the voice of children themselves, in their diaries and autobiographies and in literature written expressly for them.[2] Such a search is based on an illusion about both the nature of childhood and of history. Children, I submit, are constructed in particular social settings; there can be no authentic voice of childhood speaking to us from the past because the adult world dominates that of the child. Thus, while we can study particular children, provided suitable materials exist, and examine general ideas about childhood, we cannot capture children's past experiences or responses in a pure form.

The desire for historical authenticity has also emerged forcefully in relation to women and the working class. The child, the woman, and the worker have all been treated as 'other', that is, as outside mainstream culture and separate from dominant social groups, and hence as not requiring the historical treatment reserved for the adult male members of elites, who become the 'norm'. In reacting against this, radical historians have sought the authentic voice of those who

not only could not speak for themselves before, but were often assumed to have no tongues. There are now lively debates about the
extent to which it is possible to bring women and the working class
back through a study of their distinctive behaviours, ideas, and writings. In a similar vein some historians of childhood claim to be giving
to the young their own, autonomous history.[3] There are, however,
different kinds of otherness involved in these three instances. For
example, the otherness of women is based on the depth of gender
difference which, however you define it, can readily be seen as constitutive of social relations in general. For the most part we understand
men and women, male and female, to be separated by a profound
gulf. The peculiarity of the otherness we assign to children is paradoxical in that we have all experienced childhood – hence to make
the child other to our adult selves we must split off a part of our past,
a piece of ourselves. This accounts for the profound ambivalence
which informs our attitudes to children and which is relived when we
become parents ourselves. It may be that women and workers have
simply spoken with the voices of the dominant discourse, although
many historians would deny this. Children, however, have inevitably
done so, since there can be no alternative for them. Their passage
into being is inexorably a coming into language, a language which is,
for the child, a given. There are no special sources available to historians or to others which avoid this trap. The quest for an authentic
other is not fulfilled by children – nor, indeed, by any other group.
Like children, both women and 'the people' have often been analogised with nature. We remain convinced that for children the com-
parison is valid, and this makes us imprisoned by it. This long-standing
analogy is reinforced by our lively biological sense of the processes of
procreation, a fresh consciousness of children – at least when babies –
as wonders of nature.

The relationship between children, childhood, and nature has existed at a number of different levels. It is as complex as our ideas
about nature itself: the state of childhood may be seen as pure, innocent, or original in the sense of primary; children may be analogised
with animals or plants, thereby indicating that they are natural objects
available for scientific and medical investigation; children could be
valued as aesthetic objects for their beauty and physical perfection –
but they could equally well be feared for their instinctual, animal-like
natures. Two fundamental points, therefore, arise out of the association between children and nature: First, the polyvalency of nature
led to a variety of concepts of childhood, and second, these diverse
meanings of childhood were deeply imbued with moral values.

Children could be used by scholars as a tool for revealing historically shifting meanings of nature. In fact, historians generally use them for different purposes, themselves products of the sentimentalising of children which the association with nature has brought. It is therefore necessary to discuss first how historians have approached these matters before considering some historical material which sheds more direct light on the matter. Throughout we should remember the power of language to shape our ideas. Historians, like everyone else, have worked from commonly held assumptions about children, without attending to the constraints – moral, cultural, and linguistic – on their own frameworks.

Historians and Children

Historians have 'discovered' children and childhood only relatively recently. It was Philippe Ariès who started the trend with his book *Centuries of Childhood*.[4] Although much criticised, it is nonetheless treated by non-historians as a definitive account which establishes certain 'truths' about the subject that are now common knowledge. The volume is a marvellously rich piece of historical writing, drawing on an impressive range of sources, some little used by historians – paintings, architecture, costume, literature, and so on. Ariès advances the thesis that in medieval society children were seen merely as small adults and treated casually. They participated in adult society because no special provisions were made for them. This situation changed, he suggests, over a long period of time, roughly the sixteenth to eighteenth centuries, with other major social transformations. The end result was a society which associated children firmly with the domestic sphere and hence with women and with education. Children came to be treated as a particular class of persons, to whom special conditions apply and for whom special provision must therefore be made. A subsidiary thesis concerns parental attitudes towards children. In times of high mortality, children were less valued as individuals, parents were more 'cruel', mourned their children less, and were generally indifferent to them. These attitudes also underwent a radical transformation, so that by the nineteenth century recognisably 'modern' emotions existed. *Centuries of Childhood* has, however, significant limitations. Ariès relies heavily on French materials, with the result that it may be illegitimate to generalise from his account. Furthermore, he simply assumes that there have been dramatic changes in the understanding and so also in the experience of childhood. He also takes it for granted that these changes are integral to larger social and cultural transformations.

There can be no doubt that there are serious shortcomings in Ariès's work, but the fundamental question remains how and why his work gripped people's imaginations so forcibly. Certainly it had novelty value; possibly he told them things they wanted to hear about children. Ariès made early modern society an 'other' with respect to children. It could be distanced, put aside, rendered safe by an account which perpetually allows readers to say 'not like us'. The flipside of this is a reinforcement of the readers' own values and attitudes, and a yardstick with which to judge how far society has come. In fact, Ariès implies a somewhat negative interpretation of modern views when he stresses the isolation and lack of sociability of the modern family in general and of women and children in particular. He often romanticised the past to celebrate traditional values. Nonetheless, Ariès may be criticised for treating the present as a norm. Whereas early modern society had no notion of childhood, we now have an elaborate one. Their absence is defined by our presence. This particular aspect of Ariès's argument has prompted much critical comment, largely in relation to the logic of historical argument.[5]

Here I want to stress another aspect of the debate. Arguments among historians of childhood have implicit value systems built into them, and judgement is passed on people long dead. This is most obvious when we look at areas that involve 'cruelty' and violence, for there is abundant historical evidence of gross physical chastisement, economic exploitation, and parental neglect. For us, cruelty to children is such an emotive topic that we lapse all too easily into confusion. Faced with evidence of infanticide, abandonment, murder, and child labour, we are at a loss as to how to construct historical arguments adequate to their explanation.[6] There is a genuine problem of imagination here. Unless scholars are willing to think deeply about violence towards children, which inevitably involves facing their own feelings, they have few options available. They can either deny the validity of the evidence or the interpretative procedures applied to it – for example, by appealing to the 'untypical' nature of infanticide – or they can seek other explanations – such as citing the ubiquity of poverty as a cause of harsh treatment of children. Those who espouse the first position often refer to the constancy of human nature in their support. It is, they imply, 'natural' for parents to love and cherish their children, and denying that this was always the case degrades the members of past societies. They have to produce counter-evidence to show that cruelty and violence were not typical.[7] Those who take up the second position generally use a form of economic determinism as their framework. Under the guiding notion of the 'family economy', they point out that shedding children could have been the only way that a family as a whole could survive.[8] Infanticide and abandonment, they argue, were forms of behaviour manifested by those pushed to extremes by hardship and degradation. Similarly, children who were sent to work, often very young, must be understood in the context of a society which took child labour for granted. This began to change only at the end of the eighteenth century, in philanthropic circles, while legislation designed to put a stop to child labour altogether did not come in Britain until the late nineteenth century and was then by no means wholly successful.

Indeed, it is hard to deny that both of these positions have some validity, although they contain refusals to imagine unfamiliar attitudes and forms of behaviour. A few historians have taken a third approach that solves some of these problems. They take the phenomena (infanticide, abandonment, murder, labour, and so on), accept their existence, and then seek to interpret them in terms of the value system of the time. They refuse the moralism implicit in so much historical writing on children. At the same time, they challenge traditional historiography by assuming that uncovering the 'meaning' that has been given to events and experiences in the past is an important and valid historical procedure.[9] It follows directly from this that those who concern themselves with material conditions must consider belief systems as an integral part of historical research. This approach also involves defending the study of 'atypical' behaviour on the grounds that it offers special insights into larger social patterns. In recent years we have come to associate the belief that the normal and the abnormal are closely linked, each existing only in relation to the other, with the work of Michel Foucault.[10] In fact, the idea that the study of deviance – defined relatively, not absolutely – reveals the norm, has existed for some time among sociologists who argue that our understanding of general social patterns may be dramatically sharpened by studying abnormal behaviour. This third approach is open to the complex position of children in past societies, and it requires the historian to be equally alive to a symbolic level.

It was implicit in Ariès's book that stages of life are historically constructed. The idea of there being definable 'ages of man' is an old one; these ages were commonly depicted in Renaissance art. But their function was not to display socially distinct categories, but to act as *memento mori*, reminding people of their own mortality as part of the larger theme of *vanitas*.[11] Historians frequently claim that 'childhood'

came to be recognised as a separate developmental category first and
then, in the nineteenth century, 'adolescence' came into existence.
The language we use to speak about such historical processes is crucial.
Were these in fact 'inventions' – that is, creations of the human mind
– or were they 'discoveries' – that is, recognitions of a state existing
outside the realm of ideas? If childhood and adolescence are inventions, then they may be understood in the same terms as other cultural
products. If they are discoveries, 'the child' and 'the adolescent' become natural, timeless categories, waiting in the wings of history for
just recognition. Discussing the problems inherent in historical language highlights the general difficulties already noted in defining
children.

These difficulties are immediately apparent if we ask the simple
questions 'What is a child?' and 'What is an adolescent?' There are no
clear-cut boundaries here – a child in one culture could be a parent
or prostitute at the same age elsewhere. There can be no neat way of
defining children simply in terms of their age. Turning to general
characteristics shared by all children provides no straightforward solutions either. What do new-borns and nine-year-olds have in common? Our answer to such a question would probably include the
following characteristics: dependence upon parents, economic and
sexual inactivity, living in the parental home, an absence of legal and
political rights. Most of these criteria do not apply to past societies.
Furthermore, different parts of a single society treat children and
childhood differently. This makes historical generalisation fraught
with difficulties, all the more so when present-day assumptions are
foisted on the past.

Many past societies had little formal apparatus for dealing with
children, hence their position was governed by contingencies. Early
modern England, it seems, operated without any clear legal definition
of 'child'. Children could be called as witnesses, if, in the opinion of
the judge, they seemed able to give testimony. With no legal controls
on age of work, a child might be self-sufficient economically at quite
a young age. Children of that era who were apprenticed, were, at
least in theory, subject to the physical discipline of their masters or
mistresses, who sometimes beat them to death.[12]

In a society at any one time, no general definition of childhood
exists, although there have been occasions when powerful sectors,
such as the law, have provided relatively coherent and systematic
accounts of what a child is, particularly in relation to rights. However,
far from lapsing into defeatism on account of the difficulty of providing general definitions, we should recognise that it opens up some

interesting possibilities. Classes, groups, and individuals are constantly negotiating and renegotiating in many different contexts what children are, using perpetual social and conceptual policing which is hard to reconstruct historically.

There is a controversial school of the history of childhood which has not been mentioned so far: psychohistory. Historians using Freudian techniques and theories inevitably place special emphasis on childhood, since psychoanalytic theory accords a privileged place to the child. For many psychohistorians this involves studying individual or collective biographies, using evidence of early experience as a major source. Although this method can help us to understand the childhood of particular individuals, it does not necessarily illuminate the historical aspects of the nature of childhood itself. This is partly because it employs a genetic model, based on biology, to explain a logic of personal development. Stressing the 'evolutionary' processes that parent–child relationships have undergone has resulted in a flat, one-dimensional history. Although it is possible to apply psychoanalytic insights to the history of childhood in a wide variety of ways, one in particular, associated with Lloyd de Mause and the journal he founded, has dominated the field. De Mause argued that societies undergo developmental processes in relation to children just as individuals do and that these can be understood psychoanalytically. Whereas in the past parents were repressive and sadistic, in more recent times they have been increasingly willing to accept the individuality of children. Parents, it seems, are growing up. The maturity of the mid-twentieth century, called the helping mode, was arrived at via five earlier modes which characterised successive historical periods: the infanticidal, abandonment, ambivalent, intrusive, and socialization modes.[13] It is frequently alleged that psychohistory reduces historical phenomena to the psychology of past individuals. It is perfectly possible, however, to apply these same ideas to groups and cognitive structures to uncover both the deep investments we have in seeing children in particular ways and the complex determinants of their lives.

Writing the history of childhood leads us to ask questions about the adequacy of our intellectual tools, calling our entire worldview into question. We must decide, for example, whether children are constructed differently by different societies, whether human nature is trans-historical, and to what extent the material circumstances of a culture guide its theories and practices in relation to children. Curious though it may seem, historians are reluctant not only to raise such matters but even to blend different approaches, as if too much else hangs on their choices. The only way to avoid the trap of a biologism according to which all parents naturally love their children or of an economic determinism in which children are either liabilities or assets to be used in family survival strategies is to examine the place of children in a given society as a whole, without exempting them from the larger multi-faceted changes all societies have undergone.

Sources and Interpretation

Historians have a wealth of material through which they can understand the child as a social and cultural product. Indeed, it is hard to think of an area of life which does not, in some way or other, bear on the nature of childhood. But some sources are more revealing than others, partly because they pertain to children and childhood quite directly. The role of educational theory and practice is the most obvious example, although historians of education have had relatively little to say about the construction of childhood, perhaps because they have conventionally given priority to the development of formal educational institutions. Of course, educational sources are limited in that schooling has paid scant attention to tiny children – hence they reveal little about children in their first years of life – and in that many are biased towards the education of boys, since in the past that of girls was often of a less formal kind. Nonetheless, we can learn much from the teaching methods used, the books provided, and the organisation of the school. Interpreting these materials can be tricky, however. If we use a present-day definition of 'good' teaching, as some historians of education do, early books for children (an eighteenth-century phenomenon) are easily dismissed as inappropriate and tedious – a value judgement with little historical merit.[14]

Those who study childhood give particular weight to autobiographies and diaries. This is part of a larger trend towards the use of such sources, discernible in many fields of social history, produced by the drive for authenticity mentioned above. This material requires scrupulous interpretation. We cannot take at face value accounts of intimate relationships provided by the participants, especially when it comes to relationships as complex and ambivalent as those between parents and children. But however these texts are used, they remain products of individual lives and may reveal little about the general state of childhood. There is an issue here of different, although related, levels of generality. It is mistaken to assume that if we aggregate numerous individual accounts we arrive at insights of a more general or abstract nature. Rather, we should seek appropriate sources which are themselves of that kind.

In this respect, medicine, like the law, is a promising area. The nature and extent of medical interest in children has been far from constant. The development of specific children's facilities (i.e. hospitals and dispensaries) was a feature of the late eighteenth and nineteenth centuries, while an organised field of medical knowledge – paediatrics – did not emerge until the later nineteenth century. There is an extensive medical literature on child-rearing which goes back at least to the seventeenth century, although it grew vastly in the eighteenth century. This literature is of particular interest because it sought to give a coherent account of children in naturalistic terms. A medical framework dictated that an internally consistent, observationally based account be produced. Significantly, this account had to be accessible to the middle-class readership to whom such works were addressed. If children raise contradictory issues for adults, then a domain dedicated to the elimination of conceptual wrinkles will prove especially revealing. Neither medical nor legal writings, however, have offered simple solutions to the conceptual complexity of the category 'child'.

Widely varied sources indicate that the general drive towards naturalism during the eighteenth century included the child – indeed, the child became a paradigm of the natural.[15] Being the heirs of this same intellectual tradition, we find it hard to step outside it and see it for what it really is – a cultural construct. To designate something as natural is not only to give it a form of otherness, but also certain kinds of priority, and to treat it as both primitive and ideal. Two things follow from the recourse to nature. First, epistemologically speaking, 'nature' is a privileged domain, in a sharp, because relatively novel, way in the late seventeenth and eighteenth centuries. Nature, because it was deemed the unique source of valid knowledge, endowed observational accounts of childhood with particular authority. Simultaneously, the medical writer's status as the possessor of natural knowledge and the child's status as natural object were affirmed. Medical practitioners, ever attentive to ways of creating and reinforcing their status, relied heavily on the validity of their knowledge in making larger claims. Second, languages of nature are highly metaphorical. We must recognise that the associations, resonances, and meanings which language, the primary analytical tool, gives rise to can never be fully determined by authors.[16]

The question of growth, especially important within a naturalistic perspective, exemplifies the difficulties people experienced in the past of finding the appropriate language. It is self-evident that children grow and at some point become adults. But how does this take place?

What other processes are similar? Can we account for emotional and intellectual growth in the same terms as physical growth? How do we know when these processes are complete? What parts of growing up are 'natural', what parts not so? Are we to characterise unnatural developments in terms of pathology, of environmental mishaps, or of parental inadequacy? Although we can, and generally have, answered these questions in biological/naturalistic terms, our responses embody social and cultural shifts. Many eighteenth-century medical writings about children insisted upon the naturalness of their development. For example, teething was redefined as a normal event, its status as disease rejected. Swaddling came to be widely condemned on the grounds that the healthy infant body does not require such human manipulation. This constituted an attack on the attitudes and customs of specific social groups. The cult of breast-feeding in this period, often associated with Rousseau, is another case where social issues – here concern about mothering and criticism of wet-nursing – were expressed in a language of nature.[17]

It was not that people suddenly changed their child-rearing habits, but that a group of middle-class professionals and intellectuals strove to rethink the nature of childhood as a part of their approach to 'nature'. This project was not confined to medicine, but also involved such areas as social and political theory and the law. Writings in these areas help us reconstruct the imaginative field childhood inhabited during that specific period. They also indicate points of tension and difficulty in relation to childhood. Rousseau's writings, for example, reveal that the role of the mother and, more generally, the nature of womanhood caused him particular problems.[18] Numerous contemporary writings tell the same story. In effect, a guarantee about the quality of mothering was sought which would certify the legitimacy of children and ensure their survival. It is certainly not coincidental that the art and literature of the period displays a considerable sentimentalisation of both mothers and young children.[19] If we took this at face value we might see no more than romanticism. Looked at with an awareness of the uses to which childhood and nature were being put, it appears rather different. It signals considerable social tension about parental roles, about who should control a child's upbringing – in fact about gender divisions in general. We could extend this analysis to include relationships between servants and children, about which there was also widespread concern.[20] When writers advise parents to police the contact between children and those who care for them, they both evoke the idea of children as natural – they are plants, for example, easily distorted or destroyed by poor gardening – and express conflicts between classes, mediated in this case through control over children.

These examples, although brief, should establish three points. First, it is impossible to separate children from their social and cultural setting; all domains contain implications for them, just as they can be used in a wide variety of arguments as emblems or symbols. Second, although our ideas about children and childhood are a product of history, it is also possible – and certainly easier – to gain a measure of distance from historical materials than from our own culture. This distance from the past, like that of anthropologists from the societies they study, is intellectually productive. It enables us to understand value systems different from our own, which should no longer be seen as the norm or as a peak of progress. Complacency is a formidable enemy. We tend to oscillate between self-congratulation for our en-lightened views of children and self-abnegation for our ill treatment of them. Third, no single type of source material provides an au-thoritative historical picture, while the value of all sources depends on their interpretation.

Two specific issues illustrate the rewards and difficulties of historical approaches: sexuality and work. Present-day attitudes towards the latter are certainly characterised by self-congratulation: We believe that in Western societies we have abolished the iniquity of economi-cally active children. A historical perspective on the fundamental change from having most children in the work force to placing all children in full-time education may be illuminating. By contrast, we have a distinctly self-punishing attitude to the sexuality of children, which goes right to the heart of current concerns. We agonise about teenage pregnancy, contraception for the young, AIDS, and incest. Sex in relation to children is popularly perceived as a crisis issue. Here too a historical perspective may be valuable.

Sexuality

We have constructed a mythical past for children. One element of this mythology is the idea that sexuality was repressed, often quite brutally, in the Victorian period, but that twentieth-century attitudes are altogether more enlightened. This fits neatly with a view com-monly expressed by historians – that the early modern period knew little sexual inhibition, hence there was no taboo associated with child-hood sexuality. Michel Foucault argued, however, that what appeared as Victorian repression was rather a compulsion to create discourses about sexuality.[21] What people apparently feared and deplored, such as children masturbating, they spoke and wrote about endlessly. For Foucault, it is essential to put the new discourses on sexuality in the context of power relations in the society as a whole; the sexuality of children is no exception to this. Since the publication of Volume One of Foucault's *History of Sexuality* (French edition, 1976, English edition, 1978), there has been a veritable explosion of writings on that subject. Many of these were written from a particular vantage point – by active members of the gay communities, for example. Scholars have also studied the male construction of female sexuality. Yet very little attention has been paid to children. This may be partly because no academic groups expressly serve their interests, and there are doubtless additional reasons. What sources are available for such an enquiry, for instance? Furthermore, in a setting where personal relations are regulated more by custom than by law, as was the case in Europe before the late nineteenth century, we might expect little comment on such matters. Whether the omission is to be blamed on the sources or on those who study them, the fact remains that historians have approached sexuality and the young through a limited range of topics: bridal pregnancy and illegitimacy, courtship customs, masturbation, and prostitution. Only in the case of masturbation were children truly involved.[22] In each case, however, the society in question had to erect some conventions, if not laws, to help its members think about whether a particular action was acceptable or not. The fact that customary controls played an important role does not mean that moral boundaries were shaky or ill-patrolled. The task of analysing the extent to which past societies understood sexual behaviour in age-related terms is just beginning. It does seem clear that criteria for judging the sexual activities of the young shifted, and that, from roughly the mid-eighteenth century on, many commentators found custom, with its strong associations with both ritual and material life, inadequate; they sought norms more rooted in 'nature'.

Although we live in a post-Freudian age, in which it is widely accepted that children possess latent sexuality, we nonetheless think of children as beings who are not actively sexual. Furthermore, we now regulate these matters by law as well as by convention. The state of childhood is one which, although preparatory for adulthood, is supposed to be free from the burden of sexual relationships. Those who attack or use children for sexual purposes violate such a deeply felt code that they are often treated as if they have forfeited their human status. Here, the conviction that it is 'unnatural' for children to have sexual relationships is scarcely amenable to purely rational analysis. The difficulty of deciding when children may be sexually active cannot be resolved in any simple way; the age of consent is a mere token in this respect. It does not prevent sexual relations by the under-aged, while by contrast many people may not experience sex until very much later. Growing up is a gradual process, hard to assess with any accuracy and varying markedly from individual to individual. We persist with a commitment to thinking in terms of the exact age of children because it appears objective, because such information is readily available, and because it is customary to do so.

The present situation, relatively speaking, is of recent origin. We may contrast it with that of eighteenth-century England, when there was little regulation of youth by any kind of institutional authority, no compulsory registration of births, little formal control on age of marriage, and only a rudimentary educational system. Contemporaries seemed uninterested in the exact age of children – for example, coroners investigating child death rarely gave a precise age, mentioning only that it was an infant, a child, or giving just an approximate age. Age was, however, becoming an issue in relation to prostitution and illicit sexual activity. The dissolute husband in Hogarth's barbed satire 'Marriage à la Mode' (1742–4) consorted with a childlike girl whom he infected with VD.[23] In condemning prostitution, the zealous philanthropist Jonas Hanway was particularly worried about the use of young girls in their early teens, despite the fact that he was less interested in immorality *per se* than in the disruption of family life occasioned by prostitution. Institutions were founded to save girls from lives of sin.[24] It is of course true that these anxieties were far more acute in relation to girls than to boys. Nonetheless, the condemnation of masturbation in the eighteenth century, which was directed principally at boys, also suggests both that sexuality and children were somehow to be separated, and that the regulation of sexual behaviour was problematic.

There were, of course, sound economic reasons why societies regulated, by whatever means, the sexual activities of the young. This may well have operated at an unconscious level. Adolescent marriage – because the girl became pregnant, for example – brought higher levels of fertility and, consequently, harsher economic burdens. Illegitimate children posed dramatic problems for their mothers, sometimes solved only by infanticide, or, less drastically, by abandonment. What past societies sought to control was not so much sexuality itself as the formation of new households and lives. Yet by the late eighteenth century a new factor had come into the equation – the association of children with nature expressed in art and literature as well as in medicine and social thinking generally. This naturalism produced a logical trap. Ideas about nature were part of larger patterns of thinking within which nature was often paired with another term, its antithesis – commonly society or culture. Eighteenth-century concepts of nature were also all-embracing, covering the whole material world, the entirety of observable reality. Separating nature from society allowed the naturalness of children – pure, innocent, asexual – to be contrasted with the uncleanness of the corrupt adult world. But an inclusive approach validated sexuality as part of nature, hence how could it be depraved?[25] These views co-existed uneasily. It is indeed hard to reconcile the belief that children are natural and asexual with the view that sexuality is integral to nature.

An excellent example is one of the most popular novels ever written, *Paul et Virginie* (1787) by Bernardin de Saint-Pierre.[26] It was an enormously powerful statement about nature. Set on Mauritius, it concerns two children who grow up together, are so close they think of themselves as brother and sister, fall in love, and yet do not marry. The reasons they do not, even at the level of the plot, are quite complex. If we ask why the writer refused to imagine such an eventuality, then we can consider the possibility that although for him romantic love was part of nature, at the same time it posed threats to a particular vision of nature. Thus, Virginie's love for Paul – and his for her – is presented in glowing terms, while her puberty is accompanied by turbulent weather mirroring her own confusion. At the point of her new sexual awareness, things begin to go wrong. She remains a virgin until she drowns in a shipwreck, frozen, as it were, at a moment of intense emotion and sexual purity.

I have used this example because, although it is hardly 'representative', it conveys exceptionally vividly the association between children and nature in the late eighteenth century and the difficulties sexuality posed to that association. Legal devices to deal with the problem, like an age of consent, are only one type of solution. They are inadequate because incapable of addressing the symbolic transformation that takes place when children become sexually active. Children themselves may not experience these changes as symbolic, but they are perceived as such at the level of group responses and mental structures. Possibly modern reactions to the sexuality of children are bound up with our conviction that sex is related to individual liberty; the rights of each person to pleasure. When children become sexually active they assert their autonomy. This autonomy is connected in our minds with the adult world and the marketplace that constitutes its environment, while sexual activity is nonetheless seen as natural. Once again, the child in its passage to adulthood is caught in the conceptual labyrinth formed from our notions of 'nature'. Similar issues arise when we consider the economic activities of children, although these are more straightforward since they have fewer troubling implications for adults.

Child Labour

Work is an exceptionally difficult concept. It has a number of different uses, and context is often the only clue to meaning. When we state that children no longer 'work' we mean that they no longer endure long hours of labour daily, under the control of an employer, for which they may or may not have received wages. Yet children are not now free to do as they please, and, although they do not receive payment for attending school, it certainly counts as 'work' in one sense. Nonetheless, few children are expected to be economically self-sufficient or to bear responsibility for others in this respect. Here, indeed, is a marked contrast with the past. It is easy to say that until the late nineteenth and early twentieth centuries the mass of the population took child labour for granted; it is much harder to assess with any accuracy the actual distribution of different kinds of work. A child could be economically active in four main ways. First, children could undertake work which was paid either in cash or in kind; or they could be apprenticed, which required a fee without providing wages, but put them in the care of masters who undertook to feed and clothe children who were indirectly bringing some economic benefit to themselves and their families. Second, children leaving home affected the family budget quite directly, either positively by no longer requiring sustenance, or negatively by withdrawing their labour. Third, children made a significant contribution when they took care of younger children to enable their parents, especially the mother, to work. Finally, they might work with the parents and so help to raise their productivity.

This was the situation until the late eighteenth and early nineteenth centuries: it was seldom condemned; indeed, contemporary commentators often stressed the simple, uncomplicated expectation that children 'do their bit'. Violence by masters against their apprentices was certainly not condoned, although it could be difficult to deal with such brutality through legal channels, but neither was it much debated in public until the 1770s. Thereafter, the debates slowly began, mostly centred on chimney sweeps. Why that particular occupation, when children undertook hundreds of different jobs? Because it was visible, it affected young children (roughly five upwards), and it had tremendous symbolic potential (black, dirt, sin, slavery, and so on). On what grounds was it deplored? Children were tender, impressionable, vulnerable, pure, deserving of parental protection, and hence all too easily corrupted by the market-place. Two main justifications existed for this characterisation of children: a Christian one, which portrayed children as in a 'sacred state of life'; and an ideological one, according to which they were somehow 'naturally' incompatible with the world of commodities.[27]

The historical moment when child labour was no longer taken for granted, even if only by a limited number of people, is particularly relevant to the leading theme of this paper: the application of concepts of nature and society to children and childhood. Although up to that point societies had regulated child labour by a variety of mechanisms, some more formal than others, these social conventions came, gradually, to seem inadequate. This sense of inadequacy was composed of many different elements. In the early days of movements critical of existing child labour practices, two features stand out. One is that legislative control of some kind was sought; the other, that children were presented as *naturally* ill-suited to heavy labour, although exactly why and how this conception arose is not yet understood. We may note that few commentators recommended the total *abolition* of child labour; they wanted it regulated and humanised.[28] Nonetheless, the logic of the arguments about the inherent vulnerability of children led to notions of and institutions for their protection. 'Better' mothering and full-time education were the centrepieces of the new view of childhood.

Conclusion

It is neither possible nor desirable to produce a summary history of children or of childhood. The very project of writing the history of these subjects is fraught with difficulties caused by the nature of the sources, by the problems intrinsic to the writing of history, and by our present-day attitudes towards and deep investments in childhood. Writing the history of children and childhood thus presents some serious challenges. One way of understanding the problems historians face is by unravelling the implications of associating children with nature. Deriving from the naturalism of the eighteenth century, this association gave rise to contradictory formulations of the essential characteristics of childhood. One of the main points of tension was how the transition from child – in the domain of nature – to adult –

in the social and cultural domain – could be conceptualised. I have focused on two themes to illustrate these issues: sexuality and work. Because past societies thought about these matters in a way so different from our own, historical materials offer us the chance to see how children fit into an unfamiliar context, and hence to infer what facets of a society most forcefully determine the nature of childhood within them. They also enable us to put the contemporary situation in perspective, appreciate its antecedents, and avoid treating it as the norm.

Yet I have sounded a note of caution on source materials, none of which unproblematically reveals historical 'truths' about children. Particular care needs to be exercised in the treatment of sources. In this essay I have suggested that analysing the language used in relation to the child is a valuable exercise. The history of institutions and legislation can also be revealing, as can direct records of the lives of children. But especially if we want to move from a social history of children to a more general history of childhood, we need a related methodological shift from material which is largely descriptive to that which is more abstract. This should provide greater insight into the structures of thinking about children at specific times. If it is the case that societies invent concepts of childhood, both consciously and unconsciously, then it is important to recognise the extent to which these mould the experience of children.

NOTES

1 R. Williams, *Keywords: A Vocabulary of Culture and Society*, 2nd ed. (London: Fontana, 1983), discusses these and many of the other concepts mentioned in this essay.

2 For example, L. Pollock, *Forgotten Children: Parent–Child Relations from 1500–1900* (Cambridge: Cambridge University Press, 1983); J. Burnett, *Useful Toil: Autobiographies of Working People from the 1820's to the 1920's* (London: Allen Lane, 1974); J. Walvin, *A Child's World: A Social History of English Childhood 1800–1914* (Harmondsworth: Penguin, 1982); P. Demers and G. Moyles, eds., *From Instruction to Delight. An Anthology of Children's Literature to 1850* (Toronto: Oxford University Press, 1982) (see esp. pp. 302–6 for a bibliography of work in this field).

3 The general interest in authenticity is exemplified by some of the contributions to *History Workshop Journal*; for the concern with giving children their own history see J. R. Gillis, *Youth and History: Tradition and Change in European Age Relations 1770–present* (New York: Academic Press, 1981; revised ed.).

4 P. Ariès, *Centuries of Childhood* (Harmondsworth: Penguin, 1973). The first French edition, under the title *L'Enfant et la vie familiale sous L'ancien régime*, was in 1960, the first English one in 1962.

5 Critiques of Ariès include A. Wilson's 'The Infancy of the History of Childhood: An Appraisal of Philippe Ariès', *History and Theory 19*, 1980, 132–53, and R. Vann's, 'The Youth of *Centuries of Childhood*', *History and Theory 21*, 1982, 279–97. Pollock, *Forgotten Children*, Chapter 1, is also critical of Ariès.

6 W. L. Langer, 'Infanticide: A Historical Survey', *History of Childhood Quarterly 1*, 1974, 353–65, and *2*, 1974, 129–34; A. Forrest, *The French Revolution and the Poor* (Oxford: Basil Blackwell, 1981), Chapter 7; I. Pinchbeck and M. Hewitt, *Children in English Society*, 2 volumes (London: Routledge & Kegan Paul, 1969 and 1973); M. D. George, *London Life in the Eighteenth Century* (Harmondsworth: Penguin, 1966, first published 1925), especially Chapter 5.

7 Pollock, *Forgotten Children*; S. Wilson, 'The myth of motherhood a myth', *Social History 9*, 1984, 181–98.

8 O. Hufton, 'Women and the Family Economy in Eighteenth-Century France', *French Historical Studies 9*, 1975, 1–22; O. Hufton, *The Poor in Eighteenth-Century France* (Oxford: Oxford University Press, 1974); K. Snell, *Annals of the Labouring Poor* (Cambridge: Cambridge University Press, 1985). M. Anderson, *Approaches to the History of the Western Family* (London: Macmillan, 1980), discusses a number of the approaches mentioned in this essay.

9 D. Sabean, *Power in the Blood: Popular Culture and Village Discourse in Early Modern Germany* (Cambridge: Cambridge University Press, 1984); H. Medick and D. Sabean, eds., *Interest and Emotion. Essays on the study of family and kinship* (Cambridge: Cambridge University Press, 1984), especially Chapter 3, by Regina Schulte on infanticide.

10 M. Foucault, *The History of Sexuality, Volume 1: An Introduction* (London: Allen Lane, 1979); M. Foucault, ed., *I, Pierre Rivière* (Harmondsworth: Penguin, 1978); P. Rabinow, ed., *The Foucault Reader* (Harmondsworth: Penguin, 1986).

11 James Hall, *Dictionary of Subjects and Symbols in Art* (London: John Murray, 1979, revised ed.).

12 George, *London Life*, Chapter 5; J. Rule, *The Experience of Labour in Eighteenth-Century Industry* (London: Croom Helm 1981), Chapter 4; Pinchbeck and Hewitt, *Children in English Society*, Chapter 9 (Volume 1) and Chapter 14 (Volume 2).

13 L. de Mause ed., *The History of Childhood* (London: Souvenir, 1976); see also *The Psychohistory Review* and *Journal of Psychohistory*, formerly *History of Childhood Quarterly*. The application of psychoanalysis to the history of childhood is also discussed in D. Hunt, *Parents and Children in History: the Psychology of Family Life in Early Modern France* (New York: Basic Books, 1980), Chapter 1 (N.B. Chapter 2 discusses Ariès); M. Poster, *Critical*

Theory of the Family (London: Pluto, 1978), especially Chapters 1 and 7; and L. J. Jordanova, 'Fantasy and History in the Study of Childhood', *Free Associations. Psychoanalysis, Groups, Politics, Culture 2*, 1985, 110–22. For an impressive defence of the value of psychoanalysis to history in general see P. Gay, *Freud for Historians* (Oxford: Oxford University Press, 1985).

14 Some standard works on the history of education are: B. Simon, *Studies in the History of Education* (London: Lawrence and Wishart, 1960); G. Sutherland, *Elementary Education in the Nineteenth Century* (London: Historical Association, 1970); W. Armytage, *Four Hundred Years of English Education* (Cambridge: Cambridge University Press, 1965). P. McCann, ed., *Popular Education and Socialization in the Nineteenth Century* (London: Methuen, 1977), is a valuable collection of recent research.

15 D. G. Charlton, *New Images of the Natural in France* (Cambridge: Cambridge University Press, 1984), especially Chapters 7 and 8; L. Jordanova, ed., *Languages of Nature. Critical Essays on Science and Literature* (London: Free Association Books, 1986), especially the chapters by Pilkington and Jordanova; J. H. Plumb, 'The New World of Children in 18th Century England', *Past and Present 67*, 1975, 64–95.

16 Jordanova, *Languages of Nature*.

17 J.-J. Rousseau, *Emile* (London: Dent, 1974, first published 1762); J. Bloch, 'Rousseau's reputation as an authority on childcare and physical education in France before the Revolution', *Paedagogica Historica 14*, 1974, 5–33.

18 J. B. Elshtain, *Public Man, Private Woman: Women in Social and Political Thought* (Oxford: Basil Blackwell, 1982), pp. 147–70; J. B. Elshtain, *Meditations on Modern Political Thought. Masculine/Feminine Themes from Luther to Arendt* (New York: Praeger, 1986), Chapter 4; J. Schwartz, *The Sexual Politics of Jean-Jacques Rousseau* (Chicago: University of Chicago Press, 1984); S. M. Okin, *Women in Western Political Thought* (London: Virago, 1980), part 3.

19 Charlton, *New Images of the Natural*, especially Chapter 8; C. Duncan, 'Happy Mothers and Other Ideas in 18th Century Art', *Art Bulletin 60*. 1973, 570–83.

20 C. Fairchilds, *Domestic Enemies. Servants and their Masters in Old Regime France* (Baltimore: Johns Hopkins University Press, 1984), Chapters 6 and 7; L. J. Jordanova, 'The Popularisation of Medicine: Tissot on Onanism', *Textual Practice 1*, 1987. Tissot was a major eighteenth-century exponent of the view that relations between children and servants should be closely scrutinised.

21 Foucault, *The History of Sexuality*, pp. 17–49; this section is also in Rabinow, *The Foucault Reader*, pp. 301–29.

22 R. H. MacDonald, 'The Frightful Consequences of Onanism: Notes on the History of a Delusion', *Journal of the History of Ideas 28*, 1967, 423–31; E. H. Hare, 'Masturbatory Insanity: The History of an Idea', *Journal of Mental Science 108*, 1962, 1–25; R. P. Neumann, 'Masturbation, Madness

and the Modern Concepts of Childhood and Adolescence', *Journal of Social History 8*, 1975, 1–27. Sexuality and the young is also discussed in E. Shorter, *The Making of the Modern Family*, (London: Collins, 1976), Chapters 3 and 4, and John Gillis, *Youth and History*.

23 See Plate 3 of William Hogarth's 'Marriage à la Mode,' conveniently reproduced in *Marriage à la Mode by William Hogarth. With a Commentary on the Pictures and a Note on the Painter by Michael Levy* (London: National Gallery, 1970).

24 [J. Hanway], *Thoughts on the Plan for a Magdalen House for Repentant Prostitutes* (London: Waugh, 1758); J. S. Taylor, *Jonas Hanway. Founder of the Marine Society. Charity and Policy in Eighteenth-Century Britain* (London: Scolar, 1985).

25 On eighteenth-century sexuality see J.-G. Boucé, ed., *Sexuality in 18th Century Britain* (Manchester: Manchester University Press, 1982) and *Représentations de la Vie Sexuelle*, a special issue of *Dix-Huitième Siècle, 12*, 1980.

26 J. H. Bernardin de Saint-Pierre, *Paul et Virginie*, first published 1787; *Paul and Virginia* (London: Peter Owen, 1982), ed. and trans. J. Donovan; P. Robinson, 'Virginie's Fatal Modesty: Some Thoughts on Bernardin de Saint-Pierre and Rousseau', *British Journal for Eighteenth-Century Studies 5*, 1982, 35–48.

27 J. Hanway, *A Sentimental History of Chimney-Sweepers* (London: Dodsley, 1785); Taylor, *Jonas Hanway*; H. Cunningham, 'Child Labour in the Industrial Revolution', *The Historian*, Spring 1987; L. J. Jordanova, 'Conceptualising Childhood in the Eighteenth Century: The Problem of Child Labour', *British Journal for Eighteenth-Century Studies, 10*, 1987, 189–99.

28 Hanway is a good example of this position. For the more general historical issues surrounding changing work patterns see N. Smelser, *Social Change in the Industrial Revolution* (London: Routledge, 1959).

2

When Does Childhood Begin?

WILLIAM RUDDICK

The question may seem straightforward, but it is conceptually, morally, and politically fraught – and difficult to answer. If, as dictionaries say, childhood is 'the state or time of being a child', there are at least four arguable answers, each with distinct conceptions of childhood – and parenthood. These alternatives are: Childhood begins

1 at birth,
2 at conception,
3 at quickening, and
4 after infancy.

I confess at the outset that I have no clear proposal to push. The merits and demerits of each answer are difficult to sum or compare. Political, metaphysical, biological, and ethical factors jostle one another. Even if we allow a single category to rule, we do not get single answers. Certain metaphysical factors (souls) favor one answer (conception); other metaphysical factors (agency) favor others (birth, post-infancy). Politically, the earlier childhood begins, the earlier parents may invoke public, or state-assisted childcare. On the other hand, the later childhood begins, the longer parents, especially mothers, retain control of their progeny.

In the light of this complexity, it may be tempting to drop childhood and to resurrect earlier accounts of the life cycle, for example, the medieval sequence of Infancy-Youth-Maturity. Some advocates of rights for children seem to want such revisions in order to curb current abuses of parental and state power. This would be an ironic twist, since childhood was allegedly introduced in recent centuries to protect children against just such abuses.[1] But it is better, I think, to retain our division of Youth into Childhood and Adolescence, and look for relief to principles of parenthood and a few distinctive child rights.

One further admission: I write throughout of '*our* concepts', '*our* practices'. This pluralizing is standard philosophical practice, Marx and Nietzsche notwithstanding. Like the royal and editorial 'we', it serves to disguise parochial judgement and to persuade without argument. For these reasons, it is especially suspect in matters in which differences of class, culture, and gender make a difference. Parent–child issues are notoriously such sensitive matters.

This admission should at least subvert the rhetorical force of the plural, even if it does not correct the underlying biases.

1 Childhood from Birth

Birth has several advantages as childhood's start. It is a biological event, and as such is the first in a series of biological changes which end with puberty, a common terminus of childhood. Biological criteria are doubly attractive: they are objective and public. There can be little disagreement about when a child is extrauterine or pubescent; birth and the development of secondary sexual characteristics are fairly public events. Moreover, children are distinguished in our thought by biological features: small size, facial and bodily proportions, and dentition. (The association of childhood and stature may explain common prejudice against shorter races and 'little people'.)

Despite their virtues, biological criteria are, however, not decisive. Although objective, puberty varies greatly in age of onset and is only roughly correlated with the social and psychological changes which are taken to define adolescence. Indeed, some psychologists set adolescence a year or two before even the earliest pubescent changes.[2]

Like puberty, birth is losing some of its significance, especially in modern hospitals. (Does a 'premie' who spends the last trimester in an intensive care incubator have two birthdays? or, like *Macbeth's* Macduff, does an infant have no birthday if delivered by Caesarian section?) Whether medical or 'natural' events, all births are social, not simply biological, events. There are usually attendants, but always an infant who comes into a world of other humans. In so doing, it becomes helpless, no longer able to draw automatically on physiological mechanisms. (Foetuses can, as it were, help themselves.) But by way of compensation, the needs of a helpless infant are public and can make demands on the psychological and moral reflexes of other people. At birth, an infant is no longer dependent on a single parent, or any parent, but only on parental care from any one of a number of potential caretakers.

So construed, birth picks up a different strand of our conception of childhood, namely, social need. To be a child is to need the aid of parents or their delegates and surrogates. A child is incapable of caring for itself and hence is dependent on older, more capable caretakers. Children's dependency, of course, changes over time. Infants may be more physically dependent; older children more psychologically dependent. But such distinctions are matters of degree (and debate). Dependency on parents and their delegates is the theme of childhood, whatever the variations. A child's diminutive size only serves to emphasize this dependency.

Likewise, puberty serves to underline the increasing independence by which adolescence, as the end of childhood, is defined. The adolescent growth spurt and hormonal flood give children the same size and configuration as parents, a biological representation of their growing capacities and desires for freedom from parental constraints and solicitude.

2 Childhood from Conception

If parental dependence, physical or otherwise, is childhood's theme, why does childhood not start before birth? Many women do regard themselves as 'being with child' from the beginning of pregnancy. They may hold this 'maternalist' attitude by virtue of eagerly skipping over intervening biological steps to hold in imagination the infant they expect. For maternalists, expectant mothers are already mothers, not women who expect to be mothers. This jump is often reinforced and authorized by religious indifference to biology: what counts is the soul, or creation by God or in God's 'image'.

In that metaphysical regard, there is no difference between an embryo and an infant; both are equally children of God. Indeed, even adults remain children of God. Religiously speaking, childhood never ends, and it is our religious task to remain childlike, in innocent awe of the Father on whom we depend for continuing life and benefits.

Although appealing and widely held, this theological Maternalism has patriarchal moral and political implications which many women, even believers, resist. Are there any secular arguments for starting childhood at conception? There was a recent attempt in the U.S. Senate to extend Constitutional protections to embryos, on the ground that they are persons. The argument turned on a dubious identification of 'human being' and 'person', as well as on a slide from 'human' in a biological sense to a wider, social sense. But even if the argument could be improved, it would not show that childhood begins at conception.[3] There is no conceptual connection between being a person and being a child. If anything, there is a conceptual incompatibility which I shall suggest below.

A less metaphysical argument might appeal to a notion of vitality

without soul, God-given or otherwise: We think of children as 'full of
life'. Such vitality does not require a soul, let alone a special human
soul. Indeed, children are said to be 'full of *animal* spirits' and are
often likened to kittens, puppies, calves and kids. Accordingly, we
might with imagination count a foetus, or even an embryo, as childlike
in its rapid growth and development. But more than mere vitality is
required to make this link: A child's vitality is the *intentional* activity
of an energetic *agent*. Neither embryos nor foetuses can be counted
as agents, unless we are willing to ascribe to them a rational soul or
mind on grounds which have nothing to do with cerebral or behavioral
development – or unless we are taken in by dubious photographic
work.[4]

3 Childhood from Quickening

By the third trimester, maternalists may experience foetal movements
as intentional, as evidence of desire and will. Before quickening in
the second trimester, there is no felt evidence. In such circumstances,
a pregnant woman can reasonably hold a very different, 'provisional'
attitude – namely, the foetus is a child-in-process, a child-in-the-
making.

This attitude is provisional in two senses: It takes thought for the
future child, and it is a conditional commitment. The obligations of
pregnancy are viewed as conditional on the state of the foetus. So
long as the pregnancy is progressing toward what obstetricians call a
'good outcome', the care and effort due the 'child-in-the-making' are
the same as those due a child at term. If, however, foetal health or
formation becomes seriously compromised in the second term, a
woman may from this viewpoint choose abortion as the termination
of a failed project. If she blames herself for the failure, she may suffer
guilt. But otherwise, the appropriate emotions would be grief and
regret. For maternalists, by contrast, the only justifications for abortion would be those for infant euthanasia. For them, an abortion is
the abandonment of a child, not of a project.

Quickening may well shift someone's view from provisional to maternalist. Would it then be a plausible intrauterine point for childhood's origin? It may not initially seem so. Besides doubts about foetal
agency, a more general objection is likely to arise: Quickening is too
personal and subjective to be a criterion. It would make each woman
the arbiter of when her child's childhood began.

But, rather than a defect, I take this to be a virtue of the quickening
proposal. Generally, people should not be forced to undertake re-

sponsibilities. If they are to be treated as autonomous moral agents, they must be allowed some control over the duration and content of those responsibilities.[5] And, autonomy apart, imposed duties are likely to be executed with resentment and lesser benefit to others. Hence, as long as women bear not only children but primary responsibility for their care, they should have latitude in deciding when maternal responsibilities begin. To decide when childhood begins is to decide when motherhood begins, and vice versa. Whatever personal and subjective leeway quickening would provide is, from this gynocentric viewpoint, fully justified.

In recent abortion law in the United States, quickening has been replaced by viability as a legal 'bright line'. (In the nineteenth century, no legal note was taken of abortion before quickening.) As a demarcation of intrauterine childhood, it too would allow women a certain leeway. Since viability depends on available medical resources, a woman could retard the time of childhood by moving from a city to the country, or advance it by a contrary journey. Nonetheless viability is a far less personal criterion: It is not based on any clear experience, and it makes physicians and their skills the primary arbiters.

For the most part, physicians tend to put childhood late in pregnancy. They all seem to allow that parturition is childbirth – the delivery of a baby. But specialists differ as to how early there is a child. Obstetrician-gynecologists are slower to speak of children in middle pregnancy than are pediatricians, a difference that persists even when they take up foetal surgery.[6] Likewise, the more optimistic foetal surgeons talk of foetal sonograms as 'pictures of children'; those who are still skeptical of these new techniques are more inclined to speak of 'foetuses' and 'sonograms'.

In general, we tend to think of those we can help as children, a point which gives some reason to take a maternalist view even before quickening, whatever one's theological views of pregnancy. The earlier in pregnancy there is a child, the earlier we can enter claims for special public assistance under the heading of 'childcare'. Likewise, the maternalist view can create earlier moral pressure on employers to reduce toxic working conditions. If employers thought of women in early pregnancy as mothers with children, they might reduce workplace hazards.

Or, alternatively, they might ban women from the workplace. (One chemical company recently gave women the option of transfer or sterilization.) This represents, as we know from abortion debates, the other side of early maternalism. The sooner there is a child, the sooner other adults feel free to limit or dictate women's options and conduct.

In general, we think it permissible to protect children from abusive parents. From the maternalist viewpoint, child abuse begins early in pregnancy. Hence, early regulation of a pregnant woman's diet and conduct would be in order. By justifying early maternal assistance, one may justify early restriction – a price we should be slow to pay.

4 Childhood after Infancy

So far I have adopted the dictionary definition of childhood as 'the state or time of being a child'. But historians and common speech favor a narrower notion which distinguishes children from infants. According to Ariès and his followers, the notion of childhood arose in Europe to separate infancy from youth and to protect children from adult usages.[7] About the age of six, children were segregated for a few years of schooling and thereby removed to some degree from the world of adult work, dress, and play. For us, infancy has a narrower meaning and shorter duration: Childhood and (nursery) school begin as early as the third year. Nonetheless, we continue to find grounds for the contrast between infant and child. Children can move about; infants can move only their limbs. Children can use or understand at least some words; infants cannot, if we take etymology seriously (from Latin: *in* not + *fari* to speak).

In virtue of children's powers of locomotion and language, we attribute to them various desires and beliefs about us and the world. Infants may be equally demanding, but children *make* demands on their caretakers. Unlike helpless infants who are entirely dependent on others to decipher as well as tend to their needs, children are undeniably full and active *agents*. And as such, they can begin to lead lives which emerge and diverge from the encompassing lives of their parents and siblings.

Many psychologists interpret this emergence as the child-agent's principal task. After the intimacy of infant nursing, the child must begin to detach itself from the maternal presence and to form the conception of a separate self acting in a larger world. Language and mobility make separation possible, but also make discipline and instruction necessary. The child's new will is unruly and its ignorance dangerous. In the traditional scenario, the child is now ready for and in need of parental authority. Enter the father, followed by the schoolmaster *in loco parentis*. ('Parent' is usually a synonym for father.)

This story favors what might be called a *logocentric* conception of childhood. From this viewpoint, childhood begins with the acquisition and response to speech, continues with school instruction and recitation, and ends with the ability to speak by and for oneself, no longer dependent on those who have previously spoken for one. Previously having had the status of beings who were (in stricter times) to be 'seen but not heard', adolescents are recognized as capable of making oaths and promises, of speaking in court or temple (witness the Jewish *bar mitzvah*, in which a boy declares his manhood by reading and commenting on the Torah in the synagogue). Such logocentric demarcations of childhood fit well with the notion of childhood as an early or even first stage in a biography – the *telling* of a life.

But, as the examples suggest, logocentric criteria also fit with practices and categories now challenged as patriarchal and sexist. To contrast the babbling infant with the speaking child is to support a distinction between the infant's suitable caretaker – warm, comforting, natural, domestic, and typically female – and the child's suitable caretaker – distant, rational, articulate, public, and typically male.[8] In short, the contrast invites the metonymic contrast between the maternal breast and paternal voice (and hand).

Moreover, if agency is the crux, we do not have to wait for language. Children learn how to get their way before verbal exchanges with their caretakers. Lives can begin before their agents can express the desires which make those lives distinct.

5 Lives without Childhood

In the light of these reflections, we may be tempted by a more radical answer – namely, childhood never begins. Perhaps childhood should be deleted from our account of the life cycle. What would be lost? Would children be worse off? Even if, as Ariès claims, childhood once saved children from premature adult usage, does it still do so in economic and political circumstances very different from those of the *ancien régime*?

We have some evidence that it does. Some children have little or no childhood because of poverty, war, or talent. Examples are boys who are dragged into the mines or onto the stage; orphaned girls who raise their younger siblings; and prodigies whose musical, mathematical, or spiritual gifts catapault them over their peers into the adult world. Are they worse off for their 'loss of childhood'?

Autobiographical complaints may not give an answer. If children without childhood are less happy, the cause may be not the loss of childhood, or the early adult responsibilities, but instead, the loss of parents or money which imposed those early responsibilities. And, as premature adults, prodigies may romanticize a childhood they never experienced but learn about at secondhand from adults with selective memories of their own childhoods. Are we to pity prodigies for spending time at the piano rather than in Hobbesian schoolyards and Dickensian classrooms?

Our question, however, is not about exceptional children or circumstances. It is about childhood as a recognized, institutionalized concept and stage of life. More extreme advocates of children's rights clearly think of childhood as a handicapping notion.[9] They claim that children would lead better lives if they were treated as 'young persons' with adult rights of domicile, work, speech, and so forth. They would not revert to medieval conditions; rather, these adult rights would protect them as they protect adults in just societies from exploitative employers, landlords, and sexual associates.

As a philosophical aside, we might note the political import of calling children 'young *persons*'. Despite recent philosophical efforts to give it specific descriptive content, personhood is a political notion, invoked to secure for disadvantaged groups equal treatment with some more favored group. The claim that women or blacks are persons is the claim that, whatever their differences from males or whites, these differences do not justify unequal standing at the bar (or polls, or altar, or . . .). This is the conceptual incompatibility between childhood and personhood which I cited earlier. As small, incapable dependents in need of parental care, children cannot be considered as persons, as equals, so long as they are thought of, or referred to, as *children*.

But is it *equal* treatment we want and demand for children, or *superior* treatment? Were children granted only the rights of adults, they would be ill-served, at least in American society, where few adults have general rights to health care or shelter. Yet even reactionary governments make special provision, however inadequate in practice, for children. Since personhood carries no particular rights, but only rights to equal treatment, a society that treats all 'persons' poorly may nonetheless treat children better.

For this reason we should be slow to drop the notion of childhood, even if disturbed by its traditional connotations of dependency, schooling, and discipline. Or, if these connotations do lead us to delete childhood from the life cycle, we should hang on to its successor, adolescence. Unlike the chronological term 'young person' (or the medieval 'youth'), 'adolescence' is a teleological term. It suggests progress toward a desirable goal, adulthood. Since the goal is desirable, those who are progressing toward it have at least some claim for help, or at least for freedom from avoidable impediments. Even if parents can keep adolescents on leading strings, they should not. We might even argue for the adolescent's *right* to mature, a right which makes claims on both the resources and forbearance of others.

But keeping adolescence, how can we make it fill the temporal gap which deletion of childhood creates? We might talk of *young persons*, aged three (we do already call them 'youngsters'). But 'three-year-old *adolescents*'? The phrase calls up images of children with precocious sexual characteristics due to tumors or to estrogen-pumped chicken in their diets. We might, however, split the years of current childhood between adolescence and infancy. If adolescence has already been expanded (by psychologists) to begin at ten years of age, we might extend it another four years. It has been noted that six-year-olds, through television, now have ready access to adult experience, however simplified or mysterious.[10]

The remaining slack could be taken up by expanding infancy to age six. Rather than focusing on verbal or other incapacities, we might draw criteria for an expanded infancy from the kinds of care infants and young children require. For example, four-year-olds as well as one-year-olds need to be protected, to have their growth fostered, and to be made responsive to the demands of others.[11] Let infancy be defined as the period in which this 'maternal care' is needed.

Expanding infancy would have several social and political advantages. First, it would subvert the traditional assumption that infant care is necessarily women's work. In an expanded infancy, infant care can clearly be men's work as well, since nursing would cease to count as the principal form of infant care. Moreover, expansion of infancy could retard social competition. As infants, children are not yet part of the public world of school and prospective careers. Longer infancy, with the suggestion of longer domestic control, might dampen and delay the anxious ambition which burdens many parents and their young children. For example, an *infant* school cannot, in principle, be easily conceived as a preparatory school, the first rung on an educational ladder to occupational success.

The political advantage of a longer infancy is similar. If, unlike children, infants are by tradition free from the 'paternal gaze' of family and state fathers, then a longer infancy may delay patriarchal scrutiny and schemes, at least in liberal societies. The fathers in totalitarian states do not wait until the end of infancy (witness Plato's *Republic* and Hitler's *Lebensborn* Program). Nor should they, if Locke and the Jesuits are right about the doctrinal importance of the first six years. A prolonged infancy might give lifelong immunity against later efforts of state indoctrination.[12]

For such immunity it would be even better to prolong infancy and retain childhood as well. Childhood can indeed invite the attention of state fathers, but adolescence demands it. In almost any state, authorities will want to ensure that those who are clearly reaching adulthood will become the right kind of adults, subjects, or citizens. In deleting childhood we might reduce parental control but increase state control of children's lives.

Instead of deleting childhood, therefore, we might look for other ways to curb those parental ambitions feared by advocates of adult rights for children. To this purpose, I once formulated a principle to moderate between two extremes of parenthood: on the one hand, narcissistic efforts at reproducing one's better self in one's children and, on the other hand, self-sacrificing provision of a maximal number of life-possibilities for children to explore.[13] On the proposed 'Prospect Provision Principle', parents following an Amish or Hasidic pattern could not limit a child's life prospects to those few which they most desire. On the other hand, the principle frees parents from a Smorgasbord program to provide a child with life-possibilities which would offend them if realized. (The Amish, for example, need not teach their children automechanics, but ought to allow them to learn mathematics or computing).

In addition to such principles of parental practice, we could seek to protect children with rights distinctively theirs. Such child-rights might include the right to mature and the more specific rights which that one entails – namely, rights to education, nutrition, and play. It may be more beneficial for children to have the right to mature – to become an adult – than to have the rights adults have (in fact, it might be better to model adult rights on children's rights than the reverse).

Although sketchy, these remarks on childhood's origin, duration, and character will, I hope, help us resist the hegemonic role which biology plays in our thoughts and theories of childhood. Although childhood is a stage of growth and development, it is also a social and political status. Children's relationships to parents and state are at least as important for this first chapter in their biographies as are stature and dentition.

NOTES

1 Philippe Ariès, *Centuries of Childhood* (New York: Vintage Books, 1962), translated from *L'Enfant et la vie familiale sous l'ancien régime* (Paris: Librairie Plon, 1960).
2 Peter Blos, *The Young Adolescent* (New York: The Free Press, 1970).

3 U.S. Senate Bill S.158 ('Human Life Bill'), with a supporting article by Stephen Galebach, *Congressional Record*, January 19, 1981.

4 For recent attempts to make foetuses look like agents in anti-abortion propaganda, see Rosalind Petchesky, 'Fetal Images: The Power of Visual Culture in the Politics of Reproduction', *Feminist Studies 13*, 1987.

5 For a related point in support of a woman's right to abortion, see Martha Brandt Bolton, 'Responsible Women and Abortion Decisions', in *Having Children: Philosophical and Legal Reflections on Parenthood*, ed. Onora O'Neill and William Ruddick (New York: Oxford University Press, 1979).

6 These observations from a conference on foetal surgery are expanded, along with related conceptions of pregnancy among physicians and their patients, in 'Are Fetuses Becoming Children?', in *Biomedical Ethics and Fetal Therapy*, ed. Carl Nimrod and Glenn Griener (Waterloo, Ontario: Wilfrid Laurier University Press, 1988).

7 Ariès, cited above.

8 See Genevieve Lloyd, *The Man of Reason: 'Male' and 'Female' in Western Philosophy* (Minneapolis: University of Minnesota Press, 1984).

9 The fullest philosophical presentation is Howard Cohen, *Equal Rights for Children* (Totowa, N.J.: Littlefield, Adams, & Co., 1980).

10 Joshua Meyrowitz, 'The Adultlike Child and the Childlike Adult: Socialization in an Electronic Age'. *Daedalus 113*, 1984.

11 These are the features of 'maternal care' as defined in Sara Ruddick, 'Maternal Thinking', *Feminist Studies 6*, 1980.

12 In the *Second Treatise of Civil Government*, Locke argues that proper exercise of parental power (equally shared by fathers and mothers) will protect children from the later appeals of patriarchal politics.

13 See 'Parents and Life Prospects', in *Having Children*, ed. O'Neill and Ruddick.

3

Thinking about Children

JUDITH HUGHES

1 Women and Children First

Of all the wrongs which adults inflict upon children, it might be expected that denying them the vote would figure rather low in any ranked ordering. Set beside data about the physical and mental abuse of children, their exploitation and deprivation, and the sheer inanity of some of our social and educational provision for them, juvenile suffrage does not look like a high priority for reform. Yet it is this question more than any other which has occupied the attention of philosophers who have recently rediscovered children as fitting subjects of debate. One reason for this is, no doubt, a genuine belief that the enfranchisement of children would lead to an improvement in their situation; the exercise of the vote would, it may be thought, enable them to elect representatives who would speak for them from their point of view and who would be obliged, in order to retain their votes, to secure reforms which children themselves would like to see. But utilitarian arguments are not all; another reason for the interest has little to do with children and much to do with a critique of liberal democracies whose foundations are perceived as fatally flawed so long as they permit the exclusion of any group in society from full political status and involvement.

The argument has been conducted on both sides with a dreary predictability reminiscent of the early debates on animal rights when the philosophical sport of characteristic hunting was in full cry. Can animals (children) think and reason? Can they make choices or claims? Can they know what their interests are, or, indeed have interests? What, in short, are they *like*? Bad arguments on one side about deficient cognitive capacities in children are matched by equally bad ones on the other which rely on the simple fallacy of supposing that although there are inadequate reasons for excluding children from full political status, there can be no adequate reasons for doing so.

Feminist philosophers and political theorists have tended to avoid this debate. They have, on the whole, been more concerned with analyses of mothering and gender roles or questions about the impact of child-bearing and -rearing on women's political status. Both of these preoccupations do, of course, rest on the assumption that children exist roughly in the way we think they do: as people who require time, attention, care, and protection in a way adults do not. The commitment to providing these things is one which, in our society, is made mainly by women and is in no way altered by evidence from weighty studies as to the precise age at which children can distinguish local councillors from members of parliament. It also tends to produce a certain cynicism in women who rightly suspect that proposed liberal reforms such as allowing children to decide whether or not to go to school, or rehabilitating the sick, disabled, or handicapped within the community will leave them as the practitioners of those reforms. Their experience of real children leads to an ambivalent stance in which both classical theories about children's inability to reason until they are ten and liberal theories about childhood being a modern invention with no basis other than adult oppression are in turn assumed or rejected. This can, however, lead to some embarrassment. Women philosophers are well aware that many of the arguments used to deny political rights to children were also used to deny those rights to women. As a recently enfranchised group themselves, they have no interest in repeating old fallacies or maintaining old prejudices. But these have a habit of recurring in many guises. In particular, modern writers are fond of describing the political enfranchisement of children as a natural and inevitable follow-on to the enfranchisement of women and blacks, a move which women and blacks may care to ponder. We did not spend a couple of centuries arguing that we were not children but adults simply to be told that, in that case, children are too. This version of the identity of indiscernibles needs to be firmly debunked particularly in the minds of those whom we call friends.

Something has gone very wrong indeed in our thinking about children when the alternatives seem to be either to write them off as non-persons or to deny that socially, intellectually, morally, or politically they exist at all. Since the difficulties appear to reside in the very terms in which the debate is conducted, it is unsatisfactory simply to pick holes in the respective arguments. If we want to think about children rather than about theories about children then we certainly should not start from here.

For that reason I am not concerned with arguing for or against children's rationality or autonomy. In any case, these are not themselves concepts which are above suspicion of partiality, a point which

has not escaped the notice of contemporary feminist philosophers.[1]
If rational is what nineteenth-century gentlemen are, then children
no less than women will come to grief in the rationality stakes. But
even if such charges can be met, theorising about the characteristics
required for membership of a *polis* is indeed 'politically heartless'
(Cavell 1979, p. 25), since it is the point rather than the consequence
of having such criteria that some will be excluded from membership.
Cavell's model of political maturity – as tied to the notion of who you
are in a political community, who speaks for you, and for whom you
can speak – is much more helpful for thinking about children.

Neither do I want to enter debates about the actual age at which
children should be allowed to vote, make contracts, or whatever. We
could only get into the same kind of double-bind as we do over rationality. Since any age we pick for any decisive purpose will not suit
all children, we can too easily slide into making the counter-intuitive
claim that age is of no relevance at all in considering how we can
interact with children. It is, however, worth noting that in our society
chronological age is accorded a significance which exceeds all bounds
of necessity. Its attraction as the determining factor for legislative
purposes on a wide range of issues is obvious and, in our large, im-
personal society, probably necessary, but that does not explain our
obsessive preoccupation with publicizing the precise ages of our children on every possible occasion and ensuring that whatever their
characters and talents they shall conform as nearly as possible to our
detailed expectations of their age groups (frequently and mistakenly
referred to as 'peer groups'). That particular obsession can no longer
be explained merely in terms of thanksgiving for their survival
through infancy and is better accounted for by reference to our apparently desperate need to appear 'scientific' by quantifying and meas-
uring everything we can and much that we can not, and a pathological
dread of appearing to make value judgements about anything at all.
That being said, the fact that 'he's only three' does seem relevant to
the reasonableness or otherwise of the demands we may make of him.
One of the main points of this chapter is to try to account for this
relevance without collapsing into the pit of characteristic-hunting
where we try to match specific abilities to exact ages.

I am concerned with the defence of the notion that there are such
beings as children who are not political adults and with showing that
we can talk about the community in which both have a place without
doing violence to either. What I say about voting is to illustrate this
larger point, but first we should consider where and how the present
arguments end in deadlock.

2 Consenting Adults

The significance which in the current literature is attached to the enfranchisement of children cannot be wholly accounted for in terms of either benevolence or respect. Underlying it are unvoiced and often unrecognized views of what it is to be a member of a *polis*, and those views colour our opinions about the status of particular practices such as voting. The reasons given for advocating the enfranchisement of children commonly include appeals to the recognition that children have interests of their own and that it is a violation of fundamental democratic principles that those with such interests should be excluded from participating in the making of laws to which they are subject. What we have here is an association model of political involvement which derives from one or another of the various forms of consent theory. In this model, groups or individuals come together in free association for mutual benefit, subjecting themselves to anything from the simple majority decision to the general will. What this presupposes is that it is possible to give or to withhold consent and this presupposition is absolutely essential. Consent theory only begins to look plausible if consent is freely undertaken and if those who so consent are themselves free beings. That is, the *polis* is a voluntary association to which people either belong or do not belong; it is a black-and-white affair, either you are a member or you are not. That is the price of freedom.

So, on one level, consent theorists have no difficulty in excluding children, not because they are stupid but because they are free in the sense that they are politically uncommitted. Locke and Rousseau make the point explicitly:

A child is born a subject of no country or government. He is under his father's tuition and authority till he come to the age of discretion, and then he is a free man, at liberty what government he will put himself under, what body politic he will unite himself to. (Locke 1960, Section 118)

Even if each man could alienate himself, he could not alienate his children; they are born men and free; their liberty belongs to them, and no-one but they have the right to dispose of it. (Rousseau 1961, p. 7)

However, there remains the difficulty mentioned above, which Locke sees very clearly. How can you be subject to laws before this consent is given, before you have yourself 'disposed' of your liberty? Locke's interest in posing this question has to do with the status of foreign visitors to a *polis*, but the same question arises in relation to

children. Locke's answer, which was to be refined and developed over
the next two centuries, is contained in the passage above. Children
may be born politically uncommitted, but there is a quite different
sense in which they are not free. The 'free' consenting adult is the
rational consenting adult; to be free is to be rational and in this sense
children are not free agents. They cannot consent until they are rational, at which time − in this sense − they become free, and until then
they cannot therefore be members of the *polis*. Nevertheless, they are
subject to its laws and we still have to account for this. The answer is
that they are not directly subject (and, indeed, the lengths to which
we go to remove children from the jurisdiction of laws which bind
adults bears witness to this belief) but are under the authority of a
father who is. Thus paternalism is endowed with another set of
justifications.

The modern liberal attack on this view begins at its end. First,
paternalism is discredited and then the debate can move back a step
and arguments about the child's fitness to consent gain a foothold,
which is where the current debate is stuck. But this argument only
makes sense if the voluntary association model is accepted by both
sides, for it is only consent theory which demands the pre-existence
of free rational beings. Once consent is replaced by utility as the basis
of liberal democratic theory this pre-condition is redundant. Mill himself did not notice this consequence, and so familiar was the belief
that children were not rational that this part of the received wisdom
simply lay unchallenged. So those who criticise Mill for excluding
children from political status are partly right to do so, but wholly
wrong in the grounds they choose for attack. Utilitarianism does not
demand the exclusion of children *a priori* as does consent theory, and
Mill has no right to take that exclusion for granted. But equally,
showing that children are rational or competent does not entail their
inclusion in a theory based on utility.

However, it is not this aspect of Mill's theory I wish to pursue; that
too would be sterile. We are as unlikely to agree whether the inclusion
of children would maximize happiness as we are to decide whether
or not they are fully rational.

We clearly need to drop this obsession with initial consent. *Pace*
Locke and Rousseau, it has frequently been noted that children are
born into societies and that by the time they arrive at adulthood their
capacity for totally unconstructed free choice is a myth. What Mill's
theory allows is the beginning of a notion of community rather than
association; one which has no need of entry qualifications but within
which freedom and autonomy are partly discovered and partly cre-

ated. It also allows for processes such as growing, developing, and maturing to take place within it, processes which those dedicated to the idea of association simply cannot handle.

3 Inventing Children

Nowhere is this inability to handle the realities of childhood more apparent than in the writings of the advocates of children's political participation. It does incalculable damage to the credibility of a view which – in spirit at least – most of us would like to applaud. It is one thing to notice that conceptions of childhood differ from age to age and society to society and quite another to make bold assertions like: 'the very idea of childhood is a European invention of the last 400 years' (Plumb 1972, p. 153); 'childhood is a fairly recent invention. ... The first children were middle class and male' (Franklin 1986, p. 10). Ariès (1962), approvingly cited as the authority for remarks such as these, had certainly read his Aristotle, who heartily endorsed the view that political maturity arrives at around thirty years of age. The point that Franklin and Plumb want to make – that some societies *handle* childhood differently, and sometimes better – is obscured by their own unnoticed allegiance to the consent model, which demands that any difference in the conditions of child- and adulthood be construed as an inferiority on the part of children by virtue of which they are excluded from participation in adult affairs. It is a problem familiar to those who have followed the discussions about the differences between men and women. The ease with which the observation that men and women are different has been converted via the formula 'women are different from men' to the judgement 'women are inferior to men' is remarkable and accounts for the otherwise incomprehensible resistance to difference theories met in some feminist writing.[2]

What prompts these extraordinary remarks is the belief that in other times or other places the activities of children and adults have not differed intrinsically as dramatically as they do in our present society. How far this is true is a matter for historians and anthropologists, but the evidence needs very careful interpretation.

It is simply misleading to produce the Ariès account (1962, pp. 98–125) of the sexual precocity of the young Louis XIII as back-up for the claim that children enjoyed free sexual expression before the invention of innocence.[3] As Ariès goes on to say, this state of affairs came to an abrupt end when at the age of seven, the young dauphin was suddenly expected to desist from such behaviour and to act properly. The reason for this was not an exaggerated respect for the sexual autonomy of infants, but a firm conviction that young children had no rationality at all, and that belief makes the child's behaviour look very different from the behaviour of adults.

Equally, it is no better to quote Shulamith Firestone's observation that 'childhood did not belong to women' (1972, p. 81) to underpin the invention of childhood theory. How we interpret it depends upon the point of view. From an educational or recreational stance it is probably true, and it was a loss. From the political angle it is false; rather we might say, it was the only thing which did belong to them. 'Childhood' and 'adulthood' are capable of being used evaluatively as well as descriptively, and the evaluation involved is not constantly negative in one direction and positive in the other. Firestone's women are disadvantaged by an absence of childhood when children *and* by its presence when adults. To say that children and adults are politically indistinguishable does not license the inference that children are treated *as if* they were adults, but only that they are treated as adults are treated. The former is evaluative, the latter descriptive. If we wish to impose a value judgement here it is no less legitimate to state the reverse. In political terms this is surely the case. When neither adults nor children are enfranchised it is merely perverse to describe this as a situation in which children are treated like adults. There may be no distinction between them, but a more plausible description of such a state of affairs would be that it was one in which adults were treated like children. It is not that we are operating here with *no* conception of childhood, but with one which includes large numbers of people who are not in fact children, and this is one of the first things they complain about. Of course, it remains to be asked whether we should treat children in certain ways, but that is not the same as asking whether we should treat children as children.

We must not assume that to treat someone as a child is to treat him in some absolute, universally identifiable way independent of the society in which he lives. All communities have ways of treating children which are different from ways of treating adults, but not all societies treat children the same. It is also worth noting that, according to Margaret Mead, since the upbringing of children is culturally evolved, in any society the method of upbringing will never suit *all* the children. The Samoans, like us, make distinctions based on age, but the Balinese make early decisions about whether a child is naughty or sober and virtuous. Mead tells us:

no recorded cultural system has ever had enough different expectations to match all the children who were born within it. . . . Neuroses . . . occur in all known societies. (1972, pp. 35–59)

So long as we live in a human society it seems that we can only get our upbringing of children more or less right for most of them, and what is more or less right is going to depend very largely on the nature of any particular society. But whatever it is like, we cannot escape the fact that we will take up some attitudes to children as children and we should first consider what we mean by this. What is it to treat a child as a child? Must what is insulting to an adult – being treated as a child – be insulting to the child? Of course it will if 'being treated as a child' is interpreted as 'being treated badly' or 'like a fool', for no one is going to go on record as advocating the ill-treatment of children, and children *qua* children are not fools.

4 Doing As We Do

> Nothing is more serious business for a child than knowing it *will* be an adult – and *wanting* to be, i.e. *wanting to do the things we do* – and knowing that it can't really do them yet. What is wrong is to say what a child is doing as though the child were an adult, and not recognize that he is still a child playing, above all growing. (Cavell 1979, p. 176; italics in original)

Margaret Mead (1972, p. 45) tells us that in fishing and hunting societies boys of five or six shoot with bows and arrows. This looks like a simple example of the kind of thing which libertarian theorists[4] would approve of – namely, children doing as adults do in those societies. Is this true? Is the child doing as the adult is doing? There may be little difference in the actions performed and, as the child grows, little to choose between the relative competence of child and adult, but is the child, however competent, doing as his father, however incompetent, is doing when he takes up his bow?

To answer this we must look beyond the activity itself to a much wider context into which the activity fits, in which it has significance, means what it means, entails what it entails. There *may* be perceptible differences in the situation; the child may be confined to a limited area, within sight or earshot of adults, or his arrows may be untipped or his bow less finely strung, or his range of targets may be circumscribed by custom, rules, or taboo. In a society where five-year-olds use real bows and arrows it is unlikely that there will not be any rules governing what is permitted or acceptable. But even if there are not, wouldn't we naturally say here that the children are *playing*? We might remark on the usefulness of their play and the seriousness with which they conduct it – there is nothing essentially frivolous about children's play – but if this is not playing, then what is? What makes us say here that the child is playing and the father not?

It is nothing observable. When we say that a child is playing we are not pointing to some intrinsic feature of his activity but indicating how it is to be regarded, what criteria are appropriate in assessing the success or failure of the performance, whether assessments of certain kinds are appropriate at all, what his activity means in the community. Then we can also say that what it means in the community is not just a matter of what he is doing but of how others see what he is doing, what they acknowledge him as doing. The problem is to say why when a child does *what* an adult does we do not acknowledge that he is doing *as* an adult does. To those who believe that as soon as children can perform the actions necessary for voting or working or contracting they should be allowed to vote, work, or contract, withholding this acknowledgement from them is as perverse as withholding it from women and constitutes the same kind of oppression. But does it?

Let us consider an example. A young child of say, six or seven, bristling with anger and resentment, shouts 'I hate you' and we say to ourselves that he doesn't mean it. It is overhasty here to assume that this silent remark is a sign of bad faith. It may be; we *may* intend that his feelings are not really felt or really intense, and if we do then we are guilty of 'soul-blindness' (Cavell 1979, p. 378).

There is a perfectly obvious sense in which the child does mean it. The words and everything else in his manner and look are his expression of hatred, and only unthinking acceptance of dogma could lead us to think otherwise. Yet the child does not mean it, not in the way an adult could mean it. When I say in excuse that he does not mean it, I mean that his feelings are real, that his expression is of his feelings (he is not merely 'exhibiting hate behaviour'), but that I will not allow this to stand as a judgement on the way things are. He will have to show me more than this to compel me to let it stand, and the younger he is, the more he will have to show me. But if an adult expressed hatred to me (though it is unlikely that one would do so in just this way) I could rightly be accused of paternalism were I to refuse to let it stand (as, when women say no you must educate yourself to accept that they mean no) and that person would have to show me more than this to compel me to reject it as a judgement on the way things are.

This is part of what treating someone as a child is; not denying that he thinks or feels but rather not leaving him in the loneliness of his judgements until he has learnt much, much more about what that involves. He must learn that his hatred can hurt me and that he minds hurting me; that it can hurt him, produce resentment, and hinder forgiveness; that one day he will be taken seriously in more ways than he might now imagine or that his apology may come too late and not be believed. Until he learns all these things he cannot mean that he hates me in the way an adult can hate me. If we supposed he could, none of us would be able to bring up children at all; we would all have been destroyed by resentment before our tenth birthdays.

What children are learning here is not a series of facts, nor even an extrapolation from a series of discrete experiences. Better to say that they are learning, above all, who they are through their discovery of others, and the concept we need here is not knowledge but maturity.[5]

Now when we say that someone is immature we do not just mean that he is young – the way we might refer to a particular tree as an immature oak. Adults can be immature whatever their age, and to call an adult immature is not to compliment him on his youthfulness. When referring to character or rationality, calling someone immature embodies a value judgement which usually licenses certain inferences about an inability to handle social relationships. It does not in this sense refer to lack of knowledge or experiences. Those who do not know what is the capital of France are ignorant of the fact, whatever their age; those who scream 'I hate you' at a three-year-old are immature, whatever their age.

But age and maturity are not entirely unconnected. To call an adult immature is to criticize as well as to describe, not because being immature is in itself a fault, but because most adults have as a matter of fact learnt to handle social relationships at least well enough for the society to function, and those who have not constitute a real threat to that society. If we regarded the immaturity of children as a similar threat our relationship with them would necessarily be one of rigorous oppression, but we do not. Adults take the responsibility for maintaining social relationships and initiate children into that process precisely by *not* treating them as equally responsible agents. An adult who fails to respond to a child's anger as the anger of a child is himself immature. We do not usually have to renegotiate our relationship with a two-year-old after a vehement expression of anger the way we would have to with an adult, we simply resume it, perhaps having learnt something about our own deficiencies in the process. What makes the whole business possible is not an unrealistic expectation that the child will behave like an adult, but a realistic one that the adult will. If adults did not take this responsibility children could never learn to assume it for themselves. We do not teach children to speak by remaining silent, neither do we teach them to take their place in the community by refusing to take our own. To treat children as equals here would be a monstrous form of oppression.

Looked at this way, maturing is itself a learning process which involves the development of our understanding of whom we are in community with, where we belong in a society, and ultimately who we are in that community. It is about discovering, inventing, being shown our point of view rather than learning to make judgements on what we view. Time does not guarantee that we will learn these things successfully, and indeed there is no statable criterion of success, but without time the enterprise is doomed.

What seems to have gone genuinely wrong in our society is that because we have been inclined to equate maturity with the acquisition of particular pieces of information about that society, its very complexity ensures that the acknowledgement of maturity is deliberately delayed to give children time to accumulate that information. If that is not what maturity is – and I have been arguing that it is not – we ought to think again, and those who complain when we keep those who are not children in a state of infancy are right to do so. But it is also why the outrage shown by Patricia Hewitt (of the National Council for Civil Liberties) at the fact that the brightest maths student of modern times is not permitted to vote is comically misplaced.[6] Being good, even amazingly good, at mathematics is not dependent upon being mature; acting with political authority is.

So it would seem that to acquire maturity, children do have to learn, but what is to be learned here cannot be taught any more than learning what I am doing when I point to the grass and say 'green' can be taught. But children do learn that the grass is green, that when they call it green we accept what they say as what we say, and they learn to do as we do in a political context too. Suggestions that there should be capacity tests for membership in the political community are as 'epistemologically stupid' (Cavell 1979, p. 25) as they are heartless; who one is is not established by an ability to answer any test questions which could be devised. Who one is in a political community depends upon how one sees oneself and how one is seen by others in that community.

5 The Primacy of Institutions

It follows that our conception of how far a child is accepted as a member of a political society is more a function of the nature of that society than of changing fashions in child-rearing or philosophical theories. There have been and still are societies with institutions such that children can find their own voices within those societies. This has nothing to do with their alleged 'simplicity'; it is not a matter of the political practices being easily understood or performed. Indeed, in many such societies full political status is achieved by very few – the chiefs or the elders or the chosen ones. It has everything to do with the demands the society makes on the individual and those the individual is able and permitted to make on it.

If we consider, for example, a one-party state, where to vote is merely to enter a polling booth and to place a cross beside a solitary name, there would appear to be no good reason to exclude children from the procedure. Once the child was able to place a mark in roughly the right position and to choose whether or not to bother to do so, then nothing of much significance would follow from the action and there would be no possible excuse for excluding him. That is because the procedure itself is infantile, not because children in lenient one-party states are particularly precocious nor because the leaders of such societies have highly developed views about the autonomy of children. It is possible precisely because they do not have highly developed views about anyone's autonomy.

The name of the game changes if we now imagine a society where the duty to vote in the one-party system is mandatory. Then there is the possibility of breaking the law, of refusing to ratify the status quo and the requirement to accept the consequences of a refusal and responsibility for compliance. In such a situation, the performance required by the procedure is no more difficult, but its significance is very different. Now, to ratify *means* something; the voter must accept responsibility for his vote. Perhaps strangely, the voter in a harsh one-party state is nearer to his counterpart in a democracy in this respect than his less-pressured neighbour. Of course, he can always abdicate some of the responsibility by claiming, for example, that his vote will make no difference to the outcome since the results are rigged, but the responsibility is his to abdicate.

In a democracy the difficulties are more severe. Because, in a democracy, our votes are intended to make some difference to the outcome, the possibility of abdicating responsibility is considerably diminished. Not to vote is a positive action which affects the outcome just as surely as any vote. (The method of voting could affect the level of responsibility; proportional representation might increase it.) How we vote, and whether we vote, we are responsible not only for fulfilling or failing to fulfil our civic duty, but very directly for the sort of society we have. Vote or no vote, children of six or ten or even thirteen are not responsible for the sort of society we have and more significantly they do not, in our society, demand it.[7]

This is not just an empirical matter. Let us suppose that, say, a ten-year-old did have the vote. Would that, as some commentators seem to think, compel adults to treat them as political equals? I think not. When the Beatles were awarded MBEs (Member of the Order of the British Empire) back in the sixties there was, of course, an outcry: However good, however much they had contributed to the balance of payments, did pop-singers really merit the MBE? But there was another, quite different reaction. Outraged elderly gentlemen returned their medals to the palace, not because of the exaltation of the Beatles but because, in their eyes, the MBE had itself been devalued. It no longer meant what it had meant. It no longer represented recognition of long and devoted service to a cause; what had been a serious honour was now a frivolous reward for transient success. I am not concerned with the truth of this opinion nor with the psychology of those who held it. The point is that had this view been widely adopted then that is what the MBE would actually represent.

It is inevitable that if children in our society were given the vote, the perception of what the vote is, what it presently assumes and demands and entails, would change to accommodate children rather than children change to accommodate it. I am not saying that through ignorance, stupidity, or anything else, children would use their votes badly or fail to signify what they meant. I am saying that the enfranchisement of children in this society would change the nature of the democratic vote just as surely as universal adult suffrage changed it from an expression of privileged power to one of majority will. If we are to argue about this then the proper grounds of the argument are the possibility and desirability of this change, not the cognitive capacities of children. Further, I am saying that ten-year-olds, though they might signify what *they* mean, would nonetheless not mean what adults mean by voting in a democracy.

The question is whether the enfranchisement of children would change our perception of children or our perception of the vote, always remembering that we are talking about children and the vote in the context of a liberal democratic society. We should be careful about assuming the former. While it is true that children learn by doing, I hope I have said enough to show that what they do involves a great deal more than their actions. An apprentice plumber may very well learn how to install the central heating by doing it, but no one in his right mind would let him loose alone on such a task. We would expect his work to be supervised and checked, ratified by a master-plumber, which he is not. This is a very ordinary way of learning, but it is not a model which can be carried over to the vote. It would be essentially self-defeating were we to teach children to vote in this way; there is no equivalent here of the apprentice-piece. What children have to learn about their responsibility for the community must be learnt outside the situation in which their responsibility is expressed.

None of this entails that children cannot make political statements at all. That would be patently false. The striking schoolchildren of Soweto clearly are politically active, and we know this from our knowledge of the structures and the response of their own society. When the military are brought out against them, when they take the full, bloody consequences of their actions, when they use the only means of protest open to adults and children alike, there is no way of seeing their behaviour differently. We might contrast this with the reaction to the children's demonstrations in England during the teachers' action of 1985. Responses varied from wondering who had put them up to it to speculating about how far they would go to get a day off school. They achieved a vicarious political standing only from the angry reaction of some nervous teachers who were alarmed that their actions would produce hostility from exasperated parents. Neither of these kinds of response seems adequate to describe what these children were doing. At least some of them were undoubtedly *protesting* at the disruption of their education and to dismiss them as idle truants is as insulting as it is ill-founded. Nevertheless, in protesting they are not acting with the full political authority with which political adults in a liberal democracy can act. When mass protest becomes the norm, or the only way to bring about political change, when 'we have no choice' but this, we should fear that something is very wrong with our practices and interpretation of democracy. Rather than seeing the children's behaviour as adult we should lament when adults are obliged to react as children. However necessary it is to retain the right to protest, it is not through protest that we act with sovereignty in a democracy, and even a protest vote is not merely a way of complaining.

So, from one point of view, the demand for the enfranchisement of children requires too much. It does not allow for learning who we are in the political community before taking the full responsibility which is involved in acting with full political authority. From a different perspective, it requires too little. In democratic societies, the right to vote has certainly been considered necessary for full political status, but it has never been considered sufficient. It is an integral part of the democratic principle that a citizen should not only be entitled to elect to office but also to stand for office. The working classes and women have been asserting this principle for more than a century and current feminist scholarship has gone further to claim that mere entitlement is not enough.[8] That is the rationale of positive discrimination in the selection of candidates for office. It is oddly paternalistic to think that children should make do with anything less. The assumption that they would be satisfied with the right to vote is made plausible only by the politically naïve view that all we do when we vote is to express our interests.

If, however, we see voting as part of a much larger expression of political maturity, responsibility, and commitment then we will also accept that these things must be learnt in other contexts before they can be expressed in a performative act – and that what is learnt cannot be taught or tested, though it will surely be 'more than we know, or can say' (Cavell 1979, p. 178).

NOTES

1 The 'maleness' of philosophy is discussed fully in Jean Grimshaw, *Feminist Philosophers. Women's Perspectives on Philosophical Traditions* (Brighton: Wheatsheaf, 1986) and in Genevieve Lloyd, *The Man of Reason. 'Male' and 'Female' in Western Philosophy* (London: Duckworth, 1984).

2 For a full discussion of difference and inferiority see Mary Midgley and Judith Hughes, *Women's Choices: Philosophical Problems Facing Feminism* (London: Weidenfeld & Nicolson, 1983).

3 This is what appears to happen in Bob Franklin (1986). See references.

4 Currently, the most cited of these are John Harris, 'The Political Status of Children' (pp. 35–59) in Keith Graham, ed., *Contemporary Political Philosophy* (Cambridge: Cambridge University Press, 1982) and John Holt, *Escape From Childhood* (Harmondsworth: Penguin, 1979).

5 In the famous passage (1260a) where Aristotle makes the remark that slaves have no deliberative faculty he also tells us that women have, but that it lacks authority, and that children have but that it is immature. Aristotle, *Politics* (London: Dent, 1959).

6 This reference to Ruth Lawrence, the child prodigy who wanted to vote, occurs in the foreword to Franklin's book. See references.

7 This point forms the basis of an argument developed in Judith Hughes, 'The Philosopher's Child', in a collection with Morwenna Griffiths and Margaret Whitford as editors (in press).

8 A strong statement of this position occurs in Janine Brodie, *Women and Politics in Canada* (Toronto: McGraw-Hill Ryerson Ltd., 1985).

REFERENCES

Ariès, Phillippe (1962). *Centuries of Childhood* (London: Cape).

Cavell, Stanley (1979). *The Claim of Reason* (Oxford: Oxford University Press).

Firestone, Shulamith (1972). *The Dialectic of Sex* (London: Bantam Books).

Franklin, Bob (1986). *Introduction* (pp. 1–23) and 'Children's Political Rights' (pp. 24–51) in *The Rights of Children*, ed. Bob Franklin (Oxford: Basil Blackwell).

Locke, John (1960). *Two Treatises on Civil Government* (London: Dent).

Mead, Margaret (1972). *Culture and Commitment* (London: Panther).

Mill, John Stuart (1964). *Utilitarianism. Liberty. Representative Government* (London: Dent).

Plumb, John (1972). *In The Light Of History* (Harmondsworth: Penguin).

Rousseau, Jean-Jacques (1961). *The Social Contract and Discourses* (London: Dent).

Part II

The Child in the Democratic Polity

4

The Family, Democratic Politics and the Question of Authority

JEAN BETHKE ELSHTAIN

Political theorists who endorse a version of authority for democratic politics and the family that eschews ready-to-hand orthodoxies and contrast models face a somewhat daunting task. They must carve out discursive space in an already crowded field dominated by interlocutors adamant about what is to be salvaged and what demolished in our current social and political arrangements.[1] As part of this task, they are obliged to take some stand on the continuing 'crisis of authority' in modernity, if only to ponder whether a perpetual crisis may not be constitutive of modern life.

The architecture of this essay is as follows: I begin by assaying the 'crisis of authority' noted above. Second, I offer a brief narrative of democratic authority, the family, and politics as an inherited dilemma that continues to haunt current reflections. Third, I state a strong case for familial authority and its relationship to democratic politics that ushers in a more ambiguous endorsement of this authority in light of current challenges to the norms and practices that constitute the family.

A caveat to forestall one predictable criticism: I, of course, recognise that there is no such thing as *the* family as a constant, unchanging object that corresponds to a universal form. Families are sets of social relations which vary with time and place. But in and of itself this doesn't tell us very much that is interesting. What is interesting, for the political theorist, is 'the family' as a discursive object, a figural representation that *signifies* by its presence or its absence within a tradition of inquiry: 'the family' as a remarkably stubborn yet adaptive repository of human hopes, dreams, and conflicts; 'the family' as actual human ties and loyalties modern society either sustains or suborns; 'the family' as symbolic object to be celebrated or condemned.

The Crisis of Authority Assayed

The political and social theorists and activists who assume a crisis of authority in democracy or the family, or would precipitate a crisis to promote change, frame their discourse through such questions as: Is 'democratic authority' an oxymoron? If democratic authority is a possibility is the family compatible with it? If not, should the family be made to conform to the standards of democratic political authority? Or should we, instead, restore older notions of authority for families and politics that modernity has destroyed or eroded? Do we have too much authority or not enough? Are we in decline or do great possibilities lie ahead if we have the political will to change what must be changed? And so on.

I will explore the contours of crisis discourse as background to my defense of authority, by taking up, briefly, exemplars of the restorationist and reformist/radical positions as articulated by Robert Nisbet and Jürgen Habermas respectively.

Robert Nisbet, in a number of important works, most notably *The Twilight of Authority*, argues that the loss of authority in the contemporary age culminates in the atomization of society, the breakdown of community, the rise of unreason, and opposition to the values of due process, privacy, and rights.[2] This potpourri of social ills is, for Nisbet, inseparable from the rise of liberalism and the victory of an instrumentalist and relativistic social ethos. At base, this crisis is moral, resulting when human life, public and private, is ruthlessly desacralised. According to Nisbet, this crisis of authority began *first* in the political sphere and then spread to 'other areas of institutional life'. He writes:

> By a strange law of social behaviour, decline actually causes attack. Let a government, economic enterprise, or church reach a certain point of enervation, ... and it is virtually certain that some kind of assault will be mounted on it.... It is in these terms, I believe, that we are obligated to see contemporary assaults upon the historic family and upon the ties and roles which the family has sustained for so many thousands of years.[3]

A prior weakening of the family's authority *causes* revolt against it rather than the reverse. Put under pressure from superior external forces, political and economic, the family has nearly succumbed. Precisely for this reason, it becomes a target for rebels who can mount a more effective assault against a weakened institution than they can combat the suprastructures which are the real culprits. Misguidedly, social rebels wind up deepening the crisis they hope to resolve.

Jürgen Habermas would find much of Nisbet's argument a long lament over the inability of conservatives to hold back the tides of social change. Habermas does, however, share Nisbet's sense of crisis, which, in Habermasian language, gets construed as a breakdown of 'system integration' so great it poses a threat to 'social integration'. System integration or, we might say, stability is menaced by a driven process of production and accumulation that creates intolerable contradictions within the political and socio-cultural system. In other words, old norms give way and alienation and anomie result.[4] When this confluence of forces culminates in a 'motivation crisis' that undermines allegiance to the standards of democratic order and its constitutive principles one confronts, as does the modern West, a full-blown crisis of legitimation.

The political projects that flow from each author's crisis mirror one another: Nisbet urges us to restore a resacralised exercise of traditional authority in familial, political, and economic spheres – we must rediscover belief; Habermas wants to create a social order that more fully deserves, hence receives, the critical allegiance of its members – we should carry even further rationalism's challenge to belief. Nisbet endorses mystery and murkiness in our arrangements so that they are less susceptible to arrogant tinkering; Habermas extols an 'ideal speech situation' of perfectly symmetrical, transparent discourse as a precondition for a new, authoritative consensus.

Crisis discourse presents us with a picture of wrongs to be righted. The political analyst who shares the language and rhetoric of crisis is likely to overdraw our dilemmas the better to mobilise our will in one direction or another. The attractions of this approach are many, including the promise that social ills can be cured once the sites of 'infection' are located and treated. Each wants to solve *the* problem. But that problem is, in part, one they shore up given their tacit commitment to the very old idea that there can be only one 'authority principle' operative within a political and social order if it is to be 'well governed'. Nisbet and Habermas would bring the world into line with the contours of an argument about what it ought to be or must be unless we want continuing conflicts and crises. The roots of their concern lie in the history of the uneasy relationship between democratic authority and the family.

Democratic Authority and the Family: The Construction of a Dilemma

The suspicions democrats have about traditional authority, lodged in kings and chiefs, in popes and lords, is easily understood. For democracy requires self-governing and self-regulating citizens rather than obedient subjects. Democratic authority, unlike the authority once believed to inhere in the person of the king, resides instead in the processes that enable persons to participate according to mutually defined and accepted rules in the life of their polity. Being in a position of authority in democracy is the temporary holding of an office at the suffrance of those who delegate certain powers to the office-holder.

These and other background features of democratic authority and its exercise emerged unevenly over several centuries as late medieval and early modern cosmologies faltered and slowly gave way.[5] The features I have in mind are the prejudgements and understandings that came to comprise the political culture of democracy. These include the principle that citizens possess inalienable rights. Possession of such rights empowered citizens to offer authoritative assent to the laws, rules, and practices that constitute democratic politics, including those procedural guarantees that afforded them protection against abuses of the authority they had themselves authorized.

Equality between and among citizens was assumed from the beginning on the part of democrats: indeed, the citizen was, by definition, equal to any other *qua* citizen. (Not everyone, of course, could be a citizen – another ongoing democratic dilemma.) Democratic citizenship required the creation of persons with the qualities of mind and spirit required for civic participation. This was seen as neither simple nor automatic by democratic theorists, leading many to insist upon a structure of education tied to a particular understanding of 'the sentiments'. Democratic education must result in a moral autonomy that stresses self-chosen obligations, thereby casting further suspicion upon all relations, practices, and loyalties deemed unchosen, involuntary, or 'natural'.

Within such accounts of democratic authority, the family emerged as a problem. For one does not, in the first instance, enter a family through free consent; one is born into the world unwilled and unchosen by oneself, beginning life as a helpless and dependent infant. Eventually one reaches 'the age of consent'. But in the meantime one is a child, not a citizen. This vexed democratic theorists, some of whom believed, at least abstractly, that the completion of the democratic ideal required bringing all of social life under the sway of a single democratic authority principle.

The historic period most critical as backdrop for our current conflict over authority, democracy, and the family is rooted in the sixteenth- and seventeenth-century shift from patriarchal to liberal-contractarian discourse. Patriarchalist discourse in its paradigmatic form (I have in mind Robert Filmer's *Patriarcha*) was preeminently about authority, constructing a tight case for authority as single, absolute, patriarchal, natural and political. In Filmer's world there is no drawing of distinctions between public and private, family and politics; indeed, there is no private sphere – in the sense of a realm demarcated from political life – nor political sphere – in the sense of a realm diverging from the exigencies of the private world – at all. Power, authority, and obedience are fused within the original grant of dominion by God to Adam at creation. Within Filmer's unitary theory of authority there are only subjects, save, perhaps, for the divine-right monarch alone. Each father lords it over his wife, his children, and his servants in his own little kingdom. But he, in turn, is subjected to the First Father, the lordly king.

To counter Filmer's case for God-given patriarchal authority proved easy enough for liberals and democrats where their visions of civil society were concerned but more tricky by far where transformed notions of democratic authority seemed to challenge the family. Was a familial form dominated by presumptions of patriarchal privilege, however softened in practice, suitable or legitimate within a civic world framed by presumptions of consent? If liberals ended a condition of perpetual political childhood were they required to eliminate childhood itself? A strong version of the liberal ideal, 'free' consent from birth, was deeply problematic given the nature of human infants.[6] Liberal contractarians were often cautious in carrying their politcal principles into domestic life, some contenting themselves with contractarianism in politics and economics but traditionalism in families; not, however, without considerable discursive maneuvering.[7] Filmer's caustic query to his liberal interlocutors concerning whether people sprang up like 'so many mushrooms' and his incredulous insistency, 'How can a child express consent?' continued to haunt liberals in part because they shared with Filmer the presumption that authority must be single in form if a society is to be coherent and orderly.

John Locke, more subtle than many, softened demands for relentless consistency, arguing instead for the co-existence of diverse authoritative social forms and practices. Conjugal society must come into being through freely chosen consent on the part of two adults. But 'parental' or 'paternal' power within the family (Locke recognized both but privileged the latter), could not serve as a model for the democratic polity any more than the norms constituting civil society provided an apposite model for families. Locke stripped the father-husband of patriarchal absolutism by denying him sovereignty, which included the power over life and death. That prerogative was reserved *only* to democratically legitimated public authority. A father's power was 'conjugal . . . not Political' and these two were 'perfectly distinct and separate . . . built upon so different Foundations and given to so different Ends.'⁸ The child's status was that of not-yet-adult, hence not part of the consensual civil order. But the education of the child into moral sentiments was vital to that wider order. Locke avoided the seductions of the patriarchal authority principle as an all-encompassing norm by refusing to launch a mimetic project that mirrored patriarchalism in the sense that it would substitute a full-blown, overarching liberal authority principle that turned the family into an explicit political body governed by the same principles that prevailed in liberal public life.

The lack of perfect congruence between political and familial modes of authority continued to vex post-Lockean liberal and democratic thinkers. Whether because of the position of women, who, having reached the age of consent could enter freely into a marriage relation only to find future consent foreclosed; or because the family itself was a blemish to those who foresaw the ultimate triumph of rationalism and contract in all spheres of human existence, liberals returned over and over to relations between the family and politics.

Enter John Stuart Mill, who, in contrast to Locke, insisted that familial and civic orders be drawn into a tight mesh with one another. For Mill, the family remained a despotic sphere governed by a 'law of force' whose 'odious source' was rooted in pre-enlightened and barbaric epochs. By revealing the origins of family relations, thus bringing out their 'true' character, Mill hoped to demonstrate that the continued subjection of women blunts social progress. He proposed a leap into relations of 'perfect equality' between the sexes as the only way to complete the teleology of liberal individualism and equality, to assure the promise of progress.

In his tract *The Subjection of Women*, Mill insisted that his contemporaries, male and female alike, were tainted by the atavisms of family life with its illegitimate, because unchosen and pre-rational, male authority, and its illegitimate, because manipulative and irrational, female quests for private power.⁹ The family would become a school in the virtues of freedom only when parents lived together in full and free consent, without power on one side or obedience on the other. Power, for Mill, was repugnant: True liberty must reign in all spheres. Liberty and equality were the sure and certain outcome of female citizenship.

But what about the childen? Mill's children emerge as rather abstract concerns: blank slates on which democratic parents must encode the lessons of obedience towards the end of inculcating authoritatively the lessons of freedom. Stripped of pre- or undemocratic authority and privilege, the parental union serves as a model of democratic probity.[10]

Mill's tract is interestingly contrasted to Alexis de Tocqueville's concrete observations of family life in nineteenth-century America, a society already evincing the effects of the extension of democratic – and the breakdown of patriarchal and Puritan – norms and practices. The political fathers of Tocqueville's America were fathers in a different mode, at once stern but forgiving, strong but flexible. They listened to their children and humoured them. They educated as well as demanded obedience. Like the new democratic father, the American political leader did not lord it over his people. Citizens were not required to bend the knee or stand transfixed in awe. The leader was owed respect and, if he urged a course of action upon his fellow citizens following proper consultation and procedural requirements, they had a patriotic duty to follow.

Tocqueville's discerning eye perceived changing public and private relationships in liberal, democratic America. Although great care was taken 'to trace two clearly distinct lines of action for the two sexes', women, though confined to domesticity, nowhere occupied a loftier position of honour and importance.[11] For the mother's familial role was enhanced given her essential civic vocation as the chief inculcator of democratic values in her offspring. 'No free communities ever existed without morals and, as I observed . . . , morals are the work of women.'[12]

Although the father was the family's natural head, his authority was neither absolute nor arbitrary. In contrast to the patriarchal authoritarian family where the parent not only had a natural right but acquired a political right to command his children, in a democratic family the right and authority of parents is a natural right alone, never a political one.[13] This natural authority presents no problem for democratic practices as Tocqueville construes democracy, in contrast to Mill. Indeed, the fact that the 'right to command' is natural, not political, signifies its special and temporary nature: once the child is self-governing, the right dissolves. In this way natural, legitimate paternal authority and maternal moral education reinforce a political order that values flexibility, freedom, and the absence of absolute rule but requires order and stability as well.

Popular columnists and 'child experts' in Tocqueville's America emphasized kindness and love as the preferred technique of child nurture. Obedience was still seen as necessary – to parents, elders, God, 'just government and one's conscience'. But the child was no longer constructed as a depraved, sin-ridden, stiff-necked creature

who needed harsh, unyielding instruction and reproof. A more be-
nign view of the child's nature emerged as notions of infant depravity
faded together with Puritan patriarchalism. The problem of discipline
grew more, rather than less, complex. Parents were enjoined to get
obedience without corporal punishment and rigid methods, using
reason and affection, issuing their commands in gentle but firm voices,
insisting quietly on their authority lest contempt and chaos reign in
the domestic sphere.

Tocqueville's image of the 'democratic family' sees children both as
ends in themselves and as means to the end of a well-ordered family
and polity. A widespread moral consensus existed in the America of
that era, a kind of Protestant civic religion. When this consensus began
to corrode under the force of rapid social change (and there are
analogues to the American story in all modern democracies), certain-
ties surrounding familial authority as a secure locus for the creation
of democratic citizens were shaken as well.

If no form of social authority can any longer be taken for granted
in light of continuing challenges to the norms that govern both familial
and civil spheres, a case *for* family authority – as a good in itself and
as one background feature that makes possible democratic society –
becomes more difficult to mount unless one opts for restorationism
or celebrates high rationalist hopes that the time is finally ripe to bring
the entire social order under the sway of wholly voluntarist norms.
If restorationists long for a return of traditional norms to their once
unambiguous status, the rational voluntarist option is problematic
given its implied intent to nullify the moral and social significance of
all 'unchosen' purposes and obligations. If one finds these alternatives
unrealistic, undesirable, or both, the task of articulating a defense of
familial authority within, and for, a social world whose members no
longer share one overriding conception of the good life, nor repose
deep faith in the future of human institutions, becomes ever more
exigent.

I move in two directions in the section below. First, I launch a strong
case in behalf of family authority. Second, I challenge this case by
taking note of objections to it that yield a more ambiguous set of
reflections and affirmations. Complicating the argument in this way
offers the reader an opportunity to evaluate whether or not the case
remains compelling or, alternatively, whether explicit recognition of
the arbitrary moments in that case may produce a more viable defense
that better serves the social goods at stake in the long run.[14]

Democratic Authority and the Family: The Strong Case

Familial authority, although apparently at odds with the governing presumptions of democratic authority, is nonetheless part of the constitutive background required for the survival and flourishing of democracy. Family relations could not exist without family authority, and these relations remain the best basis we know for creating human beings with a developed capacity to give authoritative allegiance to the background presumptions and principles of democratic society as adults. Family authority structures the relationship between adult providers, nurturers, educators, disciplinarians and dependent children, who slowly acquire capacities for independence. Modern parental authority is shared by mother and father. (Some readers may take strong exception to this claim, arguing that the family is patriarchal, even today, or that the authority of the mother is less decisive than that of the father, or that Mill was right. Children, however, exhibit little doubt that their mothers are powerful and authoritative, though perhaps not in ways identical to fathers.) This ideal of parental equality in relation to children does *not* presuppose an identity between mother and father. Each can be more or less a private or a public person, yet be equal in relation to children in the way here described.

What makes the family authority relationship distinctive is the sense of stewardship internal to it, the recognition that parents undertake continuing solemn obligations and responsibilities. The authority of the parent is special, limited, and particular. Parental authority, like any form of authority, may be abused, but unless it exists the activity of parenting itself is impossible. The authority of parents in relation to children is implicated in that moral education required for democratic citizenship, the creation of a democratic political morality. The *Herzenbildung* – education of the heart – which takes place in families should not, however, be one piece of an explicit political agenda. To make it such is to treat the family instrumentally, affirming it only insofar as it can be shown to serve some externally defined set of purposes. That the family underscores the authoritative rules and norms that govern the wider order may be true. But it also offers alternatives to the actual policies and programmes a democratic public order may throw up at any given point in time.

The intense loyalties, obligations, and moral imperatives nurtured in families may clash with the requirements of public order and authority. For example, young men may refuse to serve in the army because this runs counter to the religious beliefs instilled by their families. This, too, is vital for democracy. Democracy emerged as a form of revolt, and keeping alive a potential locus for revolt sustains democracy in the long run. It is no coincidence that all twentieth-century totalitarian orders laboured to destroy the family as a locus of identity and meaning apart from the state. Totalitarian politics strive to consume all of life, to allow for a single *public* identity, to destroy all private life, to require that individuals identify only with 'the group' rather than with specific others.

Family authority within a democratic, pluralistic order does not exist in a direct, homologous relation to the principles of civil society. To establish an identity between public and private lives and purposes would weaken, not strengthen, democratic life overall. For children need particular, intense relations with specific adult others in order to learn to make distinctions and choices as adults. The child confronted prematurely with the 'right to choose' – should parents abnegate their authority – or situated too soon inside anonymous, institutional contexts that minimize points of special, unique contact and trust with specific adult others, is likely to be less capable of choosing later on. To become a being capable of posing alternatives, one requires a sure and certain place from which to start. In Mary Midgley's words: 'Children . . . have to live *now* in a particular culture; they must take some attitude to the nearest things right away.'[15] The social form best suited to provide children with a trusting, determinate sense of place and ultimately a 'self' is the family. Indeed, it is only through identification with concrete others that children can later identify with non-familial human beings and come to see themselves as members of a wider human community.

Family authority is inseparable from parental care, protection, and concern. In the absence of such ties, familial feelings would not be displaced throughout a wider social network – they would, instead, be vitiated, perhaps lost altogether. And without the human ties and bonds that the activity of parenting makes possible a more general sense of 'brotherhood' and 'sisterhood' cannot emerge. If the transactions of a democratic political society are to be facilitated there must be individuals with the capacity to give authoritative adherence to the background presumptions and principles of that society. These presumptions are constituted in part by the family as the locus for the emergence of socially responsible, autonomous human beings.

The nature and scope of parental authority alters over time. Children learn that being a child is not a permanent condition. One of the lessons the family teaches is that no authority is omnipotent, unchanging, and absolute. Working through the family authority principle, as the child struggles for identity, requires that she question authority generally. Examples of authoritarian parents do not disconfirm this ideal case; they do, however, point to the fact that the family authority principle, like any constitutive principle, is subject to deformation and abuse in particular cases. If the possibility for abuse is granted, sustaining familial authority – that of both parents in their relations to children, as well as that of families in relation to the wider social order – keeps alive that combination of obligation and duty, freedom and dissent, which is characteristic of democratic life.

The stance of the democrat towards family authority resists easy characterization. It involves a rejection of any ideal of political and familial life that absorbs all social relations under a single authority principle. Families are not democratic polities. And democratic polities should not be 'familialized'. With its concreteness, its insistence on the unique and the non-instrumental, the family helps us to hold intact the respective 'good' and 'ends' of exclusive and inclusive relations and arrangements. Any further erosion of that ethical life embodied in the family bodes ill for democracy. The resulting vacuum would not be filled by some perfect democratic consensus that covered children as well as adults unambiguously. Instead one would get more coordination and control from those public and private entities, economic, political, and social, for whom democracy and all that sustains it are as much a nuisance to be combatted as an ideal and way of life to cherish.

Abusive families are a particular tragedy. The loss of the family and its characteristic forms of authority and relations would be a general débâcle from which we would not soon recover. The irony is that those who want 'more democracy' often wind up endorsing less personal, hence less directly accountable and 'attackable', forms of authority. The replacements for parents and families would not be a happy, consensual world of children coequal with adults but one in which children became clients of institutionally powerful social bureaucrats and engineers of all sorts for whom they would serve as so much grist for the mill of extra-familial schemes and ambitions.

The ideal democratic family sketched here is a feature of a democratic *Sittlichkeit*, one vital and necessary arena of concrete social life and ethical existence. But it serves as well as a 'launching pad' into more universal commitments, a civic *Moralität*. The child who emerges from such a family is more likely to be capable of acting in the world as a complex moral being, one part of yet somewhat detached from the immediacy of his or her own concerns and desires given the complex negotiations that were internalized as part of growing up.

Democratic Authority and the Family: Ambiguous Recognitions

The strong case above presumes a family that is secure, or can be made secure, in its authoritative role and serves as the bearer of a clear *telos*. This is spine-stiffening stuff. But it presupposes a wider social surround that no longer exists in its paradigmatic form, having ceased to endorse unambiguously the shouldering of family obligations and locating less honour in long-term moral burdens. The authoritative norms that sustain the case have fallen under sustained pressures that promote individualistic, mobile, and tentative relations between self and others. Modern subjects are enjoined to remain as untrammelled as possible in order to attain individual goals and to enjoy their 'freedom'. Constraints grow more onerous than they were when it was anticipated that everyone would share them – all women, almost without exception, would become mothers; all men, almost without exception, would become supportive fathers. Located inside a wider ethos that no longer affords clear-cut moral and social support for familial relations and responsibilities, young people, unsurprisingly, choose in growing numbers to postpone or evade these responsibilities.

In acknowledging these transformations, the case for familial authority is softened but not abandoned. Taking account of shifts in the social ethos does not mean that one succumbs to them as if they comprised a new authoritative norm simply by virtue of their existence. But some alterations are warranted, including articulation of less dauntingly rigorous normative requirements for being a parent than those required, or implied, by the strong argument. The changes I have in mind here are *not* facile reassurances that modern human beings can be unfettered individualists and encumbered parents in some happy, perfect, harmonious configuration. For parental authority both *constrains* and *makes possible*, locating mothers and fathers in the world in a way that *must* be different from that of non-parenting adults. This need not lock parents into a dour notion of their duty that encourages them to overstate their power to shape their children, and their responsibility for doing so. Modern ideals of parental authority should be open to such recognitions as the fact that children frequently have something to teach parents, that transformations flow 'up' as well as 'down'. The modern family is a porous institution, one open to a variety of external images and influences. Parents are no longer the sole moral guardians and one's defense of familial authority must take this into account, assessing its meaning in the structure of domestic life.

Critics of family authority might continue the challenge by claiming that the strong case falters because it can be shown to contain arbitrary elements, and that the existence of such features constitutes a *prima facie* indictment of any and all norms or practices that can be shown to contain such elements. Arbitrariness is unjustifiable and illegitimate by definition, these critics might persist, and the ideal posed above is arbitrary in several ways: it privileges procreative heterosexual unions, thereby excluding a variety of other intimate arrangements – whether 'non-exclusive', 'open' marriages and families, or homosexual unions – from its purview, and hence from any constitutitve role in the creation of social good; it maintains a notion of the child as a dependent who requires discipline and restriction, thus shoring up 'paternalism' ostensibly in behalf of children but really to deny them their rights; it limits parental social choices by stressing dependability, trust, and loyalty to the exclusion of adventure, unpredictability, and 'openness'; it constructs a case for ethical development that is self-confirming in assuming that a set of authoritative norms and persons is essential to family life.

Perhaps, however, behaviour modification is a less strenuous and more effective shaper of a child's actions. Perhaps children thrown early on out of the home and into a group context emerge less burdened by individual conscience and moral autonomy, hence are freer to act creatively without incessant, guilt-ridden ruminations about responsibility and consequence than those children reared in the family idealised in the strong case. Perhaps children who learn at an early age to be cynical and *not* to trust adults will be better skeptics, better prepared to accept the rapid changes of modernity, than the trusting, emotionally bonded, slowly maturing children in the family sketched.

Without taking a position on the substance of each of the specific challenges noted above, I concede the point about arbitrariness but reject the corollary claim that the presence of arbitrary elements within a case for family authority constitutes in itself a devastating blow to any possible defense of that authority. A reflective brief on behalf of family authority should recognise explicitly that every set of authoritative norms will contain some 'arbitrary elements within it', arbitrary 'in the sense that, while they are indispensable to this way of life, there are other forms of living... in which this special set would not be necessary.'[16] In the absence of any authoritative rules and relations, the social world would be more rather than less dominated by violence, coercion, or crass manipulation.

Take, for example, the incest taboo. Unless one accepts the arguments of socio-biologists, the incest taboo can be construed as arbitrary; indeed, a number of radical social critics have challenged it by declaring that the taboo's arbitrariness, which they translate to mean both 'illegitimate' and 'indefensible', is contrary to individual freedom of expression and action. Exposing its arbitrariness, they would liberate children from paternalistic despotism and parents from an ancient superstition. Chafing at restrictions of sexual exploration that construct strong normalizing limits and establish sharp boundaries between familial and extrafamilial sexuality, as well as between adults and children inside families, these antiauthoritarians celebrate total freedom of sexual exploration as an alternative.

The mistake on the part of the anti-incest taboo protagonists is not their insistence that we recognise the arbitrary features of our social arrangements, but their conviction that such exposure requires the elimination of the rules or practices in question. In assuming that a viable mode of social existence might come into being and flourish in the absence of authoritative restrictions, the 'antis' emerge as naïve and dangerous. They open up social life to more rather than less brutalisation, including targeting children (in the example under purview) as acceptable resources for adult sexual manipulation and coercion. Continued authoritative acceptance of the incest taboo implicates one in an arbitrary standard, true. But that standard is necessary to sustain a social good – protecting children from systematic abuse by the more powerful. Parental power is limited and constrained. Adult power, shorn of the internal moral limits of the incest taboo, would become more generalised, less accountable, and dangerously unlimited.

A second criticism along similar lines might hold that in defending the family and intergenerational ties, one privileges a restrictive ideal of sexual and intimate relations. Such privileging, being arbitrary, is unacceptable, and should cease. There is no easy way to meet the criticisms of those who believe that a society can and should stay equally open to all, or nearly so, alternative arrangements, treating lifestyles as so many identical peas in a single social pod. The advocate of such normative levelling will not be happy with a tempered response that ushers in the cautionary note that a defense of family authority not overstate the imperatives involved in a manner that construes other ways of ordering human relations as wholly unworthy of consideration. The caveats I have in mind would recognise explicitly that families in modernity must co-exist with those who live another way, whether heterosexual or homosexual unions that are by choice or by definition childless, communalists who diminish individual parental authority in favor of the pre-eminence of the group, or other alternatives.

But the recognition and acceptance of plural possibilities does not mean each alternative is 'equal' to every other with reference to specific social goods. No social order has ever existed that did not endorse certain activities and practices as preferable to others. Every social order forges terms of inclusion and exclusion. Challenges to our forms of exclusion and inclusion, as these are structured by the family, push towards a loosening but not a wholesale negation in our normative preference for intergenerational family life. In defending family authority, then, one acknowledges that one is *privileging* relations of a particular kind when and where certain social goods are at stake.

Those excluded by, or who exclude themselves from, this authoritative norm, should not thereby be denied social space and tolerance for their own practices. And it is possible that if what were at stake were, say, seeking out and identifying those creations of 'self' that enhance an aesthetic construction of life and sensibility, the romantic bohemian or rebel would get higher marks than the Smith Family of Freemont, Nebraska. Nevertheless, we should be cautious about going too far in the direction of a wholly open diversity with reference to authoritative evaluations lest we become so vapid that we become incapable of distinguishing between the moral weightiness of, say, polishing one's Ferrari and sitting up all night with a sick child. The intergenerational family remains central and critical compared to other arrangements in nurturing recognitions of human frailty, mortality, and finitude, in inculcating moral limits and constraints which are necessary to sustain the background preconditions of democratic life. A revamped case for family authority takes account of challenges to its normalizing and arbitrary features, opens it to ambiguities and paradox, and abandons along the way whatever advantage might remain in pressing a morally self-certain perspective.

The worries of historic liberal thinkers about the family's anomalous position within a civic world governed by contractarian and voluntarist norms seems, as this essay winds down, misplaced. Ironically, what such analysts *feared* is what I here *endorse*: a form of family authority that does *not* mesh perfectly with democratic authority principles yet remains vital to the sustaining of a pluralistic culture. This is an example of one of many paradoxes that social life throws up, and that political philosophers would be well advised to recognize and to nourish rather than rush to rule all 'inconsistencies' out of court in line with the requirements of some abstract system. The discordancies embodied in the uneasy co-existence of family and democratic authority sustain those struggles over identity, purpose, and meaning that are the very stuff of democratic life.

The ideal of family authority that emerges from these reflections is worthy of endorsement because it helps to keep 'the crisis of authority' alive rather than requiring discursive and political closure. To resolve the untidiness of our public and private relations by establishing a form of hegemony that either reaffirms unambiguously a set of unitary, authoritative norms, whether restorationist or revolutionary, or eliminates all such norms as arbitrary hence expungeable evils, is to jeopardize the social goods that democratic and familial authority, paradoxical in relation to one another, promise – to men and women as parents and citizens and to their children.

NOTES

1 By 'our', I mean, roughly, members of societies in the modern West. There are many other ways of organising social life that would not confront our conundrums.

2 Robert Nisbet, *The Twilight of Authority* (Oxford: Oxford University Press, 1975).

3 Ibid., p. 80.

4 Jurgen Habermas, *The Legitimation Crisis* (Boston: Beacon Press, 1973).

5 This is not to say that all features of these ontologies are, in principle, no longer available to us. Many continue to structure their lives primarily in and through such ontologies of faith, but not, I would argue, without conflict.

6 Hobbes in *Leviathan* is here, as elsewhere, an anomalous thinker, fusing absolutism with consent in all spheres, including the family, and accepting coerced 'choice' as legitimate.

7 On this subject, see Mary Lyndon Shanley, 'Marriage Contract and Social Contract in Seventeenth-Century English Political Thought', in *The Family in Political Thought*, ed. Jean Bethke Elshtain (Amherst: University of Massachusetts Press, 1982), pp. 80–95.

8 John Locke, *Two Treatises of Government*, ed. Peter Laslett (New York: New American Library, 1965), p. 357.

9 John Stuart Mill, *The Subjection of Women* (Greenwich, Conn.: Fawcett, 1970).

10 Not even Mill took the argument for consent to its *reductio ad absurdum* in some recent versions of 'children's liberation'. See Richard W. Krouse, 'Patriarchal Liberalism and Beyond: From John Stuart Mill to Harriet Taylor', in *The Family in Political Thought*, ed. Elshtain, pp. 145–72.

11 Alexis de Tocqueville, *Democracy in America*, ed. Phillips Bradley (New York: Vintage Books, 1980), 2:223.

12 Ibid., p. 209.

13 Ibid., p. 203–4.

14 William E. Connolly, 'Modern Authority and Ambiguity', *Politics and Am-*

biguity (Madison: University of Wisconsin Press, 1987), pp. 127–42, argues that ambiguity is necessary to any defense of authority in modernity.

15 Mary Midgley, *Beast and Man. The Roots of Human Nature* (Ithaca, N.Y.: Cornell University Press, 1978), p. 291.

16 Connolly, 'Modern Authority and Ambiguity', p. 138.

5

Teenagers and Other Children

RICHARD LINDLEY

In this chapter I argue that there is a strong case for extending a range of adult rights and responsibilities to all teenagers, and that our treatment of teenagers is inconsistent with a proper respect for the principles of liberal democracy. If this is true, then such an extension should become part of the political agenda in all liberal democracies. Before discussing the case of teenagers, I should say a little about what I mean by liberal democracy.

Liberal Democracy

The distinctive value of democracy is a belief in the political equality of all citizens. Although there is great controversy over what constitutes 'genuine' democracy, the following two principles are essential, as constitutive of a minimal conception of political equality. First, *All citizens have an equal right to participate in the political process.* Second, *All citizens have the right not to be treated arbitrarily.* According to this principle, if any two people or groups of people are treated differentially by the state, it is incumbent on the state to provide an explanation which shows that the treatment is based on a demonstrable relevant difference between the two.

The definitive value of liberalism is a belief in the vital importance of personal autonomy (or self-determination, I use the expressions interchangeably). It is held by liberals that individuals should be able to live their own lives according to their own conceptions of a good life, except when by so doing they stop others from doing the same.

The political systems of Western Europe, North America and Australasia all claim the moral allegiance of their citizens on the grounds that they are liberal democracies. If we combine the liberal and dem-

I would like to thank Errollyn Bruce for many ideas expressed in this paper, and Geoffrey Scarre for very detailed and helpful comments on earlier drafts.

ocratic principles set out above, we arrive at what I take to be the cardinal principle of liberal democracy:

P: Everyone is to have an equal right to the most extensive self-determination compatible with a similar self-determination for all.

This is very similar to John Rawls's First Principle of justice (see Rawls 1972, p. 60). It differs only in that I have substituted 'self-determination' for 'basic liberty', on the grounds that I believe political liberties are instrumental goods whose prime worth is that they enable people to develop and express their autonomy. As I understand the values of liberal democracy, in a just liberal democratic society all people would be able to develop, maintain, and exercise their autonomy to a maximal degree, to the extent that by so doing they did not prevent others from doing the same. This follows directly from the two values, suitably interpreted, of liberty and equality.

Since this chapter is primarily addressed to those who find *P* plausible, I shall not spend time trying to defend *P*. However, as 'autonomy' is a controversial concept, I shall say a little about what I mean by it, and why it is so important for liberal democrats.

Autonomy: What it Is and Why it Matters

'Autonomy' literally means 'self-rule' or 'self-government', and originally applied to Greek city-states which had achieved independence from rule by other city-states. The autonomy which is central to liberalism is *personal* autonomy. To be personally autonomous an individual must be free not only from direct domination by other people, but also from domination by custom or social pressure. Furthermore, an autonomous person is free from the internal disabilities of irrationality and ignorance. An autonomous individual controls his own life. Autonomy can be vitiated by failures either of belief or of action. A fully autonomous individual would act only on correct beliefs which he had rationally scrutinized, and would always do what he judged to be best in the circumstances. (For a detailed discussion of autonomy, see Lindley 1986.)

Nobody is, on this account, fully autonomous, since we are not perfectly rational, and finite intelligences cannot be omniscient. However, everyone who is able to act for reasons is more or less autonomous. The liberal belief in autonomy has two prongs: first, society should be structured to promote the widest development of autonomy; second, society should be structured to promote the widest exercise of autonomy.

There are two reasons why liberals believe it is so important to structure society in the ways mentioned above: autonomy is a highly important constituent of human happiness or well-being, and the exercise of autonomous choice is vital both for the development of autonomy and for the promotion of the other constituents of happiness. Perhaps the most eloquent defender of this liberal view of self-determination is John Stuart Mill.

Mill, being a utilitarian, accepted that happiness is the only true intrinsic good. This is consistent with his view that self-determination is intrinsically good, because he believed that self-determination is a part of happiness.

Mill was at pains to distinguish genuine happiness from mere contentment. He argued that those who understood what it was to be autonomous would prefer to retain their autonomy even if this was more painful than abandoning it. Mill described the 'sense of dignity' constitutive of a well-developed autonomy as

so essential a part of happiness of those in whom it is strong, that nothing which conflicts with it could be, otherwise than momentarily, an object of desire for them. Whoever supposes that this preference takes place at a sacrifice of happiness ... confounds the two very different ideas of happiness and content.... It is better to be a human being dissatisfied than a pig satisfied; better to be Socrates dissatisfied than a fool satisfied. (Mill 1861, p. 9)

It is probably true that most people whose autonomy is well developed would not wish to abandon it, even for large increases in pleasure. However, this does not establish that a more autonomous life would be intrinsically better for those whose autonomy is less well developed. Nevertheless, without such an assumption, it is hard to make sense of the strength of liberals' objections to state paternalism.

There are many places where Mill defends his belief that it is good for the state to allow people to live their lives according to their own values and interests. For example, in his discussion of individuality in *On Liberty* he writes:

The same things which are helps to one person towards the cultivation of his higher nature are hindrances towards another. The same mode of life is a healthy excitement to one, keeping all his faculties of action and enjoyment in their best order, while to another it is a distracting burthen, which suspends or crushes all internal life. Such are the differences among human beings in their sources of pleasure, their susceptibilities of pain, and the operation on them of different physical and moral agencies, that unless there is a corresponding diversity in their modes of life, they neither obtain their fair share of happiness, nor grow up to the mental, moral and aesthetic stature of which their nature is capable. (Mill 1859, p. 125)

In another passage, Mill argues that where the pı
people's actions on paternalistic grounds 'the odds
wrongly, and in the wrong place' (ibid., p. 140).
make their own (possibly bad) decisions is a sou
partly due to the fallibility of the would-be pate
the special knowledge of and concern for their own interests w....
individuals possess (there being enormous variety in the interests and
needs of different people), and partly because the exercise of choice
is necessary for the development and maintenance of autonomy.

The belief that individuals should be able to live according to their
own conception of a good or worthwhile life, provided that this does
not illegitimately restrict the liberty of others to do the same, is indeed
a cornerstone of liberal political philosophy. The two enemies of liberalism are moralism and perfectionism, which are really two sides of
the same coin. *Moralism*, as I define it, is the view that certain sorts of
activity should be banned because they are immoral, even though they
harm nobody, except on the grounds of their alleged immorality.
Perfectionism, as I define it, is the view that certain ways of life or sorts
of activity are so excellent that people ought to pursue them, and if
resistent, should be compelled to pursue them, even though they
benefit nobody, except on the grounds of their alleged excellence.

Restrictions on Liberty

It is in the light of a belief in the principle of maximal equal self-
determination that the strongest liberal objections to paternalism
make best sense. For example, consider Mill's famous Liberty Principle, according to which

the only purpose for which power can be rightfully exercised over any member of a civilised community, against his will, is to prevent harm to others.
His own good, either physical or moral is not a sufficient warrant. . . . In the
part [of his conduct] which merely concerns himself, his independence is, of
right, absolute. Over himself, over his own body and mind, the individual is
sovereign. (Mill 1859, p. 73)

The absolutist tone of this principle has confounded many who have
sought to reconcile it with Mill's professed utilitarianism. If, however,
we treat the principle as deriving from the belief that following it
offers the best chance of *maximising* self-determination, the problem
disappears. Anyway, this is how I take the Liberty Principle.

Given this kind of rationale, it is always open to people to propose
exceptions to the ban on paternalism. It is an empirical question

whether particular kinds of paternalistic intervention are likely to maximise people's autonomy. There are, within liberal democratic societies, two groups of people for whom widespread paternalistic intervention is practised and accepted – the mentally disordered and children. Both raise important and fascinating questions for defenders of liberal democracy. Our topic here is children. Why, should *children* be singled out for special treatment? Why should *they* be prevented from doing as they choose, on paternalistic grounds?

Mill, the champion of individual liberty, thought it obvious that his Liberty Principle should not apply to children, and justified his view with a simple commonsensical reason. Of the doctrine expressed in the Liberty Principle, that power should be exercised over members of a civilised community only to prevent harm to others, Mill wrote:

It is, perhaps, hardly necessary to say that this doctrine is meant to apply only to human beings in the maturity of their faculties. We are not speaking of children, or of young persons below the age which the law may fix as that of manhood or womanhood. Those who are still in a state to require being taken care of by others, must be protected against their own actions as well as against external injury. (Mill, 1859, p. 73)

It seems obvious that *anyone* who is in a state to require being taken care of by others should be cared for (provided that this care is effective, and does not violate the rights of anyone else). From this it follows that those who *still* require such care should receive it. The plausibility of the claim that children should be singled out for paternalistic protection against their own actions can be properly assessed only when a clear sense is given to the phrase 'in a state to require being taken care of by others'. What is it, in this context, to be in such a state?

Paralysed polio victims, dystrophy sufferers, and victims of serious road accidents are all in a state to require being taken care of by others, in the dramatic sense that without the care of others they would be unable to stay alive. Nevertheless, this dependence gives no special justification for paternalistic restrictions on their actions. Suppose, for example, that a polio victim prefers spending every evening watching television to engaging in those more edifying pursuits which we compel children to follow, such as reading history books, solving mathematical problems, and writing essays. Her dependence on others for survival would in no sense justify someone's forcing her to engage in the edifying pursuits. This is because such physical dependence does not of itself impair a person's faculty of choice, even though what is physically possible for such a person is severely limited.

The demented and the severely mentally handicapped are in a state to require being taken care of by other people, because their ability to make autonomous choices *is* severely impaired. For example, someone with Alzheimer's syndrome could very well forget where he was and be quite unaware of the dangers of walking onto a busy road. If people such as he were not 'protected against their own actions' they would not last long – not because they wish to shorten their lives, but because they no longer possess a sufficiently coherent understanding of the world to estimate even immediate, gross dangers to their safety.

We often speak of mentally ill people as needing to be taken care of by others. This is expressed in legislation which allows for the compulsory admission to hospital and treatment of patients whose illness is such that they are likely to endanger their own or other people's health or safety. Without entering into controversy over the nature of so-called 'mental illness', I would like to describe the sense in which such people need to be taken care of. Schizophrenics and manic depressives may need to be looked after by others because they are especially likely to act in a way which is contrary to their own interests, as defined by their own conceptions of a good life (even if their state allows them to retain such a conception). Their conduct is likely to be far from autonomous and if unchecked may lead to an untimely death (which raises special problems of its own), or to an overall exacerbation of current loss of autonomy. In these circumstances paternalistic restriction of liberty may actually be *required* by respect for the sufferer's autonomy.

Continual Development and Arbitrary Distinctions

Perhaps the most initially plausible objection to paternalistic restrictions on children appeals to the democratic principles of non-arbitrary treatment. According to this principle, we recall, any differential treatment of two groups or individuals by the state must be contingent upon a demonstrable relevant difference. This principle is justifiably invoked to condemn racism and sexism.

There are two children's 'liberationist' arguments which appeal directly to this principle, but despite initial attractions, neither is compelling.

According to the first, our present age-related restrictions on children's liberty are arbitrary, since, for example, there is no relevant difference between a girl of fifteen and three-quarters and a girl of sixteen, which would render the former but not the latter incapable of proper consent to a sexual relationship. 'If sixteen-year-olds can choose, why can't I?' would be a legitimate question for a girl approaching her sixteenth birthday. Because the precise location of these boundaries is arbitrary, all those on the wrong side of them suffer injustice. Although this is a plausible argument, it is less powerful than appears at first sight, and indeed leads to absurdity if pursued systematically to its logical limit.[1] Let us assume that there is at least some period in the life of a human being when he is clearly in need of the kinds of paternalistic protection in question. If such a person is in need of paternalistic protection (on account of developmental and experiential limitations) at, say, six months, then he is also in need of paternalistic protection at six months plus one day (for the difference one day makes will not be sufficiently dramatic to constitute a demonstrable relevant difference). The same reasoning applies to the person when he is six months and a day, and so on, right through to mature adulthood. If changes are continual (on a continuum), then a strict application of the principle of no arbitrary distinctions leads to the conclusion that everybody stands in need of paternalistic protection. Running the argument the other way, starting from a highly rational, well-informed adult, one could equally conclude that nobody – not even babies – stands in need of paternalistic protection.

This result will be familiar to those acquainted with the famous Sorites Paradox, which is sometimes illustrated by the example of a heap of sand. A heap is composed of a finite number of grains of sand, and could be constructed by starting with one grain, and steadily adding a grain at a time. If an accumulation of x grains is not a heap, it seems arbitrary to designate as a heap that same accumulation with the addition of a single grain.

Any legal entitlement or restriction is bound to be arbitrary in that it puts into different categories some cases which are in themselves relevantly similar, since the effectiveness of the law requires it to be well defined, while it deals with a spectrum of cases. Legal systems should aim to minimise arbitrary treatments (rather than abolish them), and having an age (or ages) of consent needn't be inconsistent with this goal.

According to a second liberationist argument, 'because you are a child' is not an acceptable reason for denying someone the vote, freedom to travel, the right to work for money, the right to choose where to live, or the right to buy goods on credit. It is an unacceptable reason because *many* people below the age which the law may fix as that of manhood or womanhood manifestly *do* have at least as much competence to exercise these rights as *many* adults who are legally entitled to exercise them. As alleged incompetence is the chief reason for restricting the liberty of children, it appears that children as a group are the subject of arbitrary discrimination, since their liberty is apparently restricted, not on account of some special incompetence or need but simply because they are children. Would universal competence tests offer a solution?

A defender of present ages of consent could concede that age is an imperfect measure of competence, yet argue that ages of consent offer the least awful alternative for protecting children who genuinely need paternalistic protection. As already stated, there is a need for easily identifiable boundaries. Moreover, there is unquestionably a significant correlation between childhood and incompetence. Those who believe that competence should be the *crucial* determinant of the granting of civil and political rights could have no principled objection to competence tests. However, they could object on the grounds that the tests would be hard to administer, might well lead to increased bitterness and division, and anyway would almost certainly incorporate unfair cultural bias (*vide* the controversy over IQ tests).

I shall not enter this controversy here. I shall not be arguing against ages of consent as such, but against the present ages. My central contention that many of the restrictions currently placed on older children are unacceptable – that teenagers are subject to paternalistic protection and control for too long – is independent of the two liberationist arguments discussed above.

My strategy will be indirect, in that much of what I have to say is about the good reasons for restricting the liberties of younger children. In making explicit these reasons, it becomes apparent that most of them just do not apply to teenagers, and those that do, apply with considerably reduced force.

Babies and Young Children

It is obvious that babies are still in a state to require being taken care of by others – in my first sense – for unless other people minister to them they will just die through cold, disease, or lack of sustenance. They are unable to care for themselves. However, they also need taking care of for reasons not dissimilar to those which justify paternalistic intervention in the lives of the demented and the severely mentally handicapped. None of them has sufficient understanding of the world around them to be able to estimate even the most immediate dangers.

What about younger children? In a paper such as this it is inevitable that the categories used to identify different periods of childhood will be vague (they are not intended to describe discrete phases which can be distinguished with scientific rigour). By younger children I mean all those in the period between babyhood and adolescence, roughly from two to twelve years old.

At the start of this period, it is clear that the child is in need of the care of others in the same senses in which babies need care. However, throughout young childhood enormous changes take place. For example, by the age of ten (if not earlier), children have a reasonable ability to judge the speed of oncoming traffic and may cross even busy roads on their own in comparative safety. Long before this age children are aware of the dangers caused by traffic. Non-mentally-handicapped ten-year-olds are clearly different from babies, the demented, and the severely mentally handicapped in that they can protect themselves against most immediate hazards other than those relating to abuse by other people.

Furthermore, by the age of ten, a non-handicapped child is certainly not physically helpless. There are no developmental obstacles in the way of such people dressing themselves, shopping for and cooking their own food, keeping themselves clean, and so on. They are certainly not dependent in the way the paralysed or severely infirm are. They are not, in that sense, in a state to require being taken care of by others.

Throughout this period children develop a set of likes and dislikes, attractions and aversions, and definite opinions about what they want to do. Yet there are, and nearly everyone thinks there should be, severe paternalistic restrictions on young children, even though children are not, in relevant respects, similar to the demented or the severely mentally handicapped. Are they, perhaps, relevantly similar to schizophrenics, depressives, or manics?

In some respects they are. For example, particularly younger young children are susceptible to violent emotional changes (including temper tantrums). These turbulences might well lead a child to make decisions which will (almost certainly) be regretted very soon after they are made. Early in the morning a seven-year old has an argument with her father. She exclaims, 'I don't want to go to school today.' 'You've got to go', says her father. She goes, and once she has set off for school, is quite happy to go, whereas if she had not gone she would have been bored and miserable at home.

Although young children have an increasingly good understanding of the world around them, their decision-making is especially likely to be impaired by their being in the grip of powerful, changeable emotions, which make it very difficult for them to act on autonomous judgements about what would be the best thing to do (from their own point of view). This is likely to diminish in the later stages of young childhood.

Perhaps the crucial handicap of young children which justifies widespread paternalistic interference in their lives is their inability (through ignorance) to make *informed* decisions about what is best for them. This inability should not, however, be exaggerated. Young children may decide they don't want to go to school on a particular morning on irrational grounds, or they might resist going on a camp because they have no idea what a good time they would have, or they might want to spend all their savings on a useless but well advertised toy. However, they are by no means incapable of making intelligent, rational, comparatively autonomous decisions about a whole range of trivial and important matters. It is all too easy for adults to underestimate the capabilities of children, as is demonstrated in Margaret Donaldson's book *Children's Minds* (1978), which conclusively refutes the Piagetian assumption that children in pre-school and early school years are literally incapable of taking account of the points of view of other people. We should not forget that the cardinal value of liberal democracy requires any power wielder to be able to produce a non-arbitrary reason for any restriction of the liberty of anyone – child or adult.

John Holt, in his polemical work *Escape from Childhood* (1975), proposes that the rights, duties, privileges, and responsibilities of adult citizens should be available to any young person, of whatever age, who wants to make use of them. He includes the following in his comprehensive list:

1 The right to equal treatment at the hands of the law – i.e. the right, in any situation, to be treated no worse than an adult would be.
2 The right to vote, and take full part in political affairs.
3 The right to be legally responsible for one's life and acts.
4 The right to work, for money.
5 The right to privacy.
6 The right to financial independence and responsibility – i.e. the right to own, buy, and sell property, to borrow money, establish credit, sign contracts, etc.
7 The right to direct and manage one's own education.
8 The right to travel, to live away from home, to choose or make one's own home.
9 The right to receive from the state whatever minimum income it may guarantee to adult citizens.

10 The right to make and enter into, on a basis of mutual consent, quasi-familial relationships outside one's immediate family – i.e. the right to seek and choose guardians other than one's own parents and to be legally dependent on them.

11 The right to do, in general, what any adult may legally do. (Holt 1975, p. 15–16).

I get the impression that John Holt's views are taken seriously by very few politicians and educational theorists. Although I do not agree with his proposals (in respect of younger children, at any rate), I think Holt should be treated seriously. He is proposing an enormous increase in the liberty of a group of people whose freedom is currently seriously curtailed. Within the tradition of liberal democratic morality, wherever there is a restriction of liberty, the restricters must (if their restriction is morally acceptable) be able to justify the restriction through non-arbitrary reasons (sexism, racism, and ageism are automatically excluded).

What's Wrong (and Right) with Holt's Proposals

The first proposal differs from the rest, since it simply states that children should not be treated any worse by the law than any adult would be. With this, it is hard to disagree, although there is bound to be controversy about what it means to be treated 'worse'. In particular, the law currently offers certain 'protections' to young people (for example in England children cannot legally be criminals below the age of ten) which some liberationists regard as an unwarranted paternalistic denial of their full status as persons. The last proposal is so general, that it includes, and extends beyond, the others. Taken literally, it is implausibly wide-ranging, and I shall not consider it separately here.

By proposal 5 (the right to privacy) Holt means not only the legal right to be free from arbitrary seizure and search, but, more interestingly, the right to privacy in the child's own home, and the right to privacy of thought. The proposal that children be free from *arbitrary* search and seizure is surely acceptable on the grounds that nobody should be subject to arbitrary treatment. Privacy of thought is problematic, if taken literally, since on the one hand thoughts are inevitably private, whilst on the other, the only way of ensuring that one's thoughts are completely private (in the sense of inaccessible to others) is through complete social isolation, which few would want for more than limited periods. Holt in fact means by 'privacy of thought' the modest idea of being able, without fear of punishment, to tell parents or teachers to mind their own business when they seek personal information from the child about what she has done or how she is feeling. I am not aware of any plausible arguments against children having this right, except that because parents are legally responsible for their children's actions, they could arguably have a right within the scope of this legal responsibility to know what their children have been getting up to (this may raise questions about how broad this scope should be).

The other right to privacy which Holt speaks of is a right to a private space. What he specifically discusses is a child's right to exclude other people (notably parents) from his bedroom. This is clearly not a right which children in impoverished families, who have to share a single room, would enjoy. Holt is not, however, arguing that everyone should have their own room, but rather that children should have just as much right as adults to their own private space. Furthermore, I am sure that Holt would concede the reasonable point that nobody has an *absolute* right to exclude all others from their private space – for their private space might contain a great threat to others, who would then be entitled to defend themselves. However, the fact that they are children should not be used as a reason for denying people a private space.

This is all very plausible, but Holt's proposal glosses over the fact that children, especially younger children, are likely to be relevantly different from the older people with whom they might cohabit. For example, young children are particularly likely not to look after their own (or other people's) property. Suppose you, the parent, suspected your child was playing with matches in his own room; I believe you should have the right to enter the room, even against his wishes, and to stop him from behaving dangerously, by coercion if he was not open to persuasion. This right is most likely to be used against young children, because they are particularly likely not to realise the dangerous consequences of their experiments (accidents involving young children in the home occur with alarming frequency). However, the intrusion into the child's private room is not ultimately justified by appeal to the fact that he is a child, but rather to the child's ignorance of danger, and to the likely awful consequences of non-intrusion. One should be allowed to go into any cohabitee's bedroom if one believed with good grounds that the person was likely, through ignorance or incompetence, to endanger himself, the property, or other members of the household.

Holt's other proposals (2 to 4, and 6 to 10) are all for enabling rights whose recognition would allow any child who wanted to, to make life-affecting decisions which are currently unavailable to children. These proposals are far more controversial than 1 and 5, since they could have dramatic effects on the lives of everyone.

For example, the enfranchisement of all children who wanted the vote would, so it is argued, greatly affect the manifestoes of any political party which would have a chance of being elected. The right to buy and sell property, to borrow money, establish credit, and so on, would greatly affect the business system, perhaps by making business people very reluctant to continue selling on credit terms. The right to live away from home might well seriously weaken the already shaky foundations of family life. Whether or not any or all of these consequences would be on balance harmful or beneficial is a difficult question, but nevertheless one which should not be ignored.

Of special relevance to liberal democratic theory is whether or not the restrictions on children's liberty deny to children an equal right to the maximum degree of self-determination compatible with a similar right for others. If the restrictions currently imposed on the liberty of children are to be justifiable in liberal-democratic terms, it must be the case either that the restrictions actually protect children's rights to self-determination, or that they are necessary to protect the equal rights of others to self-determination.

Protection of Children's Rights to Self-determination

There is a temptation among those concerned with the protection of children's rights to assume that any restriction on their liberty which does not apply to adults must be wrong, on the grounds that it constitutes an unfair attack on the child's right to self-determination. But this assumption is unwarranted.

First, the decisions of young children in the restricted areas are likely to be especially defective. For example, a four-year-old is unlikely to appreciate the consequences of assuming 'financial independence and responsibility', despite having a desire to be able to spend money. A young child is, in this respect, similar to a mentally handicapped adult.

Second, it is particularly likely that a young child would, if unrestricted in the relevant areas, act in a way which, in the long-term, would be antithetical to her self-determination. There are two ways in which this could be so: by failure to develop the capacity for self-determination, or by creating circumstances in which the opportunities for exercising self-determined choices are curtailed.

Mill's consequentialist arguments against paternalistic interference with autonomous choices in order to protect the agent – even where such interference has as a goal the promotion of the agent's overall autonomy – have considerable plausibility. However, these arguments apply with much less force to young children, because their choices are likely to be far less autonomous than those made by older people. This is partly because of their ignorance of the nature and consequences of complex institutional acts such as voting or buying goods on credit, and partly due to their particular susceptibility to violent and frequently changing emotions.

Let us now briefly consider voting. My two-year-old from time to time utters the words 'Maggie, out, out, out!' I think he picked up the phrase from observing a political demonstration, possibly on television. Suppose we agree with Holt that my son, like anyone else, should be allowed to vote, as long as he wants to. It would be comparatively easy (I think) for me, the parent, to derive a notional consent from him that he would like to vote, and to persuade him that he should vote for a particular candidate (perhaps the one who is also inclined to say 'Maggie, out, out, out!'). Although my two-year-old could probably be taught to put a cross in the right place on the ballot form, it is by no means clear that such an act would constitute a genuine choice to help elect a particular candidate to parliament.

Or consider the 'right to direct and manage one's own education'. A child reaching the age of five (the age at which most children have to start school) is more than likely to be reluctant to go to school, particularly on the first day, and during the first month of school. Such a child might, if asked and allowed to decide, choose not to go to school, preferring instead the familiar security of home. Once again, such a choice would be severely impaired, because such a child would have no grasp of what she would be missing in rejecting education. The child's decision to stay at home would not constitute a meaningful choice to direct her own education.

Although it is not clear what the effects of their non-autonomous voting would be for young child voters' long-term autonomy, it is clear that allowing five-year-olds to decide whether they will go to school and what they will learn would actually reduce their chances of *developing* autonomy. Furthermore, a lack of education is most likely to reduce a person's chances for the *exercise* of autonomy later. Allowing young children complete financial control of their resources, although

it would hasten the development of their autonomy, might well lead
to autonomy-reducing impoverishment. For a young child is particularly likely to spend unwisely, having a severely misguided conception of financial realities.

If there is clear evidence that a person's intended choice is seriously
impaired, and would likely lead to a reduction in his overall autonomy,
then it is not inconsistent with a proper respect for his right to self-
determination to restrict his choice (or choices) in the area of incompetence, *provided the intervention is not a greater threat to the person's
autonomy than would be the impaired choice.* I believe that for many areas
of young children's lives these conditions are met, although for each
area where paternalistic restrictions are being considered, it is necessary to ask seriously whether this is so.

Protection of Adults' Rights to Self-determination

The liberal-democratic principle requires that *all* citizens have an
equal right to maximal self-determination. This entails that it may be
legitimate to restrict one group's self-determination to protect that of
other people. This is uncontroversial, and justifies laws against coercion and the imprisonment of one citizen by another. Its rationale –
a belief in the vital importance of self-determination – also legitimates
restrictions on the freedom of those who unwittingly may threaten
other people's self-determination.

If young children (whose health and safety requires them to be
looked after during the day) were able to direct and manage their
own education, they would (inadvertently perhaps) restrict their parents' (usually their mothers') chances to exercise autonomy throughout the day. If young children were allowed to receive from the state
the minimum income guaranteed to adult citizens, this would have
to be at the expense of some adults who would receive less or who
could lose their employment altogether. The ability to buy goods on
credit is an interesting case. If young children were granted the legal
right to buy goods on credit, it is very likely that the proportion of
bad debts to those who provided those goods would increase, since
young children are especially unlikely to realise properly the implications of buying on credit (how many young children ask their parents for very large gifts, promising to pay them back out of their
pocket money, when in reality repayment by this means would be
impossible?). The costs of bad debts have to be borne by all those who
engage in transactions of goods on credit.

It could be argued that the restrictions on the self-determination of adults which would follow from the extension of adult rights to young children are far less than the present restrictions on children. If one group has almost no chances for self-determination, while another has very good chances, does not justice require, where appropriate, a redistribution in favour of the former – and are not young children, in this respect, the worst off of all? Consider an analogy with slaves. Emancipation of slaves reduced the autonomy of the slave-owners, but was required by justice for the slaves.

The obvious rejoinder to this argument is that the analogy with slavery is misleading. For childhood, unlike slavery, is a phase through which all adults have passed. The present restriction of the self-determination of children is not a case of one group of people being badly treated throughout their lives in order that another can gain an unfair advantage, since, if we consider people's whole lives, the paternalistic restrictions on children apply equally to everyone.

For this reason, I think the argument in favour of greater self-determination for children needs more than just the appeal to equal rights for all which characterises anti-sexist and anti-racist arguments. It also rests on the specifically liberal principle that more extensive self-determination is better than less – and hence that people should have the right to the *most extensive* self-determination compatible with a similar self-determination for others. People would have greater autonomy throughout their whole lives if, as children, they were less restricted by paternalistic intervention.

The argument against Holt's suggestion that the full range of adult self-determination rights should be extended to *any* child who wants such rights ultimately rests on one or both of the following claims:

1 Extending these rights to all such children would not maximise the children's overall self-determination (throughout their whole lives);
2 Extending these rights to all such children would violate the equal rights of others to maximal self-determination.

Because each of these claims appeals to consequences, any use of one of them is open to empirical challenge, and a philosophical essay such as this cannot enter into detailed empirical argument. Having said that, I believe it is most likely that many of the restrictions on the freedom of young children could genuinely be justified by appeal to one or other of the claims. There are two main reasons for this. First, young children cannot understand the social, political, and economic institutions which govern a complex society. Second, young children are especially subject to domination by violent emotional changes. The consequences of these limitations have been outlined above. They include the facts that young children find it hard, literally, to look after themselves, that they are especially likely to resist autonomy-enhancing opportunities, and that they would be especially likely to make unwise financial commitments without understanding the nature or consequences of what they were doing. These points may be summarised in the claim that young children can be said to have a coherent plan of life only in a Pickwickian sense.

Teenagers

I said at the beginning that my main concern was to argue that teenagers are treated in a way which is inconsistent with the liberal-democratic principle of equal maximal self-determination. I have so far said very little about teenagers. This is because my main argument is indirect. I have assumed that any restriction on anyone's liberty requires a non-arbitrary justification. I have argued that there are good reasons for rejecting John Holt's radical proposals to extend adults' rights and responsibilities to *all* children who want them. This is because of the serious and unavoidable impairments to the autonomy of the decision-making of young children. To render my main claim plausible, it is necessary to point out that teenagers are in fact subject to severe paternalistic restriction, and that arguments for restricting the liberty of young children do not apply to teenagers with sufficient force to justify present practice.

Currently there are severe restrictions on the liberty of teenagers to do as they choose. In the United Kingdom and the United States, nobody under eighteen is enfranchised. Children have to attend school until at least sixteen (unless their parents can demonstrate that they are providing a suitable alternative education). It is impossible in England for people under eighteen to buy goods on credit without the consent of their parents. Girls under sixteen are held in law to be incapable of consenting to sexual intercourse (as are homosexual boys under twenty-one). Children under sixteen are not allowed to gain full-time employment, nor are they allowed to leave home. These are but a few of many restrictions on the liberty of teenagers. Although there are some age-based restrictions on the liberty of eighteen- and nineteen-year-olds, the major restrictions on teenagers are on the under sixteens (especially in regard to sexual freedom, choice of abode, compulsory education, and inability to seek full-time employment), and the under eighteens (especially in regard to financial independence and the vote). It is upon these that I shall concentrate, partly because eighteen- and nineteen-year-olds are subject to far fewer restrictions, and partly because it is doubtful whether most people would regard them as children anyway.

I believe that many of the current paternalistic restrictions on the under-sixteens and under-eighteens are unwarranted, because these people do not suffer from the disabling conditions which justify widespread paternalism for younger children. I am sure that this is true in regard to the unavoidable ignorance of younger children, somewhat less so in regard to the problem of emotional instability.

Here are some examples which are intended to show that the argument for paternalistic restriction of younger children, which appeals to their unavoidable ignorance, does not apply to teenagers, even younger teenagers.

Ignorance

Whereas five-year-olds have no understanding of the nature and purpose of school, teenagers, after eight years of schooling, cannot seriously be said not to know what school is like. Many teenagers find school irrelevant to their interests, do not enjoy it, and apparently gain very little from it. The results are widespread disaffection within the classroom and high levels of truancy. The disaffection in the classroom makes it nigh impossible for teachers to encourage critical enquiry in their pupils, the paramount aim being quiet, if not peace. This seriously limits the chance for school to help pupils to develop their own powers of self-determination, and indeed leads to widespread truancy (see Jeffs 1986).

Closely related to compulsory education is the ban on full-time employment for children. One of the main justifications for restricting child labour was to protect children from the most appalling exploitation by adults during the industrial revolution. Once again, whilst it is true that five-year-olds are not developmentally capable of understanding what is entailed in a labour contract, teenagers face no such obstacle. Admittedly they are likely to be less experienced than, say, twenty-year-olds but, equally, twenty-year-olds are likely to be less experienced than thirty-year-olds. If teenagers are especially likely to be exploited by unscrupulous adult employers, justice would require that the exploiters rather than their victims be restricted. If people between the ages of thirteen and sixteen were allowed to seek full-time employment, they would certainly need some protection against exploitation, perhaps in the form of a minimum wage and rigorous health and safety standards. Admittedly this would restrict the liberty of the employers, but it would be justified in the name of maximal equal rights of self-determination.

What about the right to live away from home? Again, it is obvious that teenagers are developmentally capable of making a genuine choice to live away from home and of managing to look after themselves. In her disturbing book about child prostitution Gitta Sereny (1986) reports that:

In America, an annual figure of between 750,000 and one million runaways is generally accepted (the media has often inflated it). The West Germans report around 20,000 runaways under sixteen.... In England and Wales... the figure of juveniles reported missing fluctuates from year to year between 13,000 and 15,000. (p. xiii)

Most runaways do return within forty-eight hours. However, in the United States and West Germany, ten percent apparently remain runaways for indefinite periods. According to Gitta Sereny a lot of them drift into child prostitution, frequently owing to financial necessity. The fact that most survive even that extraordinarily harsh and dangerous life is a testimony to their strength, ingenuity, and flexibility. If teenagers below the present age of majority were *allowed* to live where they chose, the tragic problem of the runaways would almost certainly be reduced.

Closely related to the right to live where one chooses is the right to express one's sexuality. It is illegal for a boy to have sexual intercourse with a girl under sixteen, even if she wants a sexual relationship with him. This is 'justified' on the grounds that the ignorance of younger teenagers makes it impossible for them to give genuine consent to sex. Once again, teenagers are in a very different situation from young children. It is quite usual for a girl to reach sexual maturity at thirteen or fourteen and to want a sexual relationship at that age. Admittedly, teenagers are comparatively inexperienced, and they may be ignorant about contraception, the risks of pregnancy, the nature of sexual feelings, and the burdens of motherhood. The ignorance could be remedied by fuller and more sensitive sex education. The inexperience is remedied – by experience.

The strongest argument in favour of an age of consent of sixteen for girls is the need to protect them from sexual exploitation. Once again, there is an injustice in the restriction having to fall on the young person because of the possible delinquency of adults. A joint working party on pregnant schoolgirls and schoolgirl mothers advocated the abolition of a general age of consent:

The law should simply prescribe that consent will be presumed to be absent if the subject of the alleged sexual assault, irrespective of his or her age, is, for reasons of physical or psychological immaturity or because he/she is suffering from a mental disability, incapable of giving real consent. (Joint Working Party on Pregnant Schoolgirls 1979, para. 314)

Although such a change might be very difficult to put into practice, at least it has the merit of giving young teenagers the chance to exercise more control over their own lives.

Finally, let us consider the vote. Whilst two-year-olds are developmentally incapable of understanding what an election is, there is no developmental reason why thirteen-year-olds could not register a meaningful vote. A study by Olive Stevens (1982) showed that, by the age of 11, children from a wide variety of backgrounds were able to understand key political concepts and issues. Admittedly many teenagers are ignorant of even the main political issues of the day; but where the ignorance is due to lack of education rather than to developmental obstacles, it is wrong for it to be used as a basis for perpetual disenfranchisement of a group. An educational system which gave top priority to self-determination could include political education (different from indoctrination) within first schools as part of a programme to encourage people to take an interest in controlling their own lives.

Emotions

As I argued above, one of the most powerful reasons for restricting the liberty of younger children is that they are especially prone to domination by violent emotional change, which severely vitiates the autonomy of their choices. Does this reason not apply to teenagers?

It should, first of all, be conceded that adolescence (roughly the period between thirteen and seventeen) is a period of emotional upheaval and very intense feelings (see Hadfield 1962, ch. 5). However, the kind of emotional instability during adolescence is relevantly different from that which besets younger children.

Younger children are particularly subject to whimsicality in that suddenly they desperately want something for no good reason, and then equally suddenly lose interest in it. Although they seek gratification, the objects of their gratification change very rapidly, and cannot, as I claimed above, be said to have sufficient cohesion to constitute a plan of life. The aim of such a plan is to 'permit the harmonious satisfaction of [a person's] interests' (Rawls 1972, p. 93).

By the time a child is thirteen, he or she is very likely to have sufficient stability and conceptual competence to be able to have the objectives of a plan of life. An important reason for the intense emotionality during adolescence is the desire to assert one's own independence, to live – for the first time – according to one's own plan of life. Although a person's conceptions of what constitutes a good life are likely to change more during adolescence than later in life, the changes are not so rapid or whimsical as to invalidate the claim that teenagers do have a plan of life. After all, adolescence is a time of great seriousness, and life-affecting decisions need not be taken for frivolous reasons. And let us not forget that for adults the criteria of *competence* for making one's own life-affecting decisions are weaker than those for making choices which would, on reflection, be the *best*.

In the end the case for extending adult rights and responsibilities to teenagers (or reintroducing them), rests on the claim that such a strategy would, overall, increase people's control over their own lives. It would be impossible to demonstrate such a claim in a philosophical essay. I do hope, however, that this paper has shown that the claim should be taken seriously, and that the onus of proof must rest firmly on the shoulders of those who wish to maintain our present paternalistic restrictions on teenagers.

NOTE

1 I am indebted to Roger Fellows for this argument. See also B. Williams (1985).

REFERENCES

Donaldson, M. (1978). *Children's Minds* (London: Fontana).

Franklin, B., ed. (1986). *The Rights of Children* (Oxford: Blackwell).

Hadfield, J. A. (1962). *Childhood and Adolescence* (Harmondsworth: Penguin).

Holt, J. (1975). *Escape From Childhood: The Needs and Rights of Children* (Harmondsworth: Penguin).

Jeffs, T. (1986). 'Children's Rights at School', in *The Rights of Children*, ed. Franklin.

Joint Working Party on Pregnant Schoolgirls and Schoolgirl Mothers (1979). *Pregnant at School* (National Council for One-Parent Families/Community Development Trust).

Lindley, R. (1986). *Autonomy* (London: Macmillan).

Mill, J. S. (1859). *On Liberty*. All quotations from John Stuart Mill are taken from *Utilitarianism, On Liberty, and Considerations on Representative Government* (1972) (London: J. M. Dent).

Mill, J. S. (1861). *Utilitarianism.* In *Utilitarianism, On Liberty, and Considerations on Representative Government* (1972) (London: J. M. Dent).

Rawls, J. (1972). *A Theory of Justice* (Oxford: Oxford University Press).

Sereny, G. (1986). *The Hidden Children* (London: Pan Books).

Stevens, O. (1982). *Children Talking Politics: Political Learning in Childhood* (Oxford: Martin Robertson).

Williams, B. (1985). 'Which slopes are slippery?' In *Moral Dilemmas in Modern Medicine*, ed. M. Lockwood (Oxford: Oxford University Press).

6

Justice between Generations

GEOFFREY SCARRE

1 Justice and the Young

What kind of social, political, and economic relationships should exist
between members of part-contemporary generations within the same
society? What kind of demands for support or services can older
citizens justly make of younger ones, and what claims can young
people legitimately lay against their elders for a share in the rights
and the privileges, the powers and the wealth of their common society?

Such questions are part of a complex of interrelated problems about
justice between generations. Other questions, which have perhaps
attracted more attention from philosophers in recent years, concern
the relations between *non*-contemporary generations: What sort of
provision should we make for people who will be alive after we are
dead? What sort of world must we leave for the twenty-first, or the
twenty-fifth, century? My limited concern in the present paper is to
enquire what justice requires for the young, and particularly young
adults, in their dealings with their older part-contemporaries. Given
the intimate connection of the issues in this area, other problems of
intergenerational justice will inevitably be raised in the course of the
discussion, but subordinately to this main theme.

My topic has not figured very high on the agenda of most political
philosophers. It is true that over the centuries there has been discussion, often rather complacent, of the correct relations between parents
and children within the family setting, while a favourite traditional,
if now somewhat old-fashioned, question for political theorists has
concerned the extent to which the structure of the just state mirrors
that of the just family. But more systematic attention to the moral
and political implications of the fact of generational flux has been less
common, despite this flux being one of the most familiar features of
our human life. The co-existence of people of different ages within

I should like to thank Richard Lindley for invaluable criticisms of an earlier draft of
this essay.

the same community, whose needs and interests are not necessarily compatible, actually raises sharp questions of justice which do not deserve to be neglected. Yet many writers have either treated these questions merely *en passant*, or left what they thought of them (if anything) to be inferred from their general principles.

In *A Theory of Justice*, John Rawls comments that the problem of justice between generations (he has chiefly in mind, I think, justice for people who do not yet exist) 'subjects any ethical theory to severe if not impossible tests' (1972, p. 284). Why should the subject of intergenerational justice be thought to raise such peculiar difficulty? (Aren't most problems in political philosophy very hard?) The root of the trouble is that it is easier, and therefore more common, to design a theory of justice to accommodate the requirements of a fixed personnel than a changing one; to theorise, in other words, as if all we had to deal with were the distributions of goods, political rights, and privileges among a population which was conveniently static in membership. Thus, most theories of distributive justice attempt to describe morally defensible recipes for allocating goods, desirable honours, and other privileges in the normal situation wherein demand outstrips supply (if the supply of such goods were infinite, there would be no need for such a theory, for each individual could acquire as much as he liked while leaving as much and as good for others). Usually theorists of distributive justice talk as if the task were to adjudicate between the conflicting claims to those goods and positions made by a single, unvarying set of people who are quite artificially supposed to represent all the claimants who need to be considered.

But the personnel of a human society is not fixed and unchanging; people are constantly being born, growing up, aging, and dying; generations succeed each other, and the identity of claimants to a society's goods and privileges is altering all the time. An empirically adequate theory of distributive justice needs to have a theory of *re*distributive justice as an integral component; it needs to describe fair mechanisms for transferring positions and goods from older to younger members of society. There would be no call for an account of redistributive justice if the supply of things in demand were sufficiently great for the young to be allocated at least what they needed (and more, perhaps) without any interference with the holdings of their seniors. Unfortunately, older and younger people must be regarded as competitors for goods and positions in short supply, and the situation from the point of view of justice is complicated by the fact that the young may make claims for things which their elders had earlier acquired quite justly.

How are such claims to be received? Are demands to benefit from redistributions to be turned down on the ground that what is justly acquired by someone is his to keep unless or until it is his pleasure to alienate it? Political thinkers, even those of a liberal stamp, have sometimes talked as if this were so. Locke said that men are, by their natures, in 'a *State of perfect Freedom* to order their Actions, and dispose of their Possessions, and Persons as they think fit, within the bounds of the Law of Nature, without asking leave, or depending on the Will of any other Man' (1698, p. 309). But a principle of this strength is very hard to defend. To see this, consider the case of refugees driven by war or persecution to seek sanctuary within the territory of some other (non-poverty-stricken) society. No matter how just the previous distribution of goods within that host society had been, it would be monstrous if its citizens refused to grant the refugees even the bare necessities of life on the ground that previously just allocations of goods remained just. But the young people of a society have a *prima facie* much more extensive claim than refugees could have to a substantial share of the goods and advantages of that society. They are not outsiders temporarily thrust on a community, but insiders growing up within it who will become part of its citizen body. In a property-owning democracy, the young must be integrated into the ranks of enfranchised, property-owning citizens if the society is to continue at all; they need to feel that they have a stake in their community, and that its interests in large degree coincide with their own. The problem of fair distribution within a society is therefore an essentially diachronic one, demanding a recognition of the constant flux of legitimate claimants for goods and privileges.

This is not meant to imply that the problem of justice for the young is merely one of fairness in distribution. Justice between part-contemporary generations requires not only an equitable pattern of allocation and reallocation of goods, honours, and privileges, but also that young people be given a fair share in the decision-making processes of their society, both as these specifically affect themselves and as they regulate the life of the whole community. Here, too, the root of the difficulty is that the young enter a world whose character has been determined by their forbears; its power structures are already in place and the capacity of a new generation to frame things anew is severely limited. Once again it is easy to spot the inadequacy of much political theorising to cope with the problems of the young; again one sees philosophers of politics forgetting to take account of the fact of changing membership of society, and of the built-in advantages which older-established citizens have over younger ones.

From the point of view of a young adult, what is the cash value of the claim to which western democracies pay lip-service that there can be no just government without the consent of the governed? There is 'nothing more evident', wrote Locke, 'than that Creatures of the same species and rank, promiscuously born to all the same advantages of Nature, and the use of the same faculties, shall also be equal one amongst another without Subordination or Subjection' (1698, p. 309). In practice, a young citizen knows little but subordination and subjection. Nowadays, admittedly, he obtains in his late teens the important right to vote for national and local government representatives. But he has had no say in the general political, social, and economic arrangements of his society, which have been presented to him as a given; he has been party to no social contract which has brought these arrangements into being, and his capacity to mould them closer to his heart's desire is very slight. Those young people who do eventually rise to positions of power and influence are, in fact, normally those who are most content to accept and work within those power structures which they have had no part in making.

The young person's impotency to settle much about the conditions under which he lives is especially apparent when he comes to seek paid employment. In contemporary circumstances, he may be altogether frustrated in his search for work, and even if he finds some, it may well not be the sort he desired. Once in work, he must follow his employer's instructions and he has little say about the character, the working conditions, the rewards, or the objectives of his labour. That many young people do not rebel against these limitations on freedom – regarding them, perhaps, as inescapable – should not be taken to imply that they tacitly consent to the restrictions placed on them. For genuine consent presumes unconstrained choice, which is notably absent here.

At this point someone might object that it is wrong, or at best misleading, to place so much emphasis on the disadvantages suffered by the young. Many members of senior generations are socially and economically underprivileged too, the young having no monopoly of disadvantage, while it is not true that all young people are worse off than all older people. Reshaping the conditions within which they live and work is as impossible for many people in middle life as it is for most of the young, while the oldest members of society (particularly those from the less affluent social classes) often have to face serious financial and other hardships.

So why single out the young for special attention here? Partly because the disadvantages of the young have too often gone unnoticed by philosophers, while the problems of the poor and the underprivileged in general have been discussed many times before. I do not wish to argue that the young are the only subjects of injustice, and I do not deny that some young adults, owing to their special talents, opportunities, or favourable family background, may quickly overtake many older citizens in wealth and social influence. But I suggest that there are certain obstacles – social, political, and economic – which unjustly hinder the course that most young people travel as they assume their positions in the citizen body. These obstacles are a legitimate, and should be an important, concern of political philosophy. (So too, incidentally, should be the problems faced by the old, though they are not the topic of the present essay.)

Moreover, many of the disadvantages faced by older citizens are nothing more nor less than the consequences of the disadvantages they suffered when young. Those who fail in early years to gain a satisfactory foothold on the social ladder may find themselves forever excluded from the more desirable social positions. The economic and social subservience endured by many middle-aged or elderly people is very often not at all independent of their constrained position in earlier years. Lack of autonomy to choose one's road entails a lack of autonomy to settle one's destination. Those looking for ways to promote greater justice in society might do worse than to begin by tackling the problems of the young, from which many of the problems of older people flow.

2 The Social Contract and the Flux of Generations

The facts of the succession of generations and of the presence of part-contemporary people within a society pose problems which political philosophy cannot ignore if it is to be adequate to the real human condition, and not content simply to prescribe arrangements for idealised and non-existent societies. Yet the problems of intergenerational justice are easier to indicate than to solve. It is easy to say that political philosophers should show more awareness of the need to accommodate their theories to the passage of generations through a society. It is much more difficult to provide a detailed blueprint of acceptable social arrangements.

I shall concentrate on the problem of justice for the young as it presents itself to political philosophy of a liberal stamp. Liberals, I shall assume, are keen to maximise freedom, but as they look upon individuals as morally of equal value (so that one person's freedom is not intrinsically less worth promoting than another's), they are likely to favour a strong degree of equality in society and the restriction of an individual's freedom only where its indulgence would constrain the like freedom of other people. This, of course, is a very rough and ready statement of liberalism; it will be refined a little as I proceed. In stressing the importance of equality to the liberal conception, I am distinguishing liberalism from what may better be termed 'libertarianism'.[1] A liberal's ideals are unlikely to be realised in a society in which there is not a strong measure of distributional and participatory equality among the citizens. On the face of it, then, a liberal's principles should encourage him to favour a set of social arrangements which have a tendency to equalise the distribution of goods and privileges among younger and older people. He will wish to remove or reduce the constraints on the freedom of the young that arise from the fact that, in general (though there are exceptions), they have an inferior rate of occupation of positions of social and economic power.

But does this mean that a liberal ought to be committed to large-scale redistributions of wealth and positions of influence from older to younger people? Should he be willing not merely to moderate, but entirely to discard, Locke's principle that what a person has justly acquired he is entitled to keep? Need he believe that an employer has no right to lay down unilaterally the conditions and objectives of a young apprentice's labour, but should consult him about these in recognition of his right to self-determination? Should he favour a form of society which is far less directive of its young people than most western states generally are, one which enables the young to play a much larger role in the management of governmental, educational, cultural, religious, and other institutions – e.g. by such processes as accelerated promotion, and abandoning the custom of making the young wait for dead men's shoes? Possibly a consistent liberal ought to adopt such policies, but liberalism to date has not been conspicuous for holding them.

In considering how a consistent liberalism should treat the young, we begin to see why Rawls said that the problem of justice between generations presents almost impossible tests for an ethical theory. Like most political philosophies, liberalism seems to have been designed with little thought for the existence of the young of the species, and with scant concern for the fact of generational change. That favourite theoretical model of liberalism, the social contract, has an inbuilt tendency to lead attention away from the idea that subjects of justice are changing individuals, and to represent them, quite artificially, as a fixed population who determine just social arrangements by agreeing on a set of these equitable with respect to their own interests. The point here is not that actual societies have not generally (or maybe ever) been brought into existence by such a contractual device; the complaint is rather that, historical or hypothetical, a social contract pictured as drawn up by a single set of self-interested individuals at a point in time is not a sensitive device for identifying principles of just relations between members of different generations.

This problem for the liberal contract notion besets it in all its versions, from that of the judicious Hooker to that of the no less judicious Rawls. The former had an interesting answer to give to the question of why a social contract made by men at one time should be binding on their successors:

And to be commanded, we do consent, when that Society whereof we are part, hath at any time before consented, without revoking the same after by the like Universal Agreement. Wherefore, as any Mans Deed past is good as long as himself continueth; so the Act of a Publick Society of Men done Five hundred years sithence, standeth as theirs, who presently are of the same Societies, because Corporations are Immortal; we were alive in our Predecessors, and they in their Successors do live still. (1676, p. 88)

This is ingenious, but unconvincing. If some genuine sense could be given to the conceit that we were alive in our predecessors, who made certain contractual arrangements for the society of which we too are part, then it might be possible to say that the successors to a set of original contractors were themselves a party to the contract. There does not, however, seem to be any remotely literal sense in which we were alive in our predecessors (note that Hooker uses the term 'predecessors' rather than 'ancestors', but the complaint stands even if we take into account the genetic connection between ourselves and our ancestors), nor does Hooker's phrasing have any very obviously compelling significance read metaphorically. It is in addition a complete non sequitur to conclude that the inhabitants of societies are immortal because societies are.

Rawls is considerably more realistic in his recognition of the problem of obtaining justice for the generations which succeed the generation which makes the contract. In the Rawlsian 'original position', the contracting parties are in a state of ignorance as to their social position, their personal talents, temperament, and abilities, and any other features which, if known to them, would be likely to bias their choice of principles of justice towards their own special interests (1972, sect. 24). Among the things they do not know is to which generation they belong – though they *do* know that they are contemporaries, and are entering society at the same time (ibid., pp. 137, 292). But now, as

Rawls acknowledges, there seems nothing in the nature of the contract to encourage them to think about the interests of members of later generations:

Since the persons in the original position know that they are contemporaries ...they can favor their generation by refusing to make any sacrifices at all for their successors; they simply acknowledge the principle that no one has a duty to save for posterity. (Ibid., p. 140)

Though Rawls is specifically discussing the issue of how a just savings principle might be motivated, his problem is one aspect of a broader one for contract theories. Why should the contracting parties worry about the interests of later people and agree to constraints on their own capacities to acquire and retain goods, positions, and powers for the sake of subsequent generations?

In Rawls's view, it is necessary to step outside the basic contract structure to cope with this difficulty. There has to be added in a 'motivation assumption' to the effect that people will naturally care for their immediate successors: 'The parties are regarded as representing family lines, say, with ties of sentiment between successive generations' (ibid., p. 292; cf. p. 140). If they possess this sentiment of benevolence towards their children, the contracting parties will ensure that the contract they agree to is not biased entirely in favour of their own generation.

It is reasonable to agree with Rawls that such benevolent feelings do exist, and that they can play a role in restraining senior generations from neglecting the interests of younger ones. But it is doubtful whether feelings of this kind can provide anything like an adequate guarantee of justice for the young. There are several considerations to fuel scepticism here. To begin with, the love or concern which people have for members of later generations tends to be directed fairly narrowly on individuals within their own family lines (as Rawls himself seems to admit) rather than on younger members of society in general. It follows that the protective impact of the benevolent impulses will also be narrowly focused, and if people feel disinclined to exploit or neglect their own descendants, they may have no such qualms with regard to those of others. Most young people are not one's own descendants or members of one's own family, and an original contractor's desire to agree to arrangements which protect his own children may well be overborne by his desire to be allowed to exploit or neglect the much greater number of other people's. In any case, not everyone has children, and those who do do not always hold them in any very special affection. But even where people genuinely love their children and other younger members of their families, that love may not be enough to prevent their failing to allow its objects full scope for self-determination. Even young adult offspring can often be subjected to heavy pressure to maintain their lifestyles in conformity with the patterns laid down by older relatives.

Historical experience offers further powerful evidence that Rawls's 'motivation assumption' is too weak to do the work he requires of it. Sentiments of benevolence towards the young have not prevented a great deal of harsh treatment and exploitation of even the youngest and most vulnerable members of the community. The sorry tale of child labour under appalling conditions in factory and sweatshop, of child beating, child prostitution, neglect and starvation of children, even deliberate infanticide, has not yet come to its close, though admittedly in the western democracies and in some other parts of the world child abuse is less prevalent than it once was. Benevolence and affectionate sentiments are too slim a foundation for justice; too many people are without them for too much of the time, or find them smothered by their self-interest. Moralists and some psychologists have spoken of generalised feelings of benevolence or inclinations towards altruism which human beings have to one another, yet the historical record is full of instances of inhumanity.

Still, most parents probably do love their children and, as Locke pointed out, this serves to temper the rigour with which parental power might otherwise be wielded; the 'Inclinations of Tenderness and Concern' for their children which God has implanted in parents will lead them to deal justly and gently with their offspring (1698, p. 352). (Locke, incidentally, says that these inclinations easily pass over into unjustified indulgence of children by parents [ibid., p. 355]; if this is so, then parents are likely to favour unjustly their own children at the expense of other people's.) One would expect that if parents love their children, they will attempt to deal fairly with them by their lights; and that is just as well for the Lockean scheme, as the rights which it allows parents to wield over their offspring are considerable. Here again the problem surfaces of the impotence of post-contractual generations to alter the terms of the contract which governs the social arrangements which affect them. Parents lose their authority over their children once the latter have reached the 'Age of Discretion' (at twenty-one, or sooner) (ibid, p. 349), and after that time, says Locke, the son is 'equally free' with his father (ibid, p. 350). Unfortunately, this equality of liberty is more formal than substantial.

The trouble is that while Locke is keen to emphasise that it is entirely up to the young person newly arrived at years of discretion whether or not he will consent to the rules which are the conditions of entry to the citizen body of a society (ibid., pp. 358, 394), in reality he has little choice but to accept them – if he does not agree to them, where else is he to go? His position is not like that of a contracting party in the 'original position' as construed by either Locke or Rawls. He does not help to make the rules, but is faced with a take-it-or-leave-it choice: if he does not like the rules, he can go elsewhere in search of better. But in the present day, as in Locke's, moving around the world in search of a more eligible social dispensation is more easily proposed than accomplished.

Locke was well aware of the constraints to which the young adult's dependent and suppliant position subjected him, but seems to have been quite unworried by them. Young people who have reached years of discretion may indeed 'choose what Society they will join themselves to, what Common-wealth they will put themselves under' (ibid., p. 358). But – 'if they will enjoy the *Inheritance* of their Ancestors, they must take it on the same terms their Ancestors had it, and submit to all the Conditions annex'd to such a Possession' (ibid.). Locke saw quite plainly that by placing conditions on the acquisition of distributable goods, older generations who hold those goods can exert powerful control over younger ones who seek a share in them:

By this Power indeed Fathers oblige their Children to Obedience to themselves, even when they are past Minority, and most commonly too subject them to this or that Political Power. But neither of these by any peculiar right of *Fatherhood*, but by the Reward they have in their hands to inforce and recompence such a Compliance. (Ibid.).

Quite so; and Locke remarks without adverse comment that a father has the power to bestow his property 'with a more sparing or liberal hand, according as the Behaviour of this or that Child hath comported with his Will and Humour.' He drily adds that 'This is no small Tye on the Obedience of Children' (ibid., pp. 357, 358).[2] The Lockean parent loves his child; but he also loves himself, and is determined not to yield to his offspring's demand for goods and privileges except in return for obedience and service on parental terms.

Locke, then, saw young people as having the right to contract into, or to remain outside of, the citizen body of a society, but he ascribed them no rights to change or question the terms of their admission – terms which, as a reflection of the original contract which determined the social arrangements, tend to favour the interests of the present possessors of power and property. That this places the young wholly at the mercy of older citizens appears not to have troubled Locke, presumably in part because he trusted the existence of parental affection to guard against gross abuse or exploitation. Nevertheless, his picture of the father insistent on his adult offspring's conformity with his 'Will and Humour' is not a specially reassuring one, and his theory fails to address properly the problem of what protection the young person has against all older citizens other than his own parents. It is likely, too, that Locke was reconciled to his doctrine of young citizenship by his respect for the rights of property. If people who have acquired property by just means can do with it what they wish, it follows that they can bequeath it to, or alienate it from, whomever they like and on whatever conditions they choose to. Potential recipients are not obliged, of course, to agree to those conditions, but they do not, in Locke's view, have the right to insist on their modification.[3]

3 The Implications of Liberal Equality

'The long-recognized liberal principle is that each person's freedom must be . . . restricted to those actions that do not intrude upon others' comparable freedoms' (Gutmann 1980, p. 8). In this succinct summing up of the notion of liberal equality, Gutmann has captured the sense of many liberals that one person's freedom deserves equal weighting with any other's, and that an individual's freedom to acquire goods and positions should not be permitted to restrict other's freedom to acquire similar goods and positions. One should not use one's freedom to gain more than one's fair share of desirable things.

There are obvious problems of interpretation and application of this attractive-sounding principle which I shall ignore here (e.g. how, in practice, are the limits of a 'fair share' of some desirable commodity to be settled? what determines fairness in the allocation of scarce goods of which there are not enough to go round?). What I want to argue is that liberals need to devote thought to how to apply the principle diachronically as well as synchronically. Suppose, to take a rather rigorously simplified example, that a half dozen individuals have each put in a claim for a share in some hitherto unallocated asset, say a piece of land or some other natural resource. On liberal egalitarian thinking, the correct solution to this allocation problem would be to give each claimant (other things, such as his ability to work the resource, or the number of mouths he has to feed from his labour, being equal) a sixth part of the asset. In this way, one claimant's freedom to acquire a sixth share does not prevent others doing the same. But now suppose that several years later a new set of claimants for the resource comes on the scene (either 'outsiders' or the descen-

dants of the original possessors of the asset). The six original proprietors refuse to bow to the newcomers' demands for a share of the
resource; 'What I have justly acquired is *mine*', each of them says, 'and
it is up to me to dispose of it, or to refuse to dispose of it, as I please'.[4]
Clearly, the freedom of the first half dozen claimants to acquire shares
in the asset has impeded – in fact, in their own opinion it has wholly
removed – the freedom of any later claimants to acquire a share in
it. And while my example is a stylised one, it is nevertheless true that
virtually all the accessible resources of our overcrowded planet have
now been distributed (whether in first instance fairly or not), leaving
new generations in the position of propertyless beggars who have to
take what is given to them on the terms offered. This situation presents, *prima facie*, an offence to the concept of liberal equality. Could
liberalism manage to cope with the difficulties arising out of the fact
of generational flux without abandoning altogether the right of anyone to acquire a private property (normally thought of as a socialist
rather than a liberal position)?

One possible response on behalf of liberalism is to argue that this
criticism misses something important in the best liberal accounts of
equality, and consequently paints a distorted picture of the liberal
position. Equality, it may be said, is not to be understood exclusively
in terms of shares of distributable goods; at least as significant, and
perhaps more so, is equality of opportunity to participate in the
decision-making processes of one's society, as these affect social arrangements in general and one's own life in particular. Young people,
the argument could run, may for the most part be unequal with their
elders in respect of holdings of distributable goods, but difference of
generation need not adversely affect their chance to play an equal
role as politically active citizens. The vote of a twenty-year-old is worth
as much at elections as that of a fifty-year-old; nor are the young
debarred from standing for political office or applying for most other
positions of social prestige and influence. When it comes to running
his life, the young adult is no more bound to obey the will of others
than an older person is; both have the right to choose their own
lifestyle (within the law), whether their choice be conventional or
eccentric. In any case, the liberty enjoyed by the young citizen enables
him, if he uses it wisely, to attain in later years both prosperity and
influence; so even his inequality in the matter of distributable goods
is something he can outgrow. Therefore, it will be concluded, in one
extremely important sense of equality the young citizen and the older
one are equal.

This argument does not deserve to be entirely dismissed. In so far as it stands, it may give the defender of liberal equality a measure of contentment with the current state of relations between part-contemporary generations. There *is* a formal political equality between younger and older citizens, they *do* share the same rights before the law, and it *is* possible to start life poor and end it rich.

The drawback is that the equality in question is on paper only to a considerable degree. In practice young people are hampered in making full use of their formal political equality because their inequality in holdings of distributable goods places them at the mercy of the better off – who, for the most part, are older people (though, of course, not all older people are well off). If you are young, how much comfort is it to you to know that your vote is worth as much as your employer's, when he meets your complaints about pay and working conditions with the response that, if you do not like the job, there are thousands of other desperate youngsters who would be glad to take it on any terms? Of what practical use to you is your political equality if you are compelled to live in an old or inferior house (all you can afford), struggling to support a young family on your limited means, and forced to make large rent or mortgage payments to swell the income of people already far more prosperous that you are? And if, as a young citizen, you dislike many of the aspects of the society into which you have been born – say, you deplore its wastage of natural resources, its cavalier attitudes to the environment, its institutionalised selfishness, the 'rat-race' – how do you exercise your right to opt out and cultivate your own garden if you cannot afford a garden to cultivate?

There is nothing new in the observation that economic disadvantage places a brake on liberty. It is a commonplace of political philosophy that limitation of means entails limitation of effective freedom, and that 'inequities in the economic and social systems may soon undermine whatever political equality might have existed under favourable historical circumstances' (Rawls 1972, p. 226). Some of the young, especially those born into the higher social classes, may, admittedly, have little appearance of being economically disadvantaged. But even members of the *jeunesse dorée* normally have to please their elders if they are to retain their privileged position; they are economically dependent on others whose 'Will and Humour' they must consult if they are not to slip downwards in the class structure. Within each social class, the young are mostly to be found (though not necessarily alone) within the bottom, most dependent, most subservient division. Towards the lower levels of the class structure, the position of the young adult can be truly awful. In the more depressed parts of Britain in the 1980s, unemployed working-class young people look forward hopelessly to permanent exclusion from economic opportunities and to a lifetime of bowing to other people's decisions about what should be done with their lives.

As Gutmann has written:

Choice is a necessary, not a sufficient, condition of individual freedom: The alternatives from which we are able to choose must be reasonable ones, and the situation of choice must be one that facilitates, or at least does not stifle, our ability and desire to choose. (Gutmann 1980, p. 10)

The highwayman who declared 'Your money or your life' was offering a choice, but hardly presenting an opportunity for his victims to exercise self-determination. The economically constrained and socially dependent position of the young similarly, if less dramatically, imposes restrictions on their capacity to make truly free choices about how to live, what to make of themselves, and how to interact with other members of their society. In the tradition of Hobbes, Hume, and Mill, liberty is to be contrasted with opposition or constraint of any kind; and we can say of the young what Mill said of the poor of his day, that though they may not be 'enslaved or made dependent by force of law, the great majority are so by force of property' – their formal civil rights notwithstanding (Mill 1879, p. 710; quoted in Gutmann 1980, p. 66).

4 Three Objections

In this section I examine some further possible objections to the thesis that justice for the young is inadequately achieved in our contemporary western societies.

> *(A) The young have no right to feel that they are getting a raw deal from their elders. On the contrary, young people owe a heavy debt to older generations – for their upbringing and education, and for the cultural, social, economic, and political institutions of the society in which they are raised – which they cannot repay. If the young lack certain privileges which older people often enjoy, there is nothing unjust about this. For in the light of what they receive from earlier generations, they have no reasonable ground to complain if some advantages are withheld. It is gratitude, not grievances, they should direct at their elders.*

At first sight, there is a lot of force in this objection. It is quite true that in many important respects each generation stands on the shoulders of its predecessors, able to enjoy the fruits of past people's efforts, but unable to make any return for them.

Herzen remarks that human development is a kind of chronological unfairness, since those who live later profit from the labor of their predecessors without paying the same price. And Kant thought it disconcerting that earlier generations should carry their burdens only for the sake of the later ones and that only the last should have the good fortune to live in the completed building. (Rawls 1972, pp. 290–1)

Have we been looking at the problem of justice between generations the wrong way round? Is the direction of unfairness really from young people to older, and not the other way about?[5]

These questions should, I think, be answered negatively. For one thing, as Rawls remarks, it is not reasonable to talk of later generations treating dead ones unfairly, given that there is no way open to later people to repay their debts to earlier ones: 'We can do something for posterity but it can do nothing for us. This situation is unalterable, and so the question of justice does not arise' (ibid, p. 291). Nor is it helpful to confuse, as Objection A does, what a generation owes to all those generations that have gone before it, and what it owes to the one or two that have immediately preceded it. There is, for instance, nothing within our inheritance more important and useful than our *language*, but while it is people of our parents' and our grandparents' generations who teach it to us, the language itself has been in the making for hundreds of generations, and our teachers are no less indebted to those predecessors than we are. A recognition of what we owe, not to the preceding one or two generations with which we are part-contemporary, but to the sum total of human generations which have gone before us, blunts considerably the impact of Objection A. Young people have good reason to be grateful to members of part-contemporary older generations – parents, teachers, taxpayers who have supported their education, and so on – for benefits received; but it is wrong to talk as if those elders were the sole sources of the goods which the young inherit from earlier people, and wrong to represent the debt owed to those same elders as being so overwhelming as to justify all social and political disadvantages to which they subject the young. Moreover, the socialisation of children and young adults is by no means an entirely altruistic affair. Child-rearing, education and cultural induction, technical training and initiation into the world of labour benefit the established society as well as the individuals who undergo them. The smooth, continuous running of the production line turning out young workers who are competent, industrious, and reasonably content with their lot (rightly so or not), is essential to the maintenance of the social organisation – and of the standard of living of older citizens. As one so frequently hears, a society's greatest asset is its young people.

If it is far from clear that the young are more provided for than providing, it is plain enough that they are given very little say in the basic social arrangements which concern them. They are compelled to bow to the plans which older people have made for them, though in fact there is no good empirical reason for thinking that young adults (and many older children) lack the capacity to take such self-regarding decisions for themselves. But there is no 'bargain' struck between younger and older generations over the mutual provision of goods and services. In practice, it is older people who have the power to lay down the terms of the relations between the generations; and there is scant evidence that they do so without an eye to their own advantage.

> (B) *People have the right to enjoy the fruits of their labour. It may in general be true that people aged fifty are more prosperous and hold more positions of influence than people aged twenty. But if they have attained their wealth and power by many years of hard work, they are entitled to possess more of those good things than young people do.*

Objection B states a principle with which it is possible to agree, as long as certain provisos are made. A reasonable position to adopt, and a recognisably liberal one, is to allow that people have the right to possess more if they have worked more, under the restriction that their freedom to accumulate goods should not obstruct that of others to do the same. The important practical question is how much discrepancy between the holdings of different part-contemporary generations this principle actually permits. I have suggested that at present the discrepancies between the holdings of younger and older generations are too great, and that serious effects on the freedom of the young follow directly and indirectly from these differences. The root problem is the scarcity of distributable goods and positions of influence relative to the demand for them. If members of senior generations annex the lion's share of these, young people are free to acquire only what few may be left, which is unfair in itself and leaves them vulnerable to exploitation and relegation to socially marginal positions. But does this mean that the principle that labour is a ground of entitlement to possessions (cf. Locke 1698, ch. 5) is in practice vacuous in regard to goods in short supply, any acquisitions of such goods entailing unacceptable restrictions on freedom?

We need not conclude so. Not all labour is a matter of simple annexation of goods. People do not merely take into their own keeping what nature has produced; they also create new goods or improve those they already have. As Locke put it:

if we will rightly estimate things as they come to our use, and cast up the several Expenses about them, what in them is purely owing to *Nature*, and what to *Labour*, we shall find, that in most of them 99/100 are wholly to be put on the account of *labour*. (1698, p. 338)

If someone by his labour brings into being more, or better, goods than were in existence before, it is fair to let him enjoy the use and possession of them, providing only that he does not employ them in a way which threatens the freedom of others; for his greater-than-average share of goods has not been obtained by drawing an inequitably large amount from the common stock. The same goes, *mutatis mutandis*, for the creation of new social roles or positions, though here the restriction against limiting the freedom of others requires specially careful attention. In general, it may be said that members of older generations have the clearest title to a greater-than-average share of those of their goods and positions which they have created or improved upon by their own efforts.

> (C) *It is unreasonable to complain that the young are treated unjustly. Youth is a stage which everyone has to undergo and, anyway, one grows out of it. No subset of human beings is being specially singled out for unfair treatment; everyone has to pass through the same phase of life, and no one stays young for ever.*

Objection C is only speciously plausible; its conclusion that the young are not treated unjustly is not supported by its (correct) premises. It is true that youth is a natural phase in everyone's life, and that one does not remain young always. In these respects, being young is unlike being black, or a woman, or homosexual. But whether people in any of these categories are treated unjustly depends entirely on the quality of the treatment they receive, and not on facts about the scope of membership of the category, or how long they remain within it.[6] Even if everyone suffered equally in youth from discriminatory treatment, that would not make that treatment unobjectionable. Similarly, if nature were to alter, and everyone went through a phase of being black, or if people born black eventually became white, the liberal conscience would, and rightly, still be disposed to condemn anti-black discrimination as evil.

It might be said that, for all that, whatever injustices the young suffer, there is a prospect of compensating good fortune later in life, when they have put off their disadvantaged condition: something which someone who is black, say, can never do. But it is better for a person not to suffer injustice at all than to suffer it first and be compensated for it afterwards. And no one has the right to compel another person to suffer just because he is prepared to make it up to him at a later date. The chance of compensating good fortune in later life is in any case, as we have seen, an uncertain one and, to the extent that it depends upon or involves unfairness to the young of a new generation, in itself unjust.

5 Routes to Reform

What sort of changes should a consistent liberal favour in the social dispensation as it affects those who have recently emerged from childhood? It is hardly possible to lay down a detailed set of proposals applicable even to all western democracies, still less to all kinds of human societies, given the wide differences which exist in empirical conditions and available resources. Still, some hints as to the direction desirable reforms might take in a democracy like Britain may suggest some of the rough characteristics that routes to reform might have in other societies as well.

Of the greatest importance would be measures designed to give young adults a greater say in the running of their own lives. Young workers, apprentices, students, and trainees of all sorts should be accorded new rights to take part in the planning of their activities in factory, office, and university. To ensure that they will use this new authority wisely, they will need to have access to extra educational resources so that they will be able to understand adequately the likely consequences of their decisions.

They should also be encouraged to offer constructive suggestions about ways of improving the general social, political, and economic environment, and there could be institutional innovations to ensure that legislators and other holders of power were forced to take their proposals seriously. Young people are naturally inclined to criticise the policies of their elders, and it might be objected that their criticism is frequently unrealistic, destructive, or extreme. That it often takes this character, I suggest, shows their anger and frustration that what they have to say goes so largely unheeded, rather than their incompetence to plan wisely. If the young were given a more responsible role in society's policy-making, so that their energy and freshness of outlook could complement the more experienced, but often complacent and conservative, perspectives of the older people who now dominate decision-making, youthful contributions might sometimes startle

by their originality, but would be less likely to appal by impracticality
or intemperance. An increased presence of young people in positions
of authority in government, the professions, the civil service, trade
unions, industrial management, and so on, could well lead to a greater,
rather than a smaller, degree of pragmatism in public affairs. It would
certainly represent a much more thoroughgoing form of democracy.

Liberalism should also favour state intervention aimed at procuring
for young citizens a more equitable share of distributable goods. Such
intervention could include the redistribution through taxation of a
measure of wealth from better-off older people to the young, the
supplying of higher quality and cheaper housing than many young
people can afford today, and much more vigorous action to ensure
that the young can secure worthwhile and long-term paid employment. The object of such intervention, it needs to be stressed, is not
to remove all challenges from the lives of the young, to make life
effortless and easy for them, but to free them to respond to the more
life-enhancing challenges their society has to offer. It adds nothing
to the quality of life at any age to have to worry about unemployment,
or how to meet heavy rent or mortgage payments, or the high cost
of food, fuel, and clothing. People who are burdened with such anxieties cannot give a high priority to self-improving social, cultural, and
recreational activities. Nor do they have much motivation to exert
themselves for the betterment of a society which they see as antago-
nistic to, rather than supportive of, their individual interests.

Difficult though it may be for those who are not of the same generation to form fraternal feelings for one another, it is part of the
liberal ideal of citizenship that those who enjoy the status of citizen,
regardless of age, should want to work for the common good, and
not merely for personal advantage. Brothers, as Rawls has said, 'do
not wish to gain unless they can do so in ways that further the interests
of the rest' [i.e. of the family] (1972, p. 105). Not merely justice for
the young, but the interests of the general community demand that
the spirit of brotherliness should bind together the generations. Fraternal feeling, however, is hard to sustain in a climate of gross material
and social inequalities between the generations.

If these proposals for reform seem unduly radical, that is because
in order to see their fairness we have to make considerable adjust-
ments to the way we look at youth and its position within the greater
society. A mere century ago, proposals to give women increased social
and political rights were seen by many people (including many
women) as outrageous and revolutionary, but today their justice is
questioned by very few. In a similar way, reforms concerning the

young may in the future appear to be unequivocally demanded by justice, no matter how strange some may find them now.

The arguments of this essay have been mounted from nothing more leftwing than a conception of liberal equality. Although liberalism of this kind is presently coming under heavy attack from the libertarian 'new Right' in Europe and North America, its ideals still provide a basic underpinning of the western democratic polities, and I believe that it is not too late to appeal to those ideals in seeking to promote an improvement in the condition of the young. For those of us who remain loyal to the notion of a free, equal, and fraternal democratic society, it must be a priority to extend our liberal sympathies to the young, and to work towards securing for them the status of full and first-grade citizens.

NOTES

1 I am influenced in my statement of the liberal position by Gutmann (1980).
2 The immediate source of this thought may have been Pufendorf, whose works, according to Laslett in his Introduction to Locke (1698, p. 90), greatly assisted Locke in the composition of the *Two Treatises of Government*. Pufendorf wrote: qui vult ex paternis bonis sustentari, ac in ea deinceps succedere, necessum est, ut ad familiae paternae rationes sese attemperet; quam moderari utique penes patrem est (1673, p. 167).
3 For Locke's view of property, see Macpherson (1962).
4 If the proprietors are familiar with the philosophical literature, they might cite in defence of their stance such works as Locke (1698) and Nozick (1974).
5 I do not mean to imply that there cannot be intergenerational unfairness in *either* direction. It is quite consistent to argue that the young are treated unjustly and that many old or elderly people are too.
6 It will be noted that my rejoinder to Objection C does not presuppose the acceptance of a Parfitian 'Reductionist View' of persons (*cf*. Parfit, 1984, Ch. 15). Such a view – which I have no space to discuss here – would, however, be incompatible with maintenance of the Objection.

REFERENCES

Gutmann, Amy (1980). *Liberal Equality* (Cambridge: Cambridge University Press).
Hooker, Richard (1676). *Of the Lawes of Ecclesiastical Politie* (London: R. White).
Locke, John (1698). *Two Treatises of Government*, ed. Peter Laslett (New York, Scarborough, and London: New American Library, 1965).
Macpherson, C. B. (1962). *The Political Theory of Possessive Individualism: Hobbes to Locke* (Oxford: Oxford University Press).

Mill, J. S. (1879). Chapters on Socialism, in *Collected Works*, ed. J. M. Robson, Volume V (Toronto: Toronto University Press, 1967).

Nozick, Robert (1974). *Anarchy, State and Utopia* (Oxford: Blackwell).

Parfit, Derek (1984). *Reasons and Persons* (Oxford: Oxford University Press).

Pufendorf, Samuel (1673). *De Officio Hominis et Civis juxta Legem Naturalem* (Lund: Vitus Haberegger).

Rawls, John (1972). *A Theory of Justice* (London, Oxford, and New York: Oxford University Press).

7

Children and the Mammalian Order

STEPHEN R. L. CLARK

I

The following argument can be constructed to suggest that children are marginal people:

1 They do not, or do not yet, exercise the distinctively human capacities of rational debate and decision-making;
2 therefore, no sane adult decision-maker would take a child as her exemplar, or think a child's life-plans (such as they are) a serious option for herself;
3 therefore, they cannot, as children, play any part in the processes whereby the rules of the Great Game are settled, or particular moves made;
4 therefore, those who do decide upon the rules do not need to take any account of what children, as such, would want;
5 therefore, any account that is taken of the welfare or expressed preferences of children must be merely sentimental;
6 therefore, good liberals, whose political programme excludes legislation that imposes any special sentimental or moral ideals on their fellow citizens, should have particular difficulty with child-welfare legislation.

That children below 'the age of reason' have no rights in their own right is a necessary consequence of any doctrine that limits the class of rights-holders to the class of recognizably and actually rational entities, entities whose deliberate co-operation is needed if any corporate action is to be undertaken, and whose forbearance can only be purchased by reciprocal forbearance. If there were, as Hume remarked, a race of creatures intermingled with ours that could never make us feel the impact of their displeasure, and could never be expected to keep any bargain that we thought to strike, we should not owe them justice, even if we owed them compassion (Hume 1902, p. 190: *Principles of Morals* 3.1.152). It would be pointless to require that we use them justly, in accordance with such rules of fair-dealing as we might be able to reason out together, for, like children, they cannot play the game on such terms.

Hume placed no necessary restrictions on the sort of laws a legislative body might enact: on his terms, child-welfare legislation or even laws protecting a child's purported 'rights' (or the rights that would be hers when she was grown) would be perfectly proper. What mattered was the 'usefulness' of such laws from the point of view of the general utility. Good 'liberals', on the other hand, often believe or find it useful to imagine that the authority of the state is drawn from some form of social contract, real or (more probably) notional. Adult inhabitants of the region over which the state claims authority either do understand or rationally should understand that they all stand to gain if necessary communal decisions can be made without undue violence, and therefore agree (or should agree, or must be presumed to have agreed) that they will submit to state authority lest worse befall. 'In nature', before any such agreement, no one does wrong by seeking to maintain her own existence and prosperity, at whatever expense to others. Each such adult individual only has a reason to do or refrain from doing anything if she can see such a reason, if there are goals of her own that require such action or inaction. 'Social contract theorists', ever since Democritus (see Cole 1967), have argued that the dangers and difficulties of such a 'natural' life are such that every rational adult would soon see the advantages of forming a social group, even if there were occasions when she lost some particular argument within the group.

We can reasonably assume that every adult individual would only agree to such a compact if it seemed likely that her interests and preferences would, in general, be given sufficient weight to rule out the possibility of her finding that she was, in effect, a slave, required to do what she was told without ever having the chance to object, to tell others what to do in her turn, or to participate in the processes of decision-making. That is all that we can assume people are bound to have agreed to, if they thought about it at all. Accordingly, the laws of our particular state must always be such as can be accepted, in the abstract, by such self-seeking individuals. In nature, people may do whatever they please to preserve their lives and livelihood. That absolute right must be abandoned on our entry into civil society, but we would not thereby abandon all our 'rights', all that we would be at liberty to do in nature. It would be absurd of any individual to put herself wholly at the disposal of others so that she had no privacy, no region within which her decision was final. Others may disapprove or despise or loath, but they have no agreed right to interfere – because it would not be rational for individuals in the state of nature to allow such a right to their chance-met companions. We establish Leviathan precisely to safeguard our lives and livelihood, and only allow it such authority as is needed to settle genuine conflicts that might otherwise escalate into outright war and the dissolution of the state.

Purely liberal or libertarian theory allows only a minimal state, charged with the duty of preventing, and punishing, the violation of right. The law has no business between a person and her morals, so long as she violates no other individual's rights of life, liberty, and the enjoyment of lawfully acquired property. What we do in 'the privacy of our own homes' or to those things that are 'our property' is for us to say. We may get drunk, break up the furniture, kick the dog, or batter the baby without violating any other adult person's rights. Nor do we violate anyone's rights by withholding our charity: civil society exists to protect our lawful enjoyments, not to demand of us that we forego such enjoyments in order to assist others. All taxation that goes beyond the minimal administrative charge for maintaining police, courts, and army is therefore unjust.

Most commentators, even those who regard themselves as liberals, are made uneasy by such a prospect. There is a great deal of existing legislation, even in impeccably 'liberal' states, that is concerned with more than the violation, or alleged violation, of the rights of adult humans. We are no longer permitted to beat 'our' dog to death on the public highway, nor 'in the privacy of our own home'. We are required to fund, through progressive taxation, all manner of 'socially valuable schemes' that go far beyond a simple protection of rights. Those liberals who wish still to insist that states exist only to protect rights, but wish to forbid cruelty to animals or require contributions to medical and other care of their fellow citizens, have to speak of the rights of animals, or of welfare rights, in addition to the simple 'liberty rights' of original liberalism. Whereas the older liberals supposed that no contracting individual could be supposed to consent to any authority beyond what was needed to preserve her own life and liberty, the modern liberal suggests that we would all rationally agree to such authority as is needed to promote the general welfare as it is defined by majority opinion. A citizen may therefore find herself funding an enterprise which seems to her unprofitable, or even immoral, and may be required or forbidden to do all manner of things that she had hitherto regarded as her own business.

Voluntary associations to provide work, pensions, medical care, library facilities, or annual paid holidays on the Black Sea would all, of course, be legitimate even under old-style liberal rules: the disagreement lies only with the question of whether any state has a right to compel people to pay for facilities they would rather not have or rather not provide *gratis*. Individuals have a duty not to injure others because that is the duty we must all be supposed to have taken on with a view to our own security. Must we also be supposed to have positive duties to help others to do whatever they want to do? The more such duties we impose on everyone the less they are at liberty, but it seems likely that we might rationally trade. It seems no more obviously rational, a welfare liberal could say, that we should agree to a merely protective state authority, than that we should agree to a more positively helpful one.

The problem is that although it is no more rational, it is also no less: one group of people might prefer one arrangement, others another. In the absence of a real, historical agreement, social contract theorists must always appeal to what we must be supposed to have agreed, what any rational creature would agree to. But there seems to be no such defined set of rules that we would be bound to accept merely in the abstract. This is especially true since the opposing pressures are resolved in obviously arbitrary ways: once it is agreed that we owe a positive debt to our fellows to behave in one way and not another, to subsidise their plans of life and not merely allow them the liberty of living without our interference, where should we, must we, draw the line? If we may not enjoy the malicious pleasure of, say, shouting racial abuse (because it seriously upsets the hearers), why is it obvious that we must never be forbidden to indulge our sexual pleasures (even though it seriously upsets the witnesses)? There is no solution in such slogans as 'So act as to maximise the number of genuinely autonomous and "human" agents', or 'satisfy as many desires as possible': either these give no one answer at all, or else the answer they are said to give is really founded on prior commitments to particular moral and other values. It is because we, the pontificating classes, approve of certain forms of life that we approve of a certain, otherwise quite arbitrary, interference in the liberties of our fellows while continuing to use old-style liberal slogans to resist their interference in our lifestyles. I do not say that we are wrong to do so: what is doubtful is that liberal ideology gives us any good ground for our discriminations.

Liberal ideology is also in a weak position with regard to supposedly non-contracting inhabitants of a region. If rights and duties in the state depend upon a real or notional consent, what of those who cannot give their consent, or can give it (eventually) only if they are treated in a certain way before they have done so? Only those with whom we, all of 'us', have good reason to come to an agreement lest worse befall (i.e. only those who could fight us if we drove them to despair) have rights, and their rights include the liberty to treat their own as they please unless they violate the real rights of others. Once again, we may have a real, voluntary compact to be nice to the 'marginal people', but we cannot complain if others do not make this bargain any more than we can complain if others do not share our sentimental attachment to wild flowers. We would not hire such people as our baby-sitters, no doubt, any more than we would hire someone who hated flowers as a florist or a park-keeper. But moral ideals that go beyond the minimum requirements of state security must, from a liberal viewpoint, be reckoned voluntary, not to be enforced on all. If baby-haters attempt to hurt my child it is my property-rights that are violated; if they hurt their own, it is only my moral conscience that is outraged – as it might be by outrageous lies, dissipation, cowardice, conceit, or greed of a kind that I nonetheless have no right to prevent or punish. Once the propriety of 'laws of manners' has been admitted, then liberalism, as ordinarily understood, is in decline.

Classical liberalism is the doctrine that 'the only purpose for which power can be rightfully exercised over any member of a civilised community, against his will, is to prevent harm to others' (Mill 1962, p. 135: *On Liberty*, ch. 1). In fact, the restriction is even tighter: the harm done to others must be a direct and unambiguous harm, accepted as such by its victims. Those who have no will in the matter, or are in no position to exercise any such will, have no such protection. Mill expressly allows that children may be required to do all manner of things 'for their own good', as that is assessed by their licensed guardians. He would certainly have opposed any such guardianship that amounted, in his view, to domestic tyranny, but it is not clear that strict liberal principles can rightly discriminate between a tyrannical use of children and a decent paternalism. If children are to be beneficiaries of the liberal rule that it be their decision that is final in all matters affecting only their own welfare, then they must have all the same rights as adults – as some libertarians propose. If, on the other hand, they are recognisably without the power, and hence the right, of rational judgement, it is not up to them to say whether they are harmed by any parental act or policy. Who then decides? What counts as harm will depend on what we suppose to be the child's destiny, her nature as a social mammal or a child of God. Generations of legislators have believed that the general welfare, and that of each particular child, is best promoted by beatings, moral exhortation, forced attendance at public executions, and the like. The goal is a society kept as law-abiding as may be and the salvation of each child's soul. Liberal commentators now decree instead that the 'hedonic' rather than the 'agonistic' mode of control is to be preferred, and that the child's welfare is to be measured by her eventual success as an adult member of a liberal society, free of prejudice, superstition, and, generally, 'illiberal attitudes'. These techniques and goals may well be laudable ones, but it is far from obvious that they are rationally agreeable to all parties, or such as would be adopted 'in the abstract', before we knew what our beliefs and attitudes were. Liberalism which gets its strength from the appearance of value-neutrality, the suggestion that only those laws are good laws that would be accepted by just anyone with a will in the matter, all too often stands revealed as the pontificating classes' own superstition. 'I am not aware', said Mill *à propos* of a proposed 'civilisade' against Mormonite polygamy, 'that any community has a right to force another to be civilised' (Mill 1962, p. 224: *On Liberty*, ch. 4). It is the identifying mark of an ideologue that she does not realise that she has an ideology, but supposes that her views are simple truths which no one but a fool or knave would dispute. Ideology is nowhere more obvious than in our treatment of children, and in the (mostly dreadful) advice offered to parents by generations of self-styled experts (see Hardyment 1983).

Those political theories, of which Mill's is indeed a good example (Mill 1962, p. 136: *On Liberty*, ch. 1), that rest upon considerations of the general welfare rather than on any presumed 'rights' that restrict communal efforts towards such a general good fare no better. If we should so act, and so legislate, as to promote the general welfare, we cannot rely upon what our view of such welfare would be in the abstract, irrespective of our culture, our upbringing, or our beliefs. Citizens would not, here and now, much care for bands of free-living children in the streets or piles of dying babies – though both have existed in the past – and may therefore argue for welfare legislation of some kind from merely self-interested motives. But what satisfies us as a life well lived is dependent on what we have been brought to believe is a life well lived. So we cannot assess child-rearing and educational practices as more or less successful in the abstract enterprise of promoting the general welfare. Those brought up one way will be happy in a different way from those brought up in another: who is happier or who spreads more happiness can only be settled if we know what happiness consists in. It is easy for us here and now to think that at the very least such happiness requires food, shelter, medical attention, friendship, and an acquaintance with the manifold life-possibilities of our society. Can we perhaps rightly enforce at least that much uniformity of practice and forbid child-rearing techniques that starve, neglect, and brutalise the child? I share the concerns of those who propose this much, but we cannot claim that the programme is in any real sense a value-neutral one, that it implies no tendentious judgements about the real destiny of the child, the guardian, or the world, that the programme is independent of the form of society into which the child may one day be initiated as an adult member. Members of child-gangs or self-supporting five-year-olds may have many virtues denied to more domesticated youngsters (see Holt 1975, p. 20). What to us is brutality may in another culture or another age be a necessary rite of passage, such that to 'rescue' the child from her oppressor is as stupid as, we think, it would be to prevent her having a painful, 'medically necessary' or 'socially important' operation. What counts as painful, or as importantly painful, depends in large measure on these larger views.

It is overwhelmingly difficult for most of us, no doubt, to imagine that a solitary, sick, malnourished, nervous child is in any sense 'better off' or 'has better prospects' than a sociable, cheerful, healthy, well-fed child. But treatment that would now be regarded as obvious child abuse has in the past been reckoned a necessary stage in the soul's salvation and the future citizen's socialisation. Swaddling clothes (so that the baby cannot move and is reduced to a state of torpor; see Hardyment 1983, p. 3), beatings, mutilations, and bogey-tales more terrifying even than modern video nasties (because seriously told to frighten the child into obedience) have all been part of the – genuinely – caring parent's armory. 'Hardly anyone will deny', said Mill, 'that it is one of the most sacred duties of the parents, after summoning a human being into the world, to give to that being an education fitting him to perform his part well in life towards others and towards himself' (Mill 1962, pp. 238–9: *On Liberty*, ch. 5). But what is that part to be? The techniques just mentioned are rational ones, in the sense that they do not subvert the agent's ends. The ends they reveal may be irrational or monstrous in a larger sense, like J. B. Watson's goal of the wholly self-reliant, physically undemonstrative child, to be achieved by a resolute refusal ever to cuddle, caress or smile upon the infant (Hardyment 1983, pp. 172–6). But to disapprove of these ends – as I do – is certainly to intrude subjective values in the sense resisted, for example, by Freeman (1983, p. 55). Either we accept that this intrusion is inevitable, or we must allow even such practices as most repel the liberal conscience.

In short: Both contractual liberalism and welfare liberalism can have little to say about children's rights. Children are marginal people who have no rights in their own right and whose welfare is determined entirely by decisions taken by others.

II

This view of children – and equivalently of other supposedly non-rational creatures – goes back at least to Stoic theory, where the outer boundaries of justice are set by the rational capacities of human beings: those who cannot deliberate, who have no rational will, have no claims in justice, own nothing, and can make no bargains. It might be admitted that good men treat the irrational with compassion, but the latter have no rights to violate, and nothing that they could mind about is much worth the wise man's concern. Children might be charming, and such as to awaken a heart-breaking affection – 'who isn't tempted', Epictetus said (*Discourses* 2.24.18), 'by attractive and wideawake children to join their sports and crawl on all fours and talk baby talk?' But no sensible person could want to be like a child, or to take the child's irrational and passing goals at all seriously. The city of the wise, which is the ideal human community, is a city that expressly excludes all those who cannot or do not live in obedience to the common law, of reason. Stoic thinkers were more consistent than most liberals in that they acknowledged that even adult human beings might be slavish or criminal, and hence no true citizens of the cosmos, to whom was owed no fair share of the world's resources nor any veto on what was to be done to them.

But although ancient opinion did generally restrict the class of rights-holders (those who would be directly wronged by enslavement, imprisonment, dispossession) to the rational adult (usually male) population, the relationship of parents and children was not a marginal one. On the contrary, 'parental affection is the germ of that social community of the human race to which we afterwards attain' (Cicero 1967, *De Finibus* 3.62).

In the whole moral sphere (*in omni honesto*) there is nothing more glorious nor of a wider range than the solidarity of mankind, that species of alliance and partnership of interests and that actual affection which exists between man and man, which coming into being immediately upon our birth, owing to the fact that children are loved by their parents and the family as a whole, is bound together by the ties of marriage and parenthood, gradually spreads its influence beyond the home, first by blood relationships, then by connections through marriage, later by friendships, afterwards by the bonds of neighbourhood, then to fellow citizens and political allies and friends, and lastly by embracing the whole of the human race. (*De Finibus* 5.65)

I am therefore within an ancient tradition in suggesting that we might profitably turn current political theory on its head. The relationship with children is not a marginal one, and children are not marginal cases. They are what the civil community is for, and the bond of parental care is the beginning of society. 'The first duty of a revolutionary is to build a society geared to children' (Adams 1971, p. 53). Although the one Stoic theme of rational contract leads to the marginalisation of 'non-rational' beings and of future generations, there is another Stoic theme that makes care for our world and our posterity the centre of moral action.

As we feel it wicked and inhuman for men to declare...that they care not if when they themselves are dead, the universal conflagration ensues, it is undoubtedly true that we are bound to study the interest of posterity also for its own sake. (Cicero, *De Finibus* 3.64)

Our duties are defined for us by what it would be wicked and inhuman to do or not to do. While liberal theorists, for good historical reasons, have sought to limit the field of enforceable duty to what we have, or rationally should have, agreed to do, the more ancient tradition precisely allowed that there were duties over and above those of voluntary association, such that (*in extremis*) anyone who violated his duties must be reckoned an enemy of God and humanity. Vervet monkeys, so it appears, can recognise whose cub it is that is crying, and expect that cub's mother to respond. The special gift of humankind is that we can (and usually do) enforce on others the demands of nature, to care for our offspring and the social bond. This gift, in its turn, is forced on us by the fact that there are those who would otherwise fail to live up to the demands of natural law. And that last fact is created, we may suspect, just by the complexity and strength of the social bond. Briefly: the more we care for others, the wider the circles of our carefulness, the greater the chance that free-loaders will be benefited by our care, and the greater the need to invent further social and cultural constraints on individual behaviour. Creatures who care only for their own offspring are caring for creatures that will in their turn care for their offspring (insofar as there is a genetically transmittable base for the behaviour); creatures that care also for cuckoos, or even for their own remoter cousins, will soon have to reinforce the merely 'natural' pressures to caring behaviour by cultural and legal means.

The point of those last remarks is to emphasise that there is a natural

error that commentators sometimes commit, of supposing that because we do in fact have laws about the proper treatment of children
we must lack a merely natural commitment to their care. There are
no laws commanding people to take care of themselves – we can take
it for granted that everyone will do just that; there are laws to control
drunkenness or drug addiction, because we know that people are not
safeguarded from such socially dangerous lapses by mere nature. If
there are laws against incest, child-beating, and murder, it is because
we might otherwise commit such acts. True enough, although perhaps
the point is not so much that we prevent what would otherwise occur
as give a meaning to what now might: but it does not follow that we
would always do so, or that the laws in question do not reinforce
natural commitments. Few people refrain from murdering their
friends because there is a law against it: the law is a reminder, the
more useful when we live in a society of relative strangers. Few people,
similarly, care for their children only because the magistrate will fine
them if they don't, or with the deliberate aim of having supporters
in their old age (one may doubt if children reared solely with this aim
would actually feel much inclination to carry it out). Laws that too
gravely contradict the natural law bring all law into disrepute. If we
can reasonably demand that parents look after their young it is precisely because they usually will, though by making the demand we
also give parents a reason, sometimes, to defy it.

The whole model of rationally self-serving individuals, who enter
society and bind themselves to a policy of mutual forbearance only
faute de mieux, is obviously flawed. The bonds of society precede legal
institutions. There seems indeed no way (except by divine intervention) that genuinely autochthonous individuals could have the cognitive and emotional apparatus to negotiate such deals, or abide by
them once made. How could we be social creatures at all if affection
for our own children were not natural (Epictetus 1.23.3)? Even the
Hobbesian state of nature included groups bound together by the
'natural lusts and affections'. Impulses to mutual aid, enjoyment of
each other's company, and shared interests in offspring are the context within which a concept of oneself develops. Why then should we
seek to restrict ourselves to a consideration of what rationally self-
serving individuals 'would' have decided, when we know perfectly
well that such individuals are a late and maverick development? Why
construct a duty to care for children on the strained supposition that
such individuals would, if they did not know whether once past 'the
veil of ignorance' they would themselves be in need of care and attention from parental figures, elect to impose some such duty on

appropriate members of society (as Blustein 1982, pp. 123ff., after Rawls 1971, p. 249)? Being what we are, we already have a natural commitment to preserve and nourish more things than ourselves.

So what is it that we are? There is a long tradition to the effect that rationality is in some way linked to social affection: 'the more intelligent, the more socially minded' (see Aristotle, *Historia Animalium* 8.589a1ff., *De Generatione Animalium* 3.758ff.). But even the belief that rationality cannot develop except in a social species does not show that rationality requires childcare on the level that human beings generally approve. Maybe we are rational because we care for our children: it does not follow that we care for our children because we are rational! On the contrary, that is a law that 'nature has taught all animals' (Justinian, *Institutions* 1.2). Pigs, so Xenophon reported, fought harder for their young than for themselves (Xenophon, *Cynegeticus* 10.23). Even amongst wild beasts, conceived as 'solitary carnivores', mothers die for their young (Aristotle, *Eudemian Ethics* 7.1235a34; see Clark 1988).

The bond of mother and children is widely perceived as natural – even to the extent of denying any moral credit to the unfortunate woman who is left alone with her parental duty. That bond by itself is enough to disprove the Diodoran thesis, adopted by Rousseau, that our human or hominid ancestors were ever solitary and brutish individuals (Diodorus 1.6). But my point is a wider one: it is not only mothers that care for the young, nor even only parents. The evidence from studies of hamadryas baboons is that we are not even the only primate species to find the young fascinating: young males regularly abduct youngsters to rear as their own: cubs are seized to act as buffers in disputes with more dominant baboons; single females, ethologically known as 'aunts', seek to take a share in child-rearing even if mother – and young– strenuously object! None of this is to say that baboons – or all humans – necessarily have any sound altruistic purpose. The independent welfare of the cub is not what marauding adults desire (see also Holt 1975, pp. 78–82). But the fact remains that it is the young who are the bonds of baboon society. It is they who mute the disputes between quarrelling adults and give them an extra reason to stick together.

It is also often the young who are the innovators. Too much popularised ethology has given the impression that the dominant males are the leaders of animal society. Better observation suggests that such dominants are merely those who could be expected to win any dispute over territory or possession. They do not necessarily 'lead'. On the contrary, it may often be the youngest of the group who literally leads, or works out the innovative tactic: the young chimpanzee who clatters empty oil-drums round the clearing to attract attentive deference; the young macaque who learns to separate sand and grain by tossing handfuls into the water. Curious and playful behaviour, conciliatory tactics in lieu of confrontational, distancing maneuvers, are the province of the young (see Clark 1982, pp. 52, 92). Because there are such creatures, who control their protectors by being 'charming' and desirable and their environment by locating new techniques that are not needed by the dominant few, the tribe (and species) of which they are a part can survive as a sociable and innovative one. 'Which is the essential dragonfly – the long-lived crawling larva, or the ephemeral winged imago?': the species could equally be represented by the child, the adult being dismissed as the degenerate modification in the later part of life to reproduce and do the necessary work (Gibson 1966, p. 438). Gibson's consciously exaggerated dictum emphasises what political theorists seem to have forgotten: as social mammals we are crucially and irreversibly marked not simply as beings that care for their young, but as beings that can extort that care. Instead of thinking of our young as marginal to the real interests and concerns and habitual practices of adult society, it is worth noticing the extent to which the rest of our society is centred on the needs and delights of the young. We are mistaken if we think that even infants are merely passive: parents, whatever self-styled experts may say, are well aware that their young have characters and purposes of their own, that it is their style that dominates the household.

It is certainly true that the young are physically at the mercy of their adults, that they are often mishandled and abused. But it does not follow that they are not, in general, in control. We 'grown-ups' attend too much to what we do, and too little to the net result of what is done. Could we not instead consider the possibility that it is the young who compel us, by example and conciliation, game and grace? Is it obvious that these 'hedonic' techniques are less effective than the 'agonistic' (see Chance 1975) or less worth choosing?

It is, obviously, not only children that can elicit the supportive love and mute the fury of their elders. 'Infantile' courting behaviour and submissive gestures towards the dominants can be seen as ways of manipulating those who are physically stronger. They work, so far as they do, because we are the sort of creatures that respond to the signals of our young. Civil communities, in short, exist as extensions of the necessary relationship of young and old. We do not seek our own individual triumph at whatever cost to our victims because even when defeated they can have recourse to infantile submission. We can be obliged to look after the weak or the poor for just the same reason: they awaken in us the same sort of parental or quasi-parental affection. The fallacy of classical liberalism is to suppose that these restraints on human behaviour must be created by cultural agreement in order to suppress the self-seeking propensities of Diodorus's solitaries. It is, on the contrary, from these habits of care and affection that civil society takes its beginning.

III

That there was never any need to construct civil society out of a pack of chance-met solitaries is obvious. It should also be obvious that there is nothing intrinsically rational about 'looking after number one', nor anything irrational about wishing others well, liking their company, and finding many of our enjoyments in their service. The creature typing these words, like the creature that is reading them, can only perform those actions as an integral part of the physical and social universe. To suppose that either of us has an existence, let alone a welfare, utterly dissociated from the existence and welfare of our fellow creatures is just silly (see Clark 1983). Even if I were like a hamadryas 'aunt', and quite unable to ask myself whether the cub I wanted to cuddle actually wanted to be cuddled by me (and to modify my impulse accordingly), I should still need happy and healthy cubs if I were ever to be prosperous. I have an overwhelming interest in the welfare of creatures that classical liberals have judged none of my business.

Once all this is admitted, it is possible to return to the attempt to isolate what counts as a strict right. As long as we had it in mind that rational adults were the central members of society, that they were the primary rights-holders, we could answer the question 'What rights do such rights-holders have?' by the simple expedient of working out what could within reason be demanded from each of them on behalf of them all. Welfare liberals, alarmed by the thought of naked laissez-faire, have tended to play down the primary claim of classical liberalism, that no one be required by law to act in ways they would not choose that everyone should act. Positive legal requirements have been added to the merely negative requirements (e.g. that one not kill or rob or threaten others) of classical liberalism. At the same time, some modern liberal thinkers have regretted 'paternalism' even in those areas where classical liberals demanded it. Whereas Mill denied any right of self-determination to those who could not be expected to exercise it rationally, some liberals (e.g. Holt 1975) have suspected that the inability of children to be self-determining is as much a cultural artefact as the once-upon-a-time imbecility of women. Even those liberals who do not go so far as to deny the validity of school-attendance laws, or to allow children the right to divorce their parents, tend to be much exercised by fear of cultural indoctrination – which is to say, by a secret wish that children be indoctrinated with the liberal ideology. Consider for a moment the irredeemably fatuous remark, attributed to one schoolteacher, that he 'does not mind what a child believes when he leaves school, as long as he believes it by being true to himself' (*Times* of London, 25 March 1987: 'Yes, I know he sells heroin, beats his common-law wife, tortures cats for fun and profit, betrays his country and cheats at cards – but he's very sincere').

But we cannot simultaneously extend the class of proper rights-holders to include children and decree that they therefore have all the rights that adults are supposed to have, any more than we can equip animals with all the natural rights that humans are supposed to have. When the set of rights-holders is enlarged, the nature of the set of compossible rights is also altered (Clark 1987). Maybe adult strangers could have absolute rights of independent action, without any corresponding rights to care. Once we acknowledge that rights take shape within the real nexus of parental and other obligations, it is clear that the rights 'we' all have are not simply those of Diodoran solitaries.

Social contract theory, in all its forms, implicitly assumes that adolescents and young adults lie at the core of society, people who can form their voluntary associations and be bound only as long as they choose to be. But such unions are the truly marginal ones – almost as marginal, indeed, as the bands of young male baboons forced out to the literal fringes of baboon society until they can make their way back to the magical centre of obligation and compelled affection. That centre is the complex network of properly adult servants or friends of the young. The right to govern one's own life as one pleases, so long as one positively offends no one else's (negative) right, is a temporary liberty, a minor compensation for being ousted from the centre. What central members of society enjoy is not that supposed right, but the more positive right and duty to participate in the growth and development of the tribe. To do so is only possible for those who submit to the law of the tribe – the law of all possible tribes – in the service of that network of relationships as it grows conscious of itself.

The notion that children, of all people, have only secondary rights was always paradoxical. Child murderers are characteristically hated and abused even by violent criminals who have themselves violated the rights of adults. The acknowledged duty of any relevantly competent citizen is to protect and save a child in distress, a duty sometimes invoked by state officials to excuse what turns out to be a clear violation of parental – and children's – rights in the name of some supposedly expert theory about the rearing of children.

These real and natural duties – of care and forbearance on the one hand and loving manipulation on the other – are mostly experienced as compulsions, cued in ways that also govern the behaviour of our non-human kin. Parental authority, as Locke argued (1965, p. 348: *Second Treatise of Government*, ch. 6), derives from parental duty, and is forfeited when those duties are not faithfully discharged (see Nozick 1974, pp. 288–90; Blustein 1982, p. 114). The good society is not the one 'we', or our adolescents, would have chosen from a position of uncultured ignorance, but the society that we and our kindred have been choosing and refining for millions of years. It is the network of historical and evolutionary rights and duties that we must work within. Children are not injured by being trained to occupy their proper roles in any one of the societies that are allowed by natural law; nor are adults injured by being required by law to do what they would generally do naturally (even if, on occasion, ineptly or sinfully). Where we are injured is in being denied the chance to take responsibility for any young, even by well-meaning liberal officials who imagine that it takes experts to rear a child. Where we are injured, even as children, is by being reared without any regard to our eventual wish and need to take responsibility for others.

Three problems remain, one theoretical and the others practical. The first is constituted simply by the popular belief that 'the naturalistic fallacy' is committed by any attempt to ground our duties on what may naturally be expected of us. Surely, it is said, what we ought to do, what as morally rational beings we would do, cannot be deduced simply from what we and our kindred generally do do? Perhaps it cannot, but there is no reason at all to think that the only proper ground for a given belief must be simply deductive. I do not strictly 'deduce' that we have duties towards our children, and our children corresponding duties and privileges in our regard, simply from the existence of the natural ties the Stoics identified. It may be imaginable that we have no such duties. It is also imaginable that nothing that we see is real: our visual perceptions can only ever be evidence of the truth of this or that dictum, never demonstrative proof. Indeed, those perceptions can only be evidence at all on the non-empirically grounded supposition that the world is such as to allow us to form true beliefs about it. The compulsions and natural habits of human-

kind are similarly evidence of what is morally required: what an irrational place the world would be (and how far from comprehensible)
if we were systematically encouraged by our given natures to mis-
perceive the moral law! In my account, the natural law is evidence,
as it was for Locke, of what God wills (see Clark 1982, pp. 103–4). If,
however, there is no such objective law, it would seem only sensible
to take as our law what we will mostly do anyway. There is, at any
rate, no fallacy in so doing, least of all the 'naturalistic fallacy' defined
by Moore (see Clark 1984).

The second, more practical issue is this: by making the adult–child
relationship the central social form, and relegating the supposedly
free adolescent to the outskirts, I may seem to be committing the same
error of taste and manners as some marriage counsellors, who make
it appear that the unmarried are the unsaved, that a fruitful marriage
is the main human sacrament. But responsibility, even for children,
comes in many forms. What is central to my claim is the notion that
we have the rights we need to meet our responsibilities, and that those
responsibilities include securing those same rights for others. The
child–adult bond is central, but not all such bonds are straightfor-
wardly parental, and even the wholly childless can and often do occupy
important slots in society.

A third criticism is related to the second: am I not being as complacent, even as offensive as David Hume in his remarks on women?

In many nations, the female sex are reduced to slavery, and are rendered
incapable of all property, in opposition to their lordly masters. But though
the males, when united, have in all countries bodily force sufficient to maintain
this severe tyranny, yet such are the insinuation, address and charms of their
fair companions, that women are commonly able to break the confederacy,
and share with the other sex in all the rights and privileges of society (Hume
1902, p. 191; *An Enquiry Concerning the Principles of Morals* 3.1.152).

Such, it is easy to suppose, are the wiles of slaves, and doubtless often
as unsuccessful as other slavish policies. Free women do not need to
charm and insinuate; would free children? Deliberate cuteness is incompatible with dignity. What children (and all of us) require is not
patronising affection, but respectful friendship.

But the case can be redescribed: even in a society that formally
acknowledged the equality of male and female, or of adult and child,
and thereby reduced the amount of cute and insinuating behaviour
that was necessary, there would be much to learn from the relationships of male and female, adult and child and adolescent. Children
revert to childish modes of conduct when their adults deny them the
right to converse on an 'adult' level, as a technique of control (see

Holt 1975, pp. 93–9; Davies 1982, pp. 118–21). But they do not therefore approve of free-wheeling laissez-aller society: freedom, adult-to-adult relationships, for them is not the adolescent departure to the edge of things, but the promise that their hopes and fears will play a part in determining social order, that friendships are possible across all social boundaries. In so far as we have failed to make a society entirely fit for children, we have failed in making the liberal dream reality. For that dream, in the end, was not one of isolated, existentially unfettered adolescents, but a world where we could respond without fear to conciliatory gestures and acknowledge that all power worth having grows from the respectful response of others. Eminently sane people, after all, can make the real, self-moving, and attentive child their pattern.

In sum: children indubitably influence and manipulate their adults, and have always done so. The efforts of 'free ephebes' and of rationalizing sages to escape the net have never wholly eliminated the control exercised by the young. The young may not be rationally autonomous in whatever sense is required by political theorists, but it is their presence, and the use of similar techniques as theirs by others, that secures something like civil peace in many human, primate, or mammalian communities. Those who insist that only rationally autonomous beings can be effective agents are blinding themselves to the manipulative success of children. Just societies must acknowledge their centrality, and the laws of those lands must be geared to reinforcing those same natural cues as normally allow the young their place and fortune. There are no abstract individuals to 'contract in' on such minimal terms as they see fit. What there is is the network of familial and friendly relationship over all the world, from which irresponsible adolescents may on occasion temporarily 'contract out'. The risk we presently run is that too many such adolescents and their functional equivalents will fail to regain responsibilities, and prefer instead those merely infantile, manipulative ways that put a burden on the working adults. In denying them the right of responsible authority, we make them outlaws or untimely dependents. In paradoxically insisting that such deracinated unfortunates are the 'real' human beings, we neglect our real situation, as well as the innovatory, conciliatory, maddening, and controlling presences of our children.

REFERENCES

Adams, P., et al. (1971). *Children's Rights* (London: Elek Books).
Aristotle (1935). *Eudemian Ethics*, trans. H. Rackham (London: Heinemann, and Cambridge, Mass.: Harvard University Press).

(1953). *De Generatione Animalium*, trans. A. L Peck (London: Heinemann, and Cambridge, Mass.: Harvard University Press).

(1965). *Historia Animalium*, (London: Heinemann, and Cambridge, Mass.: Harvard University Press).

Blustein, J. (1982). *Parents and Children* (New York: Oxford University Press).

Chance, M. (1975). 'Social Cohesion and the Structure of Attention', in *Biosocial Anthropology*, ed. R. Fox (London: Maleby Press), pp. 93ff.

Cicero (1967). *De Finibus Bonorum et Malorum*, trans. H. Rackham (London: Heinemann, and Cambridge, Mass.: Harvard University Press).

Clark, S. R. L. (1982). *The Nature of the Beast* (Oxford: Oxford University Press).

(1983). 'Gaia and the Forms of Life', in *Environmental Philosophy*, ed. R. Elliot & A. Gair (Milton Keynes: Open University Press), pp. 182.

(1984). 'Morals, Moore and MacIntyre', *Inquiry 26*, 425–45.

(1987). 'Animals, Ecosystems and the Liberal Ethic', *Monist 70.1*, 114–33.

(1988). 'Good Ethology and the Decent Polis', in *The Good of Community*, ed. H. Lesser and A. Loizou (Manchester: Gower Press).

Cole, T. (1967). *Democritus and the Sources of Greek Anthropology* (American Philological Association Monograph 25).

Davies, B. (1982). *Life in the Classroom and Playground* (London: Routledge & Kegan Paul).

Diodorus (1933). *Library of History*, Vol I, trans. C. H. Oldfather (London: Heinemann, and Cambridge, Mass.: Harvard University Press).

Epictetus (1925). *Discourses*, trans. W. A. Oldfather (London: Heinemann, and Cambridge, Mass.: Harvard University Press).

Freeman, M. D. A. (1983). *The Rights and Wrongs of Children* (London: Pinter).

Gibson, T. (1966). 'Youth for Freedom' (London: Freedom Press: 1951), in *Patterns of Anarchy*, ed. L. I. Krimerman and L. Parry (New York: Doubleday), pp. 436ff.

Hardyment, C. (1983). *Dream Babies* (Oxford: Oxford University Press).

Holt, J. (1975). *Escape from Childhood* (Harmondsworth: Pelican).

Hume, D. (1902). *Enquiries*, ed. L. A. Selby-Bigge (Oxford: Clarendon Press).

Justinian (1937). *Institutes*, trans. J. B. Moyle (Oxford: Clarendon Press, 5th ed.).

Locke, J. (1965). *Two Treatises of Government*, ed. P. Laslett (New York: New American Library).

Mill, J. S. (1962). *Utilitarianism & Other Writings*, ed. M. Warnock (London: Fontana).

Nozick, R. (1974). *Anarchy, State and Utopia* (Oxford: Blackwell).

Rawls, J. (1971). *A Theory of Justice* (Oxford: Clarendon Press).

Xenophon (1925). *Minora Scripta*, trans. E. C. Marchant (London: Heinemann, and Cambridge, Mass.: Harvard University Press.

8

The Right to Found a Family

JOHN HARRIS

The right or freedom to found a family expresses something so basic
and deep-rooted in human psychology and social practice that it seems
hardly worthy of special attention. And yet it is problematic in the
extreme. Since it is, in a way, more fundamental than even the right
to life, it is important to be clear about just what might be involved
in sustaining or denying claims about the right to found a family and
about the legitimacy of interfering with this supposed right or cir-
cumscribing it in various ways.

I must make clear that by talking of the *right* to found a family I
do not of course mean to be metaphysically tendentious about the
existence of rights, in the manner, for example, of Robert Nozick,
who asserts on the first page of *Anarchy, State, and Utopia* that
'[i]ndividuals have rights...', 'things' that are in some sense self-
evidently possessed by people and which, by their very nature, are
overriding and operate to 'trump' conflicting non-rights claims.[1] I
mean merely that when we talk about rights, we do so to signal that
we are talking about claims to the freedom to do certain things that
we take very seriously indeed. This means that where a right to do
something is recognised, it is implied that it would be wrong to interfere with a person's exercise of that right and that, if such interference were to be justified, quite extraordinarily strong reasons
would have to be produced to justify it. And, perhaps equally important, that these extraordinarily strong reasons are weighty enough
for us to regard the interests of the person whose rights are defended
as sufficiently important for holding that others have an obligation
to respect those interests.

So, is there a right to found a family? The European Convention
on Human Rights[2] has seen fit to recognise and protect such a right
and its authority has been much invoked of late in arguments about

I am much indebted to Geoffrey Scarre for his very patient and insightful editing of
this piece and for many helpful suggestions.

what aid might be called on in the legitimate exercise of that right. The occasion for this interest has been the debates surrounding the use of new techniques in medicine, particularly in human embryology, and the consequent reawakening of old debates about surrogate parents.[3]

For the record, this right, while very briefly and succinctly stated as Article 12 of the Convention is, in the Convention's formulation, profoundly ambiguous. Article 12 reads as follows:

Men and women of marriageable age have the right to marry and to found a family according to the national laws governing the exercise of this right.

It will be obvious that this article is almost totally opaque. How is it to be interpreted? Do men and women have the right to found a family independently, or only if married? Must they be of marriageable age to found a family or only of marriageable age to marry? Can national laws take away these rights or only regulate them? Is marriageable age defined by law, custom, or biology?

Clearly the European Convention on Human Rights is of little help if we wish to understand just what might be involved in respecting or even comprehending the right to found a family. What I want to do is examine the moral constraints that ought to govern the foundation of a family and in the light of these, consider the fundamental question of what rights or freedoms may appropriately be spoken of in this context. I shall assume that marriage is morally as well as biologically irrelevant to claims that may legitimately be made about the foundation of a family and I shall ignore this institution except in so far as it figures in the articulation of prejudices that should be dismissed.

My strategy will be to start by assuming that we would wish to respect the right to found a family and by reviewing the many problems involved in understanding what such a right might amount to. This will reveal a number of important moral issues that must be resolved before a coherent view of the rights and wrongs of having children can be arrived at. From this, a view about the morality of founding families will emerge.

I The Right to Found a Family

1 What Is the Point of the Right to Found a Family?

When we wish to understand whether or not we might be justified in respecting a particular right we need to know something about its point, about what interests or values it is supposed to protect.[4] There are a number of perspectives from which we might wish to defend the right to found a family, and although they overlap at many points and even collapse on occasion one into another, if we start at least with a sense of how they differ this will help us to be clear about one dimension of the issues involved. I want to start by distinguishing what we might call 'society-centred', 'adult-centred', and 'child-centred' views of family foundation.

a) Society-centred Views

These regard the family as a 'fundamental unit of society'[5] and see the right to found a family in terms of the perpetuation and protection of one of society's basic units. The point of such a right from this perspective is to serve the needs of a particular conception of society and to do so by protecting a particular conception of the family as a social unit. More loosely, society's interests might simply be served by measures which help to ensure that there *will* be a next generation, or a sufficiently populous one, by facilitating the production of children. This may also, of course, be part of an adult-centred view. And in so far as there might be a 'society view' about the sorts of children it would be socially desirable to produce, such a view might well set limitations on the right to produce, say, severely handicapped children.

b) Adult-centred Views

Such views would see the right to found a family as perhaps simply a dimension of human freedom, or, more specifically, the right might be seen as protecting adult desires for the satisfactions of procreation – child-bearing and birth or child-rearing. Relatedly the importance of founding a family might be viewed in terms of the desirability of securing succession or inheritance, or as attaching to the prestige of founding or heading a family, or in terms of the need to secure the protection of a family to provide for a secure old age. In all of these cases and others we might imagine the right claimed is for the protection of the various interests of would-be founders of families. These may not be adults in the legal sense, nor indeed in the biological sense (if there is one). They will at any event be existing individuals with views about having or looking after children.

c) Child-centred Views

The child-centred view would regard the right to found a family as securing the interests of the next generation. As with society-centred

views, this conception of family foundation might well involve constraints on the sorts of people judged fit to produce and rear children
as well as on the sorts of children it is judged right to bring into or
allow to continue in existence. It might, for example, be thought
wrong to inflict on children certain sorts of disadvantage whether
these stem from the context in which they are to be reared, the people
who are to look after them, or from handicaps it is known or can be
predicted they will possess.

Understanding just what the point of a right to found a family might
be will tell us about what might be involved in granting the protection
of such a right to various classes of individuals. Of course the legitimacy of each of these views might well be challenged, as might the
morality of enforcing them. This is another issue and one to which
we will return.
    In addition to understanding the point of a right to have children
we might need to know about what might be called the ambit of such
a right. Against whom might it be enforced or claimed and how are
conflicts of rights to be resolved?

2 What Is the Ambit of the Right?

Founding a family involves much more, and perhaps also much less,
than simply doing what comes naturally and hoping for the best.
Perhaps it is time to say something about just what might be meant
by 'founding a family'. I've persevered with this rather quaint phrase
used by the European Convention on Human Rights because it is
usefully ambiguous. However, it is time to be clear about what we
mean when talking of founding a family.

a) What Is a Family?
I'm not interested here in producing a definition of the family or
indeed in producing any watertight definition at all, but merely in
making plain what for the moment I mean by 'founding a family'. I
shall take 'founding a family' to mean something as broad as the
acquisition by a person or persons of one or more children, where
'acquisition' involves taking those children into the person's home as
full members of the household and where those acquiring the children
take on the obligation to afford them care and protection and are
consequently entitled to regard those children as in some sense 'their
own'.
    Now the paradigm, if not any longer the established way to found

a family, is for a man and a woman to marry and then lie back and think of their native land. This is probably what the European Convention envisages, and its Article 12 is designed to prevent states from putting impediments in the way of marriage or procreation by consenting couples. However, most of the rights we know of are rights possessed by individuals, and so we must ask what sort of people can claim and maybe enforce such rights, against whom or what can they do so, and in what circumstances?

b) Rights against Individuals

If we imagine what might be involved in the enforcing of the right to found a family by one individual against another we can see immediately how this right would have to be limited by other individuals' competing rights to self determination and freedom from assault. Clearly any man, for example, wishing to claim his right to found a family in the absence of a consenting partner, either in the form of a woman willing to bear or try to bear his children, or in the absence of a willing egg or embryo donor and a suitable surrogate mother, would be demanding the right to perform rape or its moral equivalent. If individuals have rights to found families which might be enforceable against other individuals this, clearly, can only mean that they have the right to attempt to found families with consenting partners of various sorts which must give way to equal competing rights of the other individuals. However, it might involve the claim that third parties should not impede legitimate attempts to found a family by, say, legislating against the use of consenting surrogates by individuals unable to have children without their assistance or by putting obstacles in the way of individuals who wish to obtain medical assistance with procreation. Or, what amounts to the same thing, by declining to provide medical assistance with procreation to some where such assistance is available to others (married couples, say) without restriction.

c) Rights against Corporations

Although the choice of a sexual and hence sometimes a procreational partner is usually regarded as a matter of individual choice, there may be many circumstances in which we might envisage rights being claimed by couples against the state or other agencies for assistance of various kinds in the foundation of a family. We are familiar with the claims that are already standard for neonatal and postnatal care and for particular types of assistance at birth as well as with 'family planning', which is not always a euphemism for attempts to avoid the foundation of a family.

Less familiar are the claims made for assistance with infertility. These may now involve the need for Artificial Insemination by Donor (AID) or In Vitro Fertilization, (IVF), and women who cannot themselves carry or give birth to a child may need the help of a surrogate mother. Some of these techniques are very costly and often require the aid not only of health care professionals of various sorts but also of amateur or professional third parties, who may be needed for the donation of sperm or eggs or even embryos, and for the lease or loan of that most valuable piece of gynaecological real estate, the womb.

Thus, claims for assistance with the foundation of a family may be very costly to satisfy and may involve the co-operation of many people and institutions. This is of course true of many of the rights claimed in complex societies. Think, for example, of the right to due process of law. This is immensely costly and demands, *inter alia*, the forced attendance of many innocent third parties as witnesses, as members of juries, or to give 'expert' opinion, as well as the co-operation of numerous professionals.

A further set of problems raised by considering the ambit of this supposed right concern precisely who can claim it.

d) Who Has the Right to Found a Family?

In addition to married couples and heterosexual couples in what are sometimes referred to as 'stable continuing relationships', homosexual or gay couples may also wish to found families, as may single people of either gender or any sexual orientation. These may even be quite young people. The recent House of Lords' judgement in *Gillick v. West Norfolk and Wisbech Area Health Authority and the Department of Health and Social Security* (All England Reports, 1985) established that the courts were not compelled to 'hold that a girl under sixteen lacked the legal capacity to consent to contraceptive advice' and that in certain circumstances that advice could be given without her parents' knowledge or consent. Of course young girls can and frequently do have children even though they are not 'legally' able to consent to sexual relations. Interestingly, this case seems to have established that whereas girls under sixteen cannot in law consent to sexual relations, they may give valid consent to medical treatment, which may of course involve much more complex considerations and the effects of which may be more far reaching. Such treatment could presumably include both AID and IVF followed by embryo transfer (the fertilization of their own eggs externally followed by the transfer of the fertilised egg to their own uterus). This judgement thus seems to establish that while it is illegal for a girl under sixteen to consent to become pregnant in the usual way via sexual intercourse, she may legally consent to become pregnant via various forms of medical intervention in a much more complex way. Thus, young girls may consent to being made pregnant by doctors but not by their lovers.

We may expect young people of both genders to begin to claim *de jure*, as well as *de facto*, 'rights' to found families on an increasing scale.

The last case we must mention briefly for the sake of completeness is that of posthumous parenting. Here, frozen eggs and sperm or frozen embryos might be left behind by men or women with a view to their being fertilised and/or implanted after the death of either or both genetic parents. Indeed, a will might request the posthumous foundation of a family and provide funds to secure it.

II Controlling Reproduction

We must now consider what legitimate reasons there might be for imposing controls or restraints upon the freedom to have children or found families. Before doing so we should remind ourselves of the claims made about having children, both in the sense of being entitled to bring them into the world and also of ensuring that they be well and properly looked after once they are here. The right to have children or found families is claimed for a number of reasons: because people badly want to have children; because it is important to individuals, to society, and to the children that they do have them; and perhaps not least because people see having children as part of the purpose and indeed the meaning of life. The claim to the freedom to have children is a very strong one, which of course is partly why it is expressed in the language of rights. Arguments as to why people should not have or should not be permitted to have children must clearly be even stronger. It will be convenient to review the arguments that are often produced in support of controlling reproduction under the three headings we have already considered (considered this time, for variety, in reverse order).

We must also be clear what might be meant by 'controls and restraints' in this context.

Controls and Restraints

It will be useful to distinguish between attempts to control reproduction or parenting – in the sense of absolute prohibitions on reproduction or of depriving parents of the custody of their children – on

the one hand, and attempts simply to hinder reproduction or parenting on the other.

It might appear that attempts to control reproduction via legislation
are doomed to failure – for how could they be enforced? But even if
any purported legislation stopped short of compulsory sterilisation,
or even compulsory abortion, it might none the less be effective.
Making it illegal for certain people or types of people to reproduce
and attaching financial penalties if they defied the legislation, coupled
with deprivation of the custody of any resulting children, might be
highly effective. But even if we rule out of court any such draconian
measures, the judicious placing of various obstacles and hindrances
in the way of reproduction might be equally effective in fact. These
are common enough already, for many individuals need help with
reproduction, and if medical services refuse their assistance to certain
individuals or types of people then they may effectively be prevented
from reproducing themselves or gaining the custody of their children.
We will return to these possibilities as we consider particular cases.

a) Child-centred Arguments

A classic formulation of the strongest argument against the freedom
to reproduce is perhaps still that of John Stuart Mill in his essay *On
Liberty*:

> It still remains unrecognised, that to bring a child into existence without a
> fair prospect of being able, not only to provide food for its body, but instruc-
> tion and training for its mind, is a moral crime, both against the unfortunate
> offspring and against society.[6]

Now of course the crimes that Mill adverts to are relatively easily
remedied as Mill is himself aware, for he continues:

> if the parent does not fulfil this obligation, the State ought to see it fulfilled,
> at the charge, as far as possible, of the parent.[7]

Thus, we need not prevent people from reproducing themselves but
should merely ensure that their children are properly educated and
cared for. However, the powerful argument that Mill introduces involves the idea that one can harm people by bringing them into existence under adverse conditions. The question arises as to how
adverse the conditions must be before this becomes true.

Clearly we must distinguish between adverse conditions that are
remediable and those which are not, and we must also distinguish
between conditions which, while technically remediable, are in fact
either unlikely to be remedied or unlikely to be remedied in time to

make a difference to the child or children in question. Equally clearly, the severity of the adverse conditions the children will have to face is also crucial.

It is likely to prove impossible to be at all precise on the question of just how adverse the conditions must be before bringing a child into the world will be properly regarded as criminal. Probably there will be considerable agreement at the extremes and a very large grey area in which we are unsure just what to think. We will be looking into this grey area in due course, but for the moment we need to clear up another troublesome issue. It is the problem of just when what we do about the creation of children counts as affecting them adversely.

It is sometimes argued that one cannot affect others adversely unless they are there to be adversely affected, in short, unless they exist. If this is right, it is clearly impossible to affect adversely children who have yet to be conceived. This seems so obviously true as to require no further discussion, and yet a simple but important argument advanced by Derek Parfit shows that this is not so. He invites us to consider the actions of two different women:

The first is one month pregnant and is told by her doctor that, unless she takes a simple treatment, the child she is carrying will develop a certain handicap. We suppose again that life with this handicap would probably be worth living, but less so than a normal life. It would obviously be wrong for the mother not to take the treatment, for this will handicap her child. . . .

We next suppose that there is a second woman, who is about to stop taking contraceptive pills so that she can have another child. She is told that she has a temporary condition such that any child she conceives now will have the same handicap; but that if she waits three months she will then conceive a normal child. And it seems (at least to me) clear that this would be just as wrong as it would for the first woman to deliberately handicap her child.[8]

It is clear from this example that our responsibility for what happens to our children extends to what we knowingly do to affect how their lives will be, whether or not those lives are in being at the time we make the relevant decisions. This is an important conclusion with ramifications far beyond our present concerns.[9] However, it also highlights a disturbing problem about just how bad the conditions adversely affecting our children must be before we are morally obliged to refrain from inflicting those conditions on them.

Suppose, along the lines of the above example, a woman learns that if she conceives a child this month it will have a minor handicap but that if she waits for three months she can conceive a perfectly healthy child. We would all judge that she should wait the three months rather than have a handicapped child. We should notice a very important feature of this case. It is that if the woman decides not to wait she will have a child that while handicapped, will have a life that is still well worth living. We can imagine that the handicap in question will be, say, the absence of one hand. Now, to be born thus handicapped is that child's only chance of being born at all – that is, it is that child's only chance of life. For the child that will be conceived three months hence, coming as it will from a different egg (let alone different sperm) will be a *different child* – not the same child minus the handicap. So, if she doesn't wait, it would be difficult to suggest that the child who results, handicapped as she will be, has been wronged by her mother, for that child will still have a life worth living and has the chance of a life thus handicapped or no life at all. So if we judge, as surely we must, that the mother in this example ought to wait, it is not because if she fails to do so she will have wronged her child but rather, that she will have done wrong. What then is the wrong she will have done? It seems that this must be understood in terms of the wrongness of bringing needless, avoidable suffering into the world, suffering that would be avoided if the woman waited for three months.

We clearly need to modify Mill's argument, for consideration of the present example makes it clear that our responsibility with regard to having children is not the responsibility to avoid harming people by bringing them into existence under adverse conditions, but the responsibility not to cause needless avoidable suffering by bringing into existence, when we need not do so, individuals who we know will suffer.

But this clarification brings a further problem in its wake. It seems clear that a mother faced with the dilemma we have been considering should not go ahead and conceive a handicapped child when she can wait and conceive a child who will be normal. But what if waiting will make no difference? What should a mother do when faced with the choice of having a handicapped child or no child (or no further child) at all?

We are surely far less confident that a woman faced with that dilemma should decide to have no children rather than have a child with a significant but still relatively minor handicap. When and why do the good reasons a woman has to postpone pregnancy to avoid bringing into the world a child who will inevitably suffer, cease to have effect? It looks as though the answer is that they cease to have effect at the point at which she can no longer regard her prospective child as replaceable. But why should this be? If she is right in thinking it wrong to add to the suffering of the world when she can avoid doing so by, in this case, postponing pregnancy and having a normal child later, why does it not remain wrong for this woman to add to the suffering of the world when the only alternative is to avoid absolutely having a child (or another child)? If she is wrong to have a handicapped child when she can *replace* it with a normal one, why does it seem less wrong, or not wrong at all, when that child is not replaceable?

It would be simple (though not easy) to say that it would be just as wrong for the mother in our present example who can have only handicapped children to go ahead and have them — and maybe this is what we should say, although we must be clear as to what *else* we would be saying if we did say so. One of the other things we would be saying, and perhaps this is partly why we hesitate here, is that certain people or certain sorts of people may not reproduce themselves. For, given the strong desire and strong interest people seem to have in having children, to prevent those who can only have handicapped children from reproducing themselves is to deny those people an important opportunity; and to deny their children the chance to exist at all.

But perhaps an easier answer is available. It is simply that, so long as the handicapped children will none the less have lives that are on balance worth living, the parents would be contributing more happiness than misery to the world by producing such children.

So, in addition to weighing the avoidable suffering that would be brought into the world by the birth of these handicapped children, we have to count in the happiness of such children also, and we have to consider the avoidable suffering to the parents who want offspring but can only produce progeny with some handicap. Faced with the prospect of the frustration of their desire to reproduce, and also with the attack upon their equal status as citizens, which would be involved in denying them an opportunity that others can freely exercise, such individuals would certainly suffer and would feel rightly that they had been victimised. And since their children, though handicapped, would still be glad to be alive, their case looks a strong one.

We can see, then, that a balance has to be struck between the suffering of those who are born handicapped on the one hand and, on the other, the harm which may be done to individuals or classes of people by preventing them from founding families. In conceding this we can see why our intuitions are different in each case we have been considering. We can understand why the person who by postponing conception can avoid the infliction of handicap on her child should do so. We can also understand that, where an individual's only chance to have a child is to have one with a certain degree of handicap, the wrong of creating avoidable suffering must be balanced against the wrong that would be done in denying people the chance to have the children they desire; children, moreover, who despite a certain degree of handicap will have lives that are worth living.[10]

b) Adult-centred Arguments

We have already reviewed some of the adult-centred reasons for founding a family and I will not go further into most of these. One of the most significant adult-centred claims about family foundation concerns more particularly the decision *not to found a family*, and centres on what have come to be thought of as *feminist* claims concerning 'a woman's right to choose'. Now, this slogan covers a large number of separate claims about a woman's control, not only over her own body, but also over the fate and sometimes the very existence of other individuals. The nature and variety of the claims that are made under this umbrella are of the first importance and it is well worth rehearsing some of the main ones. Before we do so, however, one claim that is sometimes made about the legitimacy of arguments about women's rights needs to be considered. It is the idea, often introduced by feminists, that only women are eligible to debate these issues.

Women Only! It is perhaps paradoxical that the advent of feminism, which is in essence a movement for equality, has evolved a separatist strand which not only excludes men from gatherings of feminist women – a not unreasonable and perhaps even an essential measure – but, more significantly, denies the eligibility of men to talk of, or judge, matters regarded as strictly the business of women. The main idea is, I suppose, that one is only qualified to speak of or judge what one knows, and men cannot possibly have the requisite knowledge or experience. They cannot, so the argument goes, know what it is like to be a woman – particularly, what it is like to be a woman oppressed by men. This essential lack of basic data makes men ineligible to contribute to the debate and also of course disqualifies the present author. My own special interest in rebutting this view will be obvious, but even interested parties can be right, and in this case the suggestion that men are ineligible to speak about a range of feminist issues – including those we are now addressing – is either tautological or false. False because, as Wittgenstein has shown,[11] most of the claims to knowledge that we can make, and most indeed of what passes for knowledge in education, is communicated by language rather than by personal and private experience. And anything communicated in language is in principle understandable by competent language users. If the feminists were right, then their own entitlement to speak about most things would be undermined, for most of the issues about which they (or anyone) would wish to speak require knowledge based on other than personal experience.

There is also a rather suspicious elitism about this position. If it were correct, it would deny any excluded minority from talking or making judgements about the domain from which they had been excluded, thereby disqualifying them from a valid critique of their oppressors.

Control of Reproduction. We must now take up again the question of the validity of feminist claims about 'a woman's right to choose'. Many of these claims have to do with what is often called a woman's 're-productive destiny': whether or not to have sexual relations at all, choice of partners, decisions about whether or not to take contraceptive precautions and choice of method, decisions about whether or not to have – or to try to have – children, and decisions about whether or not to have abortions. All of these claims are contested by some people and are regarded as controversial.

There are of course disputes about the age at which women may legitimately be free to have sexual relations with others, and there are also legal constraints on such matters. In marriage there are disputes about whether a woman is free to decline sexual intercourse and hence as to whether rape within marriage is legally possible. Many people besides parents may attempt to influence the choice of sexual or marriage partners and there may be cultural and racial (or racist) influences here also. The now notorious 'Gillick' case, the bare bones of which were mentioned earlier, has highlighted attempts to influence or circumscribe a young girl's ability to take contraceptive measures on her own responsibility as well as her ability to choose whether or not to have an abortion.

A woman's right to choose abortion, for example, depends not simply on establishing her competence to make autonomous choices for herself, but also on what might be termed the moral status of the foetus. And her right to choose to have children if she wants them will depend on the justifiability of bringing children into the world in circumstances that could for some reason be morally questionable.

These dimensions of the problem of understanding the morality of choosing to found a family – or of choosing not to do so – are apt to be lost in the fog of political rhetoric and religious humbug that so often surrounds discussion of these issues. For example, those feminists who are inclined to say that 'no true state of equality can exist for women in a society that denies them freedom and privacy in respect of fertility control'[12] must be entitled to claim that women would be justified in purchasing their equality, or that society is entitled to establish such equality, at the cost of the lives of the many foetuses that must be sacrificed to the establishment of such a right.[13] Equally, those who regard the life of the foetus as *sacred* must be satisfied that there are good reasons for supposing that the life of the foetus is not only valuable, but that it has a value comparable with that of the adults whose freedom and political rights its protection may threaten.

If it could be shown that the life of the foetus is sacred or that unborn children are entitled to the same protections as are afforded to adults, then a woman's right to choose would have to be balanced against the competing rights of the foetus to exist, or at least its right not to have its existence terminated at the wish of its mother. But the foetus does not possess those capacities that make its life valuable, that render it capable of valuing its own existence and hence make it wrong to deprive that individual of something that it values.[14] 'A woman's right to choose' does not then have to compete with the right of the foetus to exist, and one very powerful set of arguments against the freedom of choice for women concerning the foundation of families disappears.

Two challenges to a woman's right to opt for abortion if she wants it are often produced at this point and it would be as well, while we are on the subject, to give them the brief attention that they deserve. The two challenges usually appear in the form of demands that either the father's interests in founding a family or (usually if she is young) the girl's parents' preferences about these matters are to be given due weight. Certainly they should be given due weight, but the weight due to them is far from massive, for if the woman whose pregnancy is at issue does not want that pregnancy to continue, then to give the sort of weight that might tip the scales to the preferences of either the father of the foetus or its maternal grandparents (whatever their parental authority) would be to conclude that any of these third parties might be entitled to subject the woman most concerned to the risks and pains of continued pregnancy and childbirth against her will. It is one thing for a woman to run these risks and endure these pains voluntarily, but to be effectively forced to do so by the weight given to the preferences of her lover, husband, or parents would be to legalise assault, battery, and imprisonment to a quite unprecedented extent.

The justification for permitting the preferences of others to force these things upon a woman in the absence of arguments that refer to the need to protect the foetus seems entirely absent. We have seen then, that women capable of autonomous choice, whether or not they are of 'legal' age, may elect not to found families if that is their choice and may take whatever steps they please to this end including, if necessary, aborting the unwanted foetus. I say 'if necessary', for no rational women would regard abortion, with its attendant dangers and unpleasantnesses, as a first-line method of contraception.

If, however, a woman decides that she would like to have children, are there any moral considerations that would prove stronger than her own preferences and which should incline us to conclude that she may not in fact be entitled to do so?

Unfit Parents. There are a number of circumstances in which it is claimed that certain individuals or certain types of people might be unfit for parenthood. Some of these considerations might with equal appropriateness have been considered under the heading 'Child-centred arguments', for they depend on the supposition that these adults are 'unfit' to have children because of disastrous consequences for the children. Before moving to a consideration of these cases, we must look quickly at some circumstances in which the alleged unfitness has nothing or little to do with the consequences for the child.

1 *Harm to the Parents.* Some parents might be thought unsuitable candidates for parenthood because of the consequent risk to themselves. The clearest case is where it is known that a mother would risk her own life or risk severe damage to her own health if she were to become pregnant or continue her pregnancy, and where the child would be normal and could probably be born alive, perhaps by post mortem Caesarian section. This is not the place to examine the question of suicide nor indeed the question of autonomy. If we assume that autonomous individuals may choose even to harm themselves or end their own lives it would be hard to think that they are not entitled to do so in circumstances in which they would thereby give life to others. To conclude otherwise would also, incidentally, rule out those acts of heroism, quite unconnected with childbirth, in which someone rescues another at the cost of her own life.

Children may also threaten their parents where the disability of the potential addition to the family would strain the health

and resources of the parents. Here again this seems clearly a
matter for parental choice.

2 *Harm to the Other Children of the Family.* There are, however, some
   circumstances in which particularly demanding additional members of a family may damage the other siblings or other children
   in the family. Should parents knowing that this is likely to be the
   case go ahead and have, say, a child they know will be handicapped and thus likely to damage other children by its demands
   – or, for that matter, a specially gifted child who, they know,
   would be likely to have the same effect?

Such circumstances may constitute good reasons for parents to decide not to have any more children, and good reasons for anyone to
conclude that perhaps they ought not to have any more. But the
question for us is whether, if the parents decide that it is worth the
risk or the certainty of some damage, they should be permitted or
helped to go ahead. Do they have the right to have children in such
circumstances?

This is perhaps no great problem; the damage we are talking about
is likely to be at best speculative and at worst far from serious. It would
be hard to conclude that children are entitled to be protected from
such damage at the cost of draconian penalties against their parents
of the sort that would have to be imposed in an attempt to prevent
them from adding to their families, or indeed at the cost of consigning
such children to the – under the circumstances – gratuitous fate of
being brought up as 'orphans'.

c) Society-centred Arguments

Under this heading we must look again at those whose fitness to
become parents is challenged on the grounds of some alleged defect.
One group of people who are increasingly 'up front' about their desire
for, and intention to, have children, are homosexuals of either gender.
Of course, gay women have always been able to have children in the
normal way by finding a willing male to oblige, but with the advent
of artificial insemination and *in vitro* fertilisation, it has been possible
for lesbians to have children without compromising their sexuality.
But the necessity of their availing themselves, to a greater or lesser
extent, of technical and medical assistance with fertilisation has raised
the possibility of the denial of that assistance. And indeed it is still
rare for single women, let alone those who are openly lesbian, to be
offered the assistance of health professionals in their endeavours to
become pregnant.

It is important to be clear that when a particular and indentifiable group of people are denied the opportunity to have the children they want, or are denied the assistance in that endeavour which is standardly provided for the generality of women, they are wronged in three important and separate ways.

First, and obviously, they are denied the chance to have their own child in the way that they want, something universally regarded as a benefit both to themselves and to society, and one so great that it is often cited not only as among the most worthwhile experiences and important benefits of life, but as one that gives point and meaning to existence. To be denied this benefit, which is available to others, is certainly to be wronged.

Second, such people are wronged if they are treated in a way which is tantamount to singling them out as second-class individuals, deemed unfit for parenthood and unsafe to be offered the care of children. To treat them so is to stigmatise such individuals and to offer them a public insult from which they are unable to defend themselves and to which it is difficult to reply. This happens also when information about, and discussion of, their way of life is excluded from school education on the grounds that it is offensive or unsuitable for consideration in that context.

Finally, where against all the odds such women do manage to succeed in becoming pregnant, they are further stigmatised by being made the subjects of especially stringent scrutiny and suspicion. They – and others – notice that they are singled out from the generality of mothers-to-be, and this again does them a separate and not insignificant wrong.[15]

The justifications for imposing these disadvantages on individuals and for insulting them and stigmatising the group with which they identify would have to be strong indeed, and we will consider these supposed justifications while examining the case of those who would acquire families by methods other than those of genetic reproduction.

III Controlling Family Acquisition

Genetic reproduction is obviously not the only way of founding families. Families are also founded when people acquire the custody of children whom they treat in some sense as their own. Adoption, fostering, and surrogacy agreements are all methods by which people may absorb children into their family who are not, or are not entirely, genetically related to the 'parents'. In our society, and in most industrialised societies, it has been customary to screen adoptive and foster parents and, lately, those entering into surrogacy agreements as to their suitability for the role and responsibility of parenting. This is somewhat odd, for it implies that we think it matters that people establish that they are fit and proper potential parents before we permit them the custody of children; it implies that we care about the sort of people who propose to have children. But we do not. Anyone who doubts this has only to think of the cavalier way in which society allows any Thomasina, Dorothea, or Harriet to go out and have children without so much as a 'by your leave'. We must remember that adoptive, foster, and surrogate parenting is a tiny proportion of the total parent population, so that the percentage of parents that we bother to scrutinise for their adequacy in the role is a negligible proportion of the whole.

The alternatives seem to be these: Either it matters that people demonstrate their adequacy as parents or it does not. If it matters, then it matters not only that adoptive and foster parents do so but that all children get whatever protection it is that screening might afford. If it doesn't matter, or if we believe that screening is useless or otherwise unacceptable, then why subject adoptive and other non-genetic parents to such a process?

It may be thought that these alternatives as stated are misleading, for might it not be argued that we cannot regulate sexual behaviour or stop people from having children if they so choose, and therefore have no alternative but to allow the current unbridled procreation? But where existing children are for some reason left without natural parents willing or able to assume the role, then we have some responsibility to be careful about whom we allow to have care of them.

But this way of stating things is not quite right either. For, as we have suggested, it *would* be possible to regulate even sexual procreation by attaching various disincentives and mandatorily depriving unlicensed parents of the custody of their children – at least until they had been screened like any adoptive parents. The reason we don't do so is not because we cannot, but because we don't want to. And we don't want to for very good reasons. These reasons have to do with the importance we attach to having children and being parents – an importance already more than once spelled out in detail. They also have to do with our reluctance to place so much power in the hands of any government: a power not only to regulate the population, but an immense one of general interference. This power would enable governments not only to interfere with what is acknowledged as one of the most important human freedoms, but also would give them the ability to use that power selectively or arbitrarily to intimidate or punish individuals or sections of the population for other and ulterior reasons unconnected with the desirability of protecting children. The power would have to be quite extraordinarily comprehensive, for it is difficult to imagine what areas of life would not be relevant to forming a view about an individual's suitability for parenthood. There would be no limit to the ambit of those officials charged with screening potential parents, and so no limit to a government's power to delve into the private affairs of citizens.

Moreover, these powers would be unnecessary, for we are able to protect candidates for adoption or fostering in the same way as we do all other children – by removing from the custody of their parents any children who have been palpably ill-treated or placed in danger and by disqualifying any potential parents who have proved their unfitness by a history of damaging or ill-treating children.

There is another and very important reason why we do not screen all potential parents. It is that we haven't the first idea of what makes someone a bad parent *in advance of their actually being one.*

Nor for that matter and equally importantly, do we have the first idea of what it is for someone to be a good parent.

What I mean to imply is that we do not have the first idea of how to characterise a 'good parent' and so do not know what the description of a 'bad parent' would be, *except* in the sense that a parent who neglects, batters, or who sexually assaults her child is unfit to have the care of children. But we have no reliable way of predicting in advance of seeing the bruises, so to speak, just who these child batterers will be. Moreover, the injustice of attempting to find people 'guilty' in advance of the offence seems no less applicable to cases such as these than it does in any other areas of human affairs.

There is absolutely no evidence that homosexuals of either gender make bad parents, nor for that matter do we have any hard information as to the adverse effects on children of being brought up in single-parent families. In the absence of such information it is hard to imagine what justifications there might be for stigmatising homosexuals or single people as somehow unfit for parenting, or the justifications for placing obstacles in the way of their becoming parents or for not affording them the help of any social or medical services that they may need to call in aid in order to found families.

IV Conclusion: Decontrolling Family Foundation

The conclusion that we have reached seems to be the following: The desire to found a family – whether by procreation, adoption, fostering,

or surrogacy – is constrained only by consideration for the fate of the
children who will constitute that family.

Where the children are or will be severely handicapped, there may
be an obligation not to bring them into or allow them to continue in
a world where their existence will be genuinely terrible. Where the
handicap is something less than this – that is, where the children will
have a reasonable if restricted life, and are likely to prefer that life
to non-existence – then, if the parents can have their own children
without inflicting even that handicap, say by having healthy children
later, they should do so. Where there is no alternative for particular
parents but to have handicapped children, then so long as bringing
those children into existence would not constitute cruelty to them, the
parents may reasonably choose so to do.

People who wish to found families where the question of handicap
does not arise are entitled to do so and are entitled to all normally
available assistance unless it can be palpably shown that they are unfit
to be parents. And this unfitness must be palpable and demonstrable,
not statistical, speculative, or based on sheer prejudice.

NOTES

1 Robert Nozick. *Anarchy, State, & Utopia* (Oxford: Basil Blackwell, 1974),
  p. ix. See also Ronald Dworkin, *Taking Rights Seriously* (London: Duckworth, 1977).
2 For what it's worth! The European Convention on Human Rights can be
  found in Brownlie (see note 5).
3 Going back at least to Abraham, or to whoever set down the story of
  Abraham, whichever has the greater historicity.
4 See my *Violence & Responsibility* (London: Routledge & Kegan Paul, 1980),
  Chapter 2, and my 'The Morality of Terrorism' in *Radical Philosophy*,
  Spring 1983, for the elaboration of this point.
5 See *inter alia* European Social Charter 1961, Part I, Sec. 17, in *Basic
  Documents on Human Rights*, ed. Ian Brownlie (Oxford: Oxford University
  Press, 1971).
6 John Stuart Mill, *On Liberty*, Chapter 5, in *Utilitarianism*, ed. Mary Warnock
  (London: Fontana, 1972), p. 239.
7 Ibid.
8 Derek Parfit, 'Rights, Interests and Possible People', in *Moral Problems in
  Medicine*, ed. S. Gorovitz (Englewood Cliffs, N.J.: Prentice-Hall, 1976).
9 See my *Violence and Responsibility* (London: RKP, 1980).
10 See Peter Singer, *Practical Ethics* (Cambridge: Cambridge University Press,
   1979) for a related discussion, particularly Chapters 1 and 2.
11 Wittgenstein's famous private language argument establishes this. I cannot

hope to summarise it here. It is to be found in his *Philosophical Investigations* (Oxford: Basil Blackwell, 1953), Part I, para 243 ff.

12 See Madelaine Simms, quoted by Elizabeth Kingdom in her 'Legal recognition of a woman's right to choose', in *Women in Law*, ed. J. Brophy and C. Smart (London: Routledge & Kegan Paul, 1985).

13 150,000 abortions are performed annually in the United Kingdom and there would perhaps be even more if abortion on demand were legalised.

14 See my *The Value of Life: An Introduction to Medical Ethics* (London: RKP, 1985), Chapter 1.

15 The argument here follows the same lines as that developed in my *The Value of Life*. See note 14.

Part III

The Worth of Children

9

Child Art and the Place of Children in Society

GARETH B. MATTHEWS

> I went to a children's art museum recently. All the paintings were stuck up on refrigerators.[1]

> In the evolution of Klee's mature work the reduction of all things to basic forms was an ultimate achievement but children *proceed* from the point at which Klee finally arrived.[2]

When our younger daughter was about four years old she painted a picture that has become a family favourite. In scarlet on an off-white background, it depicts, in a simple, pyramidal form, the heads and shoulders of three human figures. We framed the picture many years ago and have hung it, from time to time, in a bedroom or family room.

During a recent house move I came across the painting again and stopped to admire its elegance and bright brashness. Though we haven't yet hung it in our new house, I can certainly imagine finding a good place for it and thinking that, of the various options open to us, hanging that particular painting in that particular place would be the very best thing we could do.

Of course there are personal reasons why my family and I like that particular painting. It reminds us of our daughter, whom we love very much. It recalls an interesting period in her life, and in our lives. And by now it is familiar to us in a way that makes it reinforce a sense of continuity in our lives.

Suppose, though, that a friend of ours who is a museum curator were to visit and to view the painting. (Let's call the painting, which now has no name, *Three Figures in Scarlet*.) Is it conceivable that a competent art collector might decide that *Three Figures in Scarlet* is a significant work of art, one worthy to be exhibited in, say, the Boston Museum of Fine Arts?

Of course anyone who tried seriously to answer that question might want more information about *Three Figures*, or about my daughter, and might want to have a look at the painting itself. But would one *need* to have more information, or to look at the painting, to answer the question? Or have I already said enough to make quite clear that the answer is 'No'? To put the question the other way around, could it be a reasonable response for the curator of a major art museum to say that she would have to look at the painting by a young child to determine whether it would be suitable for the museum's permanent collection?

Of course the Boston museum might be doing a special collection to illustrate, so to speak, the natural history of painting and drawing. The curator might want *Three Figures in Scarlet* as a fine example of some recognisable style or stage of development in children's painting. I shall explore a little later what it might mean to say that this or that work would make a good addition to a collection of children's art. For the moment, though, let's consider the bigger question. Is it conceivable that *Three Figures in Scarlet* might be a good addition to a general collection of art?

In fact, curators don't go around collecting art irrespective of category. They may find something that would make a good addition to their collection of impressionism, or Flemish art, or cubism, or Japanese watercolours, or what have you. But they collect work in categories. So even if we don't imagine our friend the curator as mounting an exhibition of children's art, we seem to have to think of her as categorising *Three Figures in Scarlet* in some way or other. Is there a recognised category in which a painting by a four-year-old might excel?

Again, the obvious category for *Three Figures in Scarlet* would be children's art. But, again, let's postpone discussing that. Is there some other category into which it might fit?

Recapitulation theories of childhood, that is, theories according to which individual ontogeny recapitulates phylogeny, suggest that *Three Figures* might be classsified as primitive art. But which primitive art? Well, suppose the style were suggestive of some of the prehistoric art of Oceania, say some of the rock or bark art of Western Australia. Perhaps interesting comparisons could indeed be made between *Three Figures in Scarlet* and certain examples of Australian rock art. But that certainly wouldn't mean that my daughter's childhood painting belongs in a museum's collection of Australian rock art – it doesn't. Nor would it fit into any other recognised category of 'primitive' or tribal art.

If it wouldn't fit into a collection of tribal art, then perhaps it should go into a modern collection. One might note, for example, similarities between *Three Figures in Scarlet* and some of the abstractionist paintings

Paul Klee did in the 1930s. Maybe it should be added to the museum's collection of abstractionism.

It is an important fact about Klee that he was interested in children's art, including, at one point, the drawings and paintings he himself had produced as a child. Indeed, the very first catalogue of his own art begins with examples of art he had produced as a child.[3] And many of his later works, including especially, I should say, many paintings from the last decade of his life, are done in a style suggestive of child art.[4] It is quite conceivable that one of these later works should be strikingly similar to *Three Figures in Scarlet*. Does that mean that *Three Figures* might be added, appropriately, to the museum's collection of abstractionism?

Not really, I think. Of course our friend, the curator, might mount a special exhibition of children's art in the company of late Klee. The point might be to help us appreciate the work of Klee done in a childlike style by laying it alongside real children's art. In a similar spirit, one might put examples of African tribal art alongside works by Picasso that were influenced by African art.[5] Again, the point would be to help us to appreciate Picasso by comparing his art with the work his art was influenced by.

Of course it might work the other way around, too. Picasso might help us understand tribal art better, and Klee might help us understand child art better. Even so, a special exhibition of Klee and children's art wouldn't tend to show that a child's painting, such as *Three Figures in Scarlet*, belongs in the museum's permanent collection of twentieth-century abstractionism, any more than the Picasso–African exhibition would suggest that early African art – or some of it – belongs in, say, the museum's collection of cubism.

The basic reason *Three Figures* doesn't belong in any of the collections established by mainline art museums is that those collections are defined historically and geographically. Striking as the similarities might be between *Three Figures* and painting or drawing in some categorised period or recognised movement, it wouldn't really belong in a collection of that art because it doesn't belong to that period or movement. Whether art should be collected in some radically different manner is a question I shall not discuss. As art *is* collected, *Three Figures in Scarlet* wouldn't belong in any collection of any established art museum.

One simple alteration in museum collections would open up the possibility of acquiring *Three Figures in Scarlet*. It would be to establish, as an addition, a permanent collection of children's art. I turn now to the question of whether it would be appropriate to establish such a collection and to the broader question of how answering the first question might help us understand better the place of children in our society and culture.

There exist already, of course, museums of childhood. Such places nourish adult nostalgia, but they also serve the more educational purpose of helping us to think about the history, sociology, and anthropology of childhood. Such a museum might reserve a wing for children's art. But the purpose of including child art would be to remind us of the phenomenon of children's drawing and painting, to exhibit something of its cultural and historical diversity, and also, perhaps, something of its cross-cultural and historical universality.

In asking whether an *art* museum, indeed a good art museum, should have a permanent collection of children's art we were, however, considering a different interest from any that would be addressed primarily by a museum of childhood. We are asking whether child art might be appropriately celebrated as art, rather than merely regarded as social and cultural artifact. Of course, doing one of those things doesn't necessarily exclude doing the other. The point, though, is that doing one doesn't necessarily *include* doing the other.

One might have expected to get some help in answering my question by looking at the persisting efforts of philosophers of art to answer Tolstoy's profoundly simple question, 'What is art?' But a little reflection will reveal that such an expectation would be unrealistic. Whether we come to accept the Imitation Theory of art, or the Expression Theory, or the Institutional Theory, or some other theory, there can be no serious question that some of the drawings and paintings of young children count as art. Indeed, it should count as a criterion of adequacy on any theory of art that it recognise at least some children's drawings and paintings as art. My question is whether among such drawings and paintings as do count as art, some are worthy of belonging to the permanent collection of a major museum. No theory intended merely to distinguish art from non-art is likely to be of much help with that question.

In more than one way, the question I am asking is a political question. In a society of children, the children might decide for themselves whether they wanted to celebrate some of the art produced by members of their own 'kind'. In our society, however, children do not have the power to make such a decision. In our society it would have to be an adult decision – a decision concerning financial resources under adult control – whether to collect children's art for a major museum.

For us, then, the question is whether we adults consider it appropriate or worthwhile to celebrate the aesthetic sensibility and artistic achievement of artistically gifted children. This, in turn, raises political questions about exploitation and about which educational ideals we choose to implement in our society. But it also has to do with whether we as adults can recognise anything of profound worth in the work of a child, even a very sensitive and gifted child.

In the aesthetic evaluation of children's art there are certainly enthusiasts as well as detractors. Aldous Huxley must be counted among the most enthusiastic of the former. In his introduction to a pamphlet of Spanish children's drawings[6] he writes that 'when left to themselves', children 'display astonishing artistic talents'. He goes on:

How sure is their sense of colour! I remember especially one landscape of a red-roofed house among dark trees and hills that possessed in its infantile way all the power and certainty of a Vlaminck.... Many of these pastoral landscapes and scenes of war are composed — all unwittingly of course, and by instinct — according to the most severely elegant classical principles. Voids and masses are beautifully balanced about the central axis. Houses, trees, figures are placed exactly where the rule of the Golden Section demands that they should be placed.

Huxley claims that 50 percent of children are 'little geniuses in the field of pictorial art', whereas among adults the percentage goes down to one in a million.

The detractors are perhaps even more easily found. I recently approached the curator of painting and sculpture at a major art museum (not, I should say, the Boston Museum of Fine Arts) with the suggestion that he mount an exhibition on the theme, 'Twentieth-Century Art and Children's Art'. I suggested he exhibit some well-chosen children's art both for its own sake and also for the relationship it would bear to the work of Klee, Miró, Dubuffet, and other twentieth-century artists whose work was influenced by child art, or at least seems to show affinities with children's art.

This curator agreed that an exhibition along such lines could have great didactic value. Indeed, he even named museums — other than his own — that might be interested in such a show. But he assured me that no children's art would ever be shown in his museum as long as he was chief curator. He would allow nothing to be exhibited there, he said, that was not first-rate art; and no children's art, he insisted, was first-rate art.

There is an identifiable position about children and the goods of childhood from which it would follow that this adamant curator was right and Huxley wrong. I suspect that some rather vague version of this position is held by many people in our society, perhaps by most people. It is given a clear statement and a straightforward defense by Michael Slote in his book, *Goods and Virtues*.[7]

Slote thinks that the goods of life are relative to the period of one's life. His claim is not just that what can be reasonably pursued as a good for childhood, or senescence, is different from what can be reasonably pursued as a good for young adulthood, or middle-age, though he also assumes that to be the case. His claim is the more interesting one that the goods of childhood and the goods of old age are less valuable, indeed much less valuable, than the goods available at the prime of life. To dramatise his point he asks us to weigh the value of good dreams. 'In a way', he writes,

> our treatment of childhood . . . is interestingly similar to the way we regard what happens in dreams. Proust tells us (roughly) that we do not reckon the sufferings and pleasures of our dreams among the actual goods and evils of our lives. . . . And just as dreams are discounted except as they affect (the walking portions of) our lives, what happens in childhood principally affects our view of total lives through the effects that childhood success or failure are supposed to have on mature individuals. Thus in cases where an unhappy schoolboy career is followed by (or, as we sometimes like to think, helps to bring about) happy mature years, we think of the later years as compensating for childhood misery, even as wiping the slate clean. (pp. 14–15)

In defence of this way of thinking Slote does several things. First, he tries to elicit from his readers the recognition that they share this view with him, even if they have not heretofore given much thought to the fact that this is indeed their view. Second, he tries to defend the view against the objection that it makes the goals, frustrations, successes, and failures of childhood irrational or perverse much in the way that the goals and frustrations of an addict, under the influence of the addiction, are perverse or irrational. And finally, in response to the objection that this view fails to account for the unity of a human life, he sketches a conception of, so to speak, the contour of human life. That conception is meant to support the idea that prime-of-life goods are much more valuable than those of any other period and even, perhaps, that childhood goods, though they 'have value for, or in, childhood', do not have 'value *ueberhaupt*', that is, value 'from the perspective of human life as a whole' (p. 17).

It seems to follow from this last point that a child's painting, though it might have great value for, or in, childhood, would probably not have value *ueberhaupt*. Since child art hardly deserves to be recognised as a distinct curatorial category in major art museums unless some of it has value *ueberhaupt*, I shall now say a little about the defensibility of Slote's view.

The devaluation of the goods of childhood that Slote both describes and commends to us is embodied, I think, in the very structure of our social institutions. It is adults, after all, and especially adults in the prime of their lives, who determine the reward-structure of our institutions and have the greatest influence in applying this structure to the individuals who get exhibitions, listings in *Who's Who*, positions on important boards, and so forth. These structures do allow homage to has-beens in their dotage; but, in general, most prizes go to achievers in the prime of life.

As far as art is concerned, our great museums embody the assessment that the celebration and appreciation of the work of great artists are among life's greater goods. But the treatment of children's art shows that we think of it as having only instrumental and personal value. It has personal value to parents, teachers, and friends associated with the child artist. It has instrumental value insofar as producing it furthers the general development of the child and, in rare cases, the further development of someone who will actually become an important artist. Otherwise, it has no value.

To justify this assignment of values Slote appeals to what is essentially a biological view of the nature and significance of childhood and old age. Here is part of what he says:

Consider how ordinary people and biologists tend to think of plants and animals over time. Within the life cycle of a given organism a distinction is typically drawn between periods of development and periods of decay, and this distinction is partly marked by treating a certain period of maturity as representing the fullest development of the organism and other periods as leading 'up to', or 'down from', it. In keeping with these distinctions, there is also a tendency to think of organisms as being most fully what they are (what they have it in them to be) during maturity, a tendency perhaps most clearly exemplified in the tradition of making general reference to organisms by their adult names rather than by names appropriate to other stages of their life cycle. (We speak of the parts of a tree's life, not of a seed's or sapling's life, of the development and decline, or old age, of a horse, but not of a colt.) (p. 36)

This biological profile suggests that the stretch of an individual organism's life that counts as maturity for that organism is also normative for it. Goods and products from earlier on are devalued as immature, whereas those that come later are devalued as belonging to senescence. Applied to the question at hand, the best reason one could have, it may seem, for refusing to establish a permanent collection of children's art in a major museum is that such art would be, perforce, immature art, and therefore inappropriate for collection alongside the most mature artistic achievements of our civilisation.

Perhaps there was a time when even the best tribal art of Oceania, Africa, and North and South America was considered primitive and therefore, as civilisations go, immature. Not many people have that attitude anymore. Artists in tribal societies are now recognised to have had traditions and apprenticeships that make it possible to distinguish mature artists and mature objects of art in a given tribal style. Moreover, the attitude towards a tribal culture embodied in the supposition that the whole culture is immature now strikes most of us both as naïve and morally offensive. Tribal art, we now think, is not, as such, immature.

We cannot, therefore, use the example of tribal art, which is represented in the collections of some of our most prestigious art museums, to question the assumption that only mature art deserves to be collected in major museums. But we can question that assumption in other ways. We could begin by asking whether Marcel Duchamp's notorious urinal, *La Fontaine*, or Andy Warhol's collection of soup cans are mature art. The notion of maturity doesn't seem to apply here.

Another relevant group of artists to consider are the so-called modern primitives. Is the art of Grandma Moses or Henri Rousseau mature art? The question seems odd. Consider Grandma Moses. Her art is unschooled; it is therefore a form of folk art. It also has about it a childlike naïveté. But, although Grandma Moses painted for the last quarter of a century of her very long life, her work did not move away from that naïveté to anything one could designate, by contrast, as mature art.

The art of a ten- or twelve-year-old who is learning to draw in an art class may be said to be immature. Perhaps it is self-consciously directed towards the satisfaction of prescribed norms and principles. Much less clear is whether the art of, say, a four-year-old could be called immature. It is not produced in a self-conscious attempt to satisfy norms or principles. But whether or not it is immature, it certainly does not count as mature art.

Does the lack of maturity in even the most aesthetically pleasing or exciting work of a four- or five-year-old automatically disqualify it from being collected alongside the best art in our culture and the other cultures we regularly celebrate? If we can assume that modern primitivists like Grandma Moses and Henri Rousseau and conceptual artists like Marcel Duchamp and Andy Warhol do deserve to be collected alongside the best art of our culture, we should conclude, I suspect, that maturity is not a necessary condition for deserving that status.

Suppose lack of maturity fails to *disqualify* children's art from being collected by a major museum. What would qualify it? That is, even if we move away from the biologically based conception of evaluation that Michael Slote relies on and allow that some of the art objects we want exhibited in even our most exalted exhibition halls cannot be called mature, we need a positive reason to select and celebrate in this way the best of children's art.

At this point it may be useful to compare child art with child philosophy. In *Philosophy and the Young Child*[8] I maintain that many young children naturally raise questions, make comments, and even engage in reasoning that professional philosophers can recognise as philosophical. Not only do they do philosophy naturally, they do it with a freshness of perspective and a sensitivity to puzzlement and conceptual mismatch that is hard for adults to achieve. The adult must cultivate the naïveté that is required for doing philosophy well; to the child such naïveté is entirely natural.

I don't mean that children, or even some children, are better philosophers than any adults are. Of course that isn't true. Other things besides a willingness to question accepted beliefs are important to doing philosophy well. But there is a freshness, an urgency and a naturalness about child philosophy that both asks to be celebrated for itself and that can help us appreciate the nature and significance of adult philosophy – or better, of philosophy itself. If one focused exclusively on the adult phenomenon, one would have only a truncated conception of what it is that moves people to ask and re-ask those age-old questions.

Might there be something analogous in child art? Might there be in the best children's art something that both asks to be celebrated in and for itself and also something that can help us appreciate the nature and significance of adult art, indeed, of art *ueberhaupt*? I think there is. If so, then child art needs to be exhibited as much as child philosophy needs to be recognised, and even published.[9]

Attempts to conceive childhood and to evaluate child culture have tended to assume either that children are merely proto-people, to be cherished and nurtured principally for their potential, or else that they are models of innocence and insight to be emulated by adults. Neither assumption is satisfactory.

Children are people, fully worthy of both the moral and the intellectual respect due persons. They should be respected for what they are, as well as for what they can become. Indeed, we can learn from them and let them enrich our lives as, much more obviously, they learn from us and let us enrich their lives. The parent or teacher who is open to the perspectives of children and to their forms of sensibility is blessed with gifts that adult life otherwise lacks.

Yet it is only in certain respects that a child's perspective is valuable to adults. Adult endeavours can have a rigour, a discipline, and a sense of history that the corresponding child efforts are bound to lack. Adult art can have a mastery of technique and a sense of style and of its place in the history of art that is not open to child art. The problem, then, is to learn how to celebrate child art for what it is and can legitimately be, without either condescension or sentimentality.

It is worth noting that both child art and child philosophy should lead us to question Michael Slote's contention that only prime-of-life goods have value *ueberhaupt*. Few children grow up to become mature artists and even fewer to become mature philosophers. For many people the art and philosophy of their childhood is never equalled, let alone surpassed, by the art or philosophy of their adult lives. If painting or doing philosophy has any non-instrumental value for them, it is their child art and their child philosophy that has such value.

So, should *Three Figures in Scarlet*, or some other work of art by a four-year-old, be added to the permanent collection of the Boston Museum of Fine Arts? I think so. Will it? That is harder to say.

Whether children's art is ever collected by our most famous art museums will depend, I suspect, on whether the currents of modernism further discredit the assumption that maturity is a *sine qua non* for an art object's being worthy of collection by a major art establishment.

If the 'maturity assumption' is widely rejected and children's art is collected seriously, that development will, no doubt, have interesting and significant social and political consequences. For one thing, our attitude towards children and towards the value-system that systematically devalues their thought, their sensibility, their experience, and the works of their creation will also change. With such change will come changes in the roles we allow to children in our society. I hope I have said enough to suggest that these developments could constitute, not only a step towards children's liberation, but a significant step towards adult liberation as well.

NOTES

1 Steven Wright, comedian, as reported in the newspaper, *The Oregonian*, Portland, Oregon, 23 January 1986.

2 J. S. Pierce, *Paul Klee and Primitive Art* (New York: Garland Publishers, 1976), p. 110.

3 O. K. Werckmeister, *Versuche ueber Paul Klee* (Frankfurt am Main; Syndikat, 1981), p. 127.

4 The intriguing and complex story of Klee's relation to children's art is very well told in the essay entitled 'Klees Kindliche Kunst', in Werckmeister's book, pp. 124–78.

5 As was done in the recent exhibition, ' "Primitivism" in 20th Century Art: Affinity of the Tribal and the Modern', at the Museum of Modern Art in New York (Sept. 1984–Jan. 1985).

6 Aldous Huxley, *They Still Draw Pictures*, published by the Spanish Child Welfare Association of America, New York, 1939, p. 3ff. I owe notice of this passage to George Boas, *The Cult of Childhood* (London: Warburg Institute, 1966), p. 100.

7 Oxford: Clarendon Press, 1983.

8 Cambridge, Mass.: Harvard University Press, 1980.

9 For a nice consideration of six child artists as artists, rather than proto-artists, see Sheila Paine, *Six Children Draw* (London: Academic Press, 1981). My own books *Philosophy and the Young Child* (see note 8) and *Dialogues with Children* (Harvard, 1984) are attempts to publish child philosophy.

10

Should All Seriously Disabled Infants Live?

HELGA KUHSE AND PETER SINGER

Modern medical technology has given us the means to sustain the lives of many seriously ill or handicapped young children who, only a decade or two ago, would have died soon after birth because the means were not available to keep them alive. But should we always try to preserve every child's life by all available means, or are there times when a young child should be allowed, or helped, to die because she is seriously ill or handicapped?

It is frequently claimed that all human beings, including handicapped newborn infants, have a 'right to life' and that it is morally wrong to base life and death decisions in the practice of medicine on the quality or kind of life in question. In this article, we shall dispute that claim and argue that quality and kind of life constitute a proper basis for medical decision-making for seriously ill or handicapped young children.

To begin, let us consider the following case. It is described by Fred M. Frohock, a professor of political science, in his recent book *Special Care*, written after he had spent four months as an observer in a modern neonatal intensive care unit of an unnamed American hospital (Frohock 1986).

Stephanie Christopher. On March 8, Stephanie Christopher was born prematurely after only 30 weeks gestation. Her main problem, however, was not her prematurity but rather a congenital disorder, epidermolysis bullosa. This disorder causes widespread and constant blistering of the skin. Lesions occur both on the outer surface of the body and on skin within the body, such as the mouth and oesophagus.

Parts of this chapter are drawn from the authors' book, *Should the Baby Live? The Problem of Handicapped Infants*, Oxford: Oxford University Press, 1985; and from an article, 'For Sometimes Letting – and Helping – Die', forthcoming in *Law, Medicine & Health Care*. The article was written as part of a larger study on 'Life and Death Choices for Defective Newborns', supported by the Australian Research Grants Scheme. We wish to thank the ARGS for their support.

Secondary growth retardation and severe anaemia are part of the syndrome.

Whilst the disease can take different forms, the prognosis is grave and many of those afflicted with it succumb to it within the first two years of life. In those who survive, the lesions may clear and they can frequently expect a satisfactory quality of life. Stephanie was put on a regime of antibiotics and had to be kept in isolation (since the major cause of death in these children is infection). She also needed an operation to clear two intestinal obstructions.

Stephanie lived for two months. During these two months, she endured much. Despite the operation to clear the intestinal obstructions, Stephanie was unable to take sufficient nourishment orally and had to be fed intravenously. But fluid oozed out through her damaged skin, and there were imbalances in hydration and nutrition. There were difficulties in suctioning Stephanie and in inserting tubes because her internal skin, like her external skin, would slough off. She was repeatedly described as a 'burns victim' – a burns victim who was burning up every day. Swathed in vaseline-soaked bandages, Stephanie was given oxygen through a mask placed close to her face, morphine to ease the pain, and another drug, narcan, to counter the effects of too much morphine.

Despite the administration of large doses of morphine, Stephanie did, however, still experience discomfort and pain. On April 8, four weeks after Stephanie's birth, Frohock recorded the following observations in his journal:

[Stephanie] is breathing rapidly, her face a few inches away from the oxygen mask. She looks like an accident victim – tired, even worn out, from some disaster that has struck her....
Stephanie is crying as the gauze is removed. Her left leg is bloody, her foot scraped raw over the ankle and on top. Her right leg looks better except for a large lesion with a scab under the area of the knee. Some of the gauzes are soaked with blood. Her hands are also bloody.... (Frohock 1986, p. 118)

There was also constantly blood in Stephanie's stools and urine.

And, ten days later, on April 18, Frohock writes:

The oxygen mask still blows into her face. She is crying, moving restlessly. Her legs and arms are wrapped in vaseline gauze.... Her body is slick with sweat and vaseline. This is pure suffering. Is there any point to it? (Frohock, 1986, p. 133)

Doctors continued to give antibiotics and oxygen to Stephanie. Also, a decision had been made that Stephanie would be stimulated manually should she stop breathing, but that there would be no resusci-

tation attempts should her heart stop. This happened on May 11, and
Stephanie died.

Should we always try to prolong every infant's life by all possible
means, or should we sometimes allow an infant to die because – even
if we might be able to sustain her life – we cannot give her an acceptable quality of life?

Sanctity of Life or Quality of Life?

People often say that every human life is equally inviolable and valuable – has 'sanctity' – and that we must not base medical decision-
making on the quality or kind of life in question. This view has
traditionally been taken by the Roman Catholic Church and was recently reiterated by Pope John Paul during his visit to Australia:

The Church . . . never ceases to proclaim the sacredness of all human life. . . .
Nothing should be done which is against life in the reality of a concrete
individual, no matter how weak, or defenceless, no matter how undeveloped
or advanced. (Pirrie 1986a)

The Protestant theologian Paul Ramsey, too, affirms the 'sanctity'
of all human life:

[T]here is no reason for saying that [six months in the life of a baby born
with the invariably fatal Tay Sachs disease] are a life span of lesser worth to
God than living seventy years before the onset of irreversible degeneration.
. . . All our days and years are of equal worth whatever the consequence; death
is no more a tragedy at one time than at another time. (Ramsey 1978, p. 191)

The view that all human life is equally valuable and inviolable is
deeply rooted in many people's pre-reflective thinking and is en-
shrined in Anglo–American law. As a Melbourne [Australia] Supreme
Court Judge, Mr. Justice Vincent, recently put it when ordering medical treatment for a baby suffering from spina bifida:

The law does not permit decisions to be made concerning the quality of life
nor any assessment of the value of any human being. . . . No parent, no doctor,
no court has any power to determine that the life of any child, however
disabled the child may be, will be deliberately taken from them. (Pirrie 1986b)

Those who take the view that all human life, irrespective of its
quality or kind, has sanctity would seem to have solved the difficult
question of how to treat seriously ill or handicapped young children;
there is no decision to be made – every child, even one like Stephanie
Christopher, has to be kept alive no less vigorously than would any
other child. Thus, if antibiotics, oxygen, intravenous feeding, and

resuscitation are commonly used in the modern hospital setting, then it is wrong to withhold these life-sustaining means from an infant just because she is handicapped, or experiences a poor quality of life. But few people, if any, ultimately take the view that all human life is equally valuable and inviolable to its logical conclusion. While their judgements that some readily available and effective life-sustaining means may sometimes be withheld or withdrawn may not explicitly refer to quality-of-life considerations, such considerations are nonetheless implicit in their judgements.

As we saw, Paul Ramsey is an advocate of the 'sanctity-of-life' view. He holds that 'all our days and years are of equal worth' and urges that we avoid quality-of-life judgements because they violate the equality of human life (Ramsey 1978, p. 191). And yet, when discussing the case of permanently comatose Karen Ann Quinlan, Ramsey quite clearly makes a quality-of-life judgement: he suggests that life-sustaining treatment may be withdrawn in this case because 'it will affect...the patient's condition in no significant respect except to prolong dying' (Ramsey 1976, p 16). But to say that treatment which would prolong life may be withdrawn *because it does not affect the patient's condition* (Karen's comatose state), is to make an implicit quality-of-life judgement; it is to suggest that treatment may be withdrawn not because it will no longer sustain the patient's life, nor because the patient is 'dying', but rather because it will sustain only a particular *kind* of life – permanently comatose human life (Kuhse 1987, ch. 4).

Implicit quality-of-life judgements are also inherent in the distinction between ordinary and extraordinary means of treatment, traditionally employed in Catholic moral theology. The Jesuit theologian Gerald Kelly has provided the now classical definition of what constitutes 'extraordinary treatment'. Extraordinary means – those that need not be used to sustain life – are 'all medicines, treatments and operations which cannot be obtained without excessive expense, pain or inconvenience or which, if used, would not offer a reasonable hope of benefit' (Kelly 1958, p. 129).

But how do we determine whether a treatment is excessively expensive, painful, or inconvenient, or whether it offers a reasonable hope of benefit? The answer to that question depends largely, and frequently exclusively, on the patient's quality of life with or after treatment. Even the Roman Catholic Church acknowledges this implicitly; in its *Declaration on Euthanasia* (Sacred Congregation for the Doctrine of the Faith 1980, p. 10) it is suggested that it might be better to replace the term 'extraordinary means' by the term 'disproportionate means'. But what is 'disproportionate' will of course vary with the patient's medical condition and with the quality and quantity of life available to her after treatment. A resuscitation attempt, for example, might be 'disproportionate' because it would extend an already burdensome life like Stephanie's by only a short period. On the other hand, if a patient were to gain another year, or ten, of normal life, then the same procedure would not be 'disproportionate'.

Leonard Weber, a Catholic theologian, has considered the question of when we should attempt to resuscitate seriously disabled infants. Weber rejects the view that such decisions should accommodate quality-of-life considerations. Rather, he says, such decisions should be based on the question of whether resuscitation constitutes an ordinary or an extraordinary means. Resuscitation would be extraordinary, or non-obligatory, in the following case:

> If, for example, the oxygen supply to the brain has been stopped and the opportunity to resuscitate only comes when it is probable that extensive damage has already been done to the brain, it should be considered an extraordinary means to attempt to restore normal blood circulation, no matter how common the procedure. (Weber 1976, pp. 92–3)

In other words, no matter how common a procedure might be, it should be considered 'extraordinary' or non-obligatory when it will extend a life that is seriously impaired or damaged. But this means, of course, that Weber – like the other writers we cited before him – is making a quality-of-life judgement.

In short, quality-of-life judgements are ubiquitous – and properly so. For the view that all human lives, irrespective of their quality or kind, are equally valuable and inviolable would, if applied consistently, have the grotesque consequence that life would have to be prolonged even in a situation where the patient would not benefit from such efforts or would be harmed by them.

One example would be the extension of an infant's life in a situation where that infant – either because it is born without a brain or has suffered severe brain damage after birth – will never be able to have conscious experiences. While such an infant will not experience pain or suffering, neither will it experience pleasure or joy – or any of the things that make life valuable. Its life would be like a dreamless sleep. Would it be of value to the infant to have its life prolonged? We think not, for the infant cannot be benefited by anything we do.

In this case, life would be of *no* value to the infant. But there are also situations where life can be of disvalue. Stephanie's life is, in our view, a case in point. Considering Stephanie's life solely from her point of view – disregarding entirely what those who watched her suffering went through, and the cost of her medical care – it would have been better if she had died shortly after her birth. Most of her life was wrought with pain and suffering, and even if she did experience some moments of pleasure or well-being, these moments could hardly have compensated her for what she endured.

Looking back over Stephanie's life now that it is over, this judgement seems undeniable, but could one argue that at the time it was in Stephanie's interests that vigorous efforts were made to keep her alive? After all, even if her chances were slim, Stephanie *might* have survived and experienced a worthwhile life. Was it therefore in her interest to endure what had to be endured? In answering that question, the fact that we are dealing with infants, rather than with older children or adults, is relevant.

Infants and Persons

Asking himself how to weigh the interests of Stephanie, Fred Frohock reflects on the distinction between competent adult patients and young children:

The quality and future of Stephanie's life are problems for everyone who comes into contact with her. No one knows how to weigh her interests in deciding whether to continue or stop her therapy. . . . She is alive. Her neurological functions are intact. . . . Yet her pain and bleak prospects might lead a rational adult to say, 'Enough' – and choose death. Stephanie cannot make this choice, nor affirm its opposite – life – as a choice. Whoever decides for her will have to make very fine decisions on benefits versus burdens, and perhaps even examine quality-of-life conditions in general, for Stephanie can have no thoughts on whether her particular life is worth living. (Frohock 1986, p. 82)

One important difference between infants and competent adult patients is thus that competent patients can express choices and act on them in a way in which infants cannot. However, Frohock's reflection that 'Stephanie can have no thoughts on whether her particular life is worth living', also points to a more fundamental difference between infants and older patients: Infants and older patients have different *kinds* of life.

Before Stephanie Christopher was born, her mother had already given birth to one other child suffering from epidermolysis bullosa. That child had lived for six weeks. To avoid the birth of another child afflicted with the disease, Ms. Christopher underwent prenatal diagnosis during the sixth month of the pregnancy that was to determine whether the child she was now carrying would suffer from this devastating disease. If the tests had been positive, she would presumably have had an abortion. The tests were inconclusive, however, and Ms. Christopher decided to continue the pregnancy. Stephanie was born a little later, when her mother was 30 weeks pregnant.

In making abortions for conditions such as epidermolysis bullosa, spina bifida, and many other handicapping afflictions available to women who want them, we are distinguishing, in our practices, between different *kinds* of life – the lives of foetuses and the lives of more mature human beings; and we draw from this the practical conclusion that different kinds of human life may be treated differently. Whereas many people would agree that foetal life may (at least sometimes) be terminated in the practice of medicine, few people would think it right for doctors to terminate the lives of competent mature patients against these patients' wishes, even if these patients were suffering from conditions that otherwise serve as grounds for abortion.

Is such a distinction between different kinds of human life – adult life and foetal life – defensible? We believe it is is. But we also believe that, as far as questions regarding the prolongation or termination of life are concerned, new-born infants are in most morally relevant respects more like foetuses than like older children or adults.

The validity of this assertion depends on the answer to a prior question: When, and why, are certain actions such as the taking of life directly wrong? The philosopher Michael Tooley has discussed that question – in the context of abortion and infanticide – more systematically than anyone else (Tooley 1983). Employing the language of rights, he suggests that for a being to have a right to something, it must have an interest in it, and, to have an interest in continuing to exist, a being must be a 'continuing self' – that is, a being which has at some time had the concept of itself as existing over time. Beings who are not 'continuing selves' do not have a right to life and it is not directly wrong to take their lives (Tooley 1983, ch. 5). We believe Tooley's argument is basically sound, and shall use the term 'person' to refer to those beings who are capable of seeing themselves as continuing selves – that is, as self-aware beings existing over time.

This, then, is the morally relevant difference between foetuses and infants on the one hand, and more mature human beings on the other: Normal adults and children, but not foetuses and infants, are persons; that is, they are self-aware and purposeful beings with a sense of the past and the future. They can see their lives as a continuing process, they can identify with what has happened to them in the past, and they have hopes and plans for the future. For this reason we can say that in normal circumstances they value, or want, their own continued existence, and that life is in their interest. The same does not apply to foetuses or new-born infants. Neither a foetus nor an infant has the conceptual wherewithal to contemplate a future and to want, or value, that future. This is, perhaps, what Fred Frohock had in mind when he wrote that Stephanie, in distinction from an adult, 'can have no thoughts on whether her particular life is worth living'.

But if an infant cannot value, or want, its own continued existence, then the loss of life for a new-born infant must be less significant than the loss of life for an older child or adult who wants to go on living. This conclusion has, as we shall see, far-reaching consequences for our treatment of seriously ill or handicapped infants.

Infants, Interests and Potential Persons

We have suggested that the death of a new-born infant or a foetus does not have the same moral significance as the death of an older child or adult because the infant is not a continuing self, capable of valuing its own continued existence. But, someone might object, there are many infants – and this includes many seriously ill or handicapped infants – who have the potential to become persons and of one day valuing their own lives in much the same way as we, who are already persons, value our lives. What makes the death of an infant so tragic in terms of this objection is that there never will be a person leading a worthwhile life. That an infant is not yet a person scarcely matters when we consider such a loss.

But frequently there can be a future person only if we inflict considerable pain and suffering on an infant. Can we justify this suffering? Many people believe the answer is 'yes'. Pointing to the successful survivors of neonatal intensive care, they will say that it was in the infants' interests to undergo the treatment. Based on this view, many people believe that the guiding principles for decision-making ought to be 'the best interests of the infant'. Life-sustaining treatment should be given to an infant if its life, with or after treatment, is likely to contain more benefits than burdens. While this view has an obvious appeal, there are a number of reasons why we should not accept it. The most important reasons have to do with the special status of infants.

Obviously, there is a tight connection between the interests a being has and the rightness or wrongness of our actions towards that being. But what *are* the interests of a new-born infant? Infants are not continuing selves and hence have no interest in their own continued existence. They do have other interests, though – momentary interests that merely require the presence of a conscious or sentient being, not the self-awareness of a person.

Infants are sentient beings. As such, they can experience pain and discomfort and be cold and hungry. They therefore have an interest in not experiencing pain and discomfort and in being warm and well-fed. But here an objection is sometimes put forth. Doctors and others sometimes say that any pain experienced by infants is less significant than the pain experienced by persons, because infants cannot remember, anticipate, or fear pain (McIntosh 1986). We regard the view that infants cannot remember or anticipate pain as entirely plausible, for if, as we have argued, infants are not continuing selves, lacking a sense of the past and the future, then it follows that they can neither remember past experiences, nor anticipate future ones – be these painful or pleasant ones. But does it also follow from an infant's inability to remember or anticipate pain that its momentary painful experiences do not count as much as the momentary painful experiences of a person? We do not think so. While a person's ability to anticipate and remember pain gives rise to some additional considerations, such considerations do not justify giving the actual experience of pain on a moment-by-moment basis a different weight in an infant and a person. If this is correct, then it follows that the moments of pain experienced by an infant must, other things being equal, be given the same moral weight as similar moments of pain experienced by a person.

Those who argue that medical decision-making for seriously ill or handicapped infants should be based on 'the best interests of the infant' may not dispute that an infant's experience of pain and suffering should count. But this suffering, so the argument frequently goes, may well be outweighed by future benefits. Those who take this view – the prestigious American President's Commission for the Study of Ethical Problems in Medicine and Biomedical and Behavioral Research, for example, in its report *Deciding to Forgo Life-Sustaining Treatment* (President's Commission 1983) – do not just look at the momentary interests of the infant (to be free from pain, warm, comfortable, and so on); they look much further ahead, to the whole future interests of the child or person into whom the infant may develop. In other words, they are asking: Will this future life in its totality contain more benefits than harms for this person?

If the issue is put like this, there will be many instances where the potential for a worthwhile life would seem to justify the infliction of some considerable suffering on an infant. There is, however, a fundamental problem in seeing life five or fifty years hence, no matter how good a life it may be, as in the interest of *this infant* now. There is, of course, a physical continuity between the infant and the later person. The former develops into the latter. Because of this, they may be said to be the same physical organism, despite the great changes that will have taken place. But there is no mental continuity, and in this crucial sense *we* are not, and never were, infants, foetuses, or embryos. Our lives as *persons* — as self-aware and purposeful beings with a sense of the past and the future — did not begin until some time after birth, when we ceased to be beings with momentary interests and became 'continuing selves'.

This undermines the claim that the existence of a person, glad to be alive, shows that a decision to continue treatment was 'in the best interests of the infant'. The infant, while still an infant, had no interest in becoming the child and adult. Its interests were much more limited than that: not to be in pain, to be warm and comfortable, and so on. If an infant has a reasonable prospect of intact survival, but in the meanwhile must experience prolonged pain and suffering, we may be keeping the infant alive not in accordance with, but *despite* the best interests of the infant. While such a decision may sometimes be justified because, among other things, it makes possible an enjoyable and worthwhile life for a child or adult, it is a mistake to assume that it can be justified by appealing to the best interests of the infant. The infant cannot be compensated for its suffering by the benefits bestowed on a potential future person. These benefits are, as it were, bestowed on someone else.

The issue of how much pain and suffering we may justifiably inflict on an infant in our attempts to keep it alive has recently been raised in a particularly stark manner in the context of infants born prematurely, at the margin of viability (Scanlon 1985, Rovner 1986). In some cases, doctors will not give anaesthetics or analgesics for invasive treatments — including major surgery — because these would put an additional strain on the infant's immature system, thereby threatening the infant's survival. While Dr. Willis McGill, chief of anesthesiology at the Children's Hospital National Medical Center in Washington, D.C., agrees that an anaesthetic should be given whenever possible for procedures that are painful and of significant duration, he none the less implies that there will be situations where such an anaesthetic will not be administered because he tries to ensure that the patient is in the best possible condition, and, as he puts it, 'It doesn't do any good to have a dead patient who doesn't feel pain' (Rovner 1986, p. 7).

One mother recently told of her horror when she discovered, almost inadvertently, that her premature son, Jeffrey – born after 26 weeks gestation and weighing less than two pounds – was awake throughout a major operation at the Children's Hospital National Medical Center. The operation included chest incisions and prying his ribs apart. The infant was paralyzed with Pavulon, a curare-type drug that left him unable to move, but totally conscious. He died six weeks after the surgery (Rovner 1986, p. 7; Scanlon 1985).

We have not recounted this case, nor that of Stephanie, to arouse horror, but rather to raise an important question that has, from our viewpoint, so far received insufficient discussion: How much suffering may we justifiably inflict on an infant who has but short-term desires and interests – an infant who cannot yet value its own continued existence? Because such painful life-sustaining procedures are never in the infant's best interest even though they may be in the interest of the person whom the infant might become, we believe that there will be some cases where the suffering of the infant – unavoidable if it is to be kept alive – may in itself be sufficient reason to forego the treatment. The situations of Stephanie and of Jeffrey may have been two such instances.

The mental discontinuity between infants and persons is one reason why we cannot justify painful treatment by simply pointing to the possible existence of a person who, five or twenty years from now, will be glad to be alive. There is, however, another reason as well. For if the argument is that it would be *wrong* to let an infant die because this would result in there never being a person leading a worthwhile life, then the same argument would lead to the condemnation not only of abortion but also of non-conception. In both cases, a person who might have existed will not exist. And from the future person's perspective, it makes but little difference whether her existence was thwarted through non-conception, abortion, or through being allowed to die in early infancy.

In Whose Interests?

So far we have sketched the philosophical difficulties that lurk behind the idea that decision-making should be based on 'the best interests of the infant'. These difficulties are one reason why we think this approach is misguided. There is, however, another – more straightforward – reason: many other factors should be taken into account – including the interests of the parents and of any children they already have.

There is no reason to assume that the momentary interests of the infant, or the interests of the person who the ill or handicapped infant might become, should automatically outweigh all these other interests. The birth of a severely handicapped infant can dramatically change the lives of the parents and siblings. It is, for example, often pointed out that the survival of a handicapped child is also the creation of a handicapped family (Simms 1983, p. 18). While that judgement may be too severe in some cases, in others it is the simple truth. To disregard these other interests altogether is incompatible with the principle of equal consideration of the interests of all those affected by our decisions – and such a principle is fundamental to ethics (Singer 1979, ch. 2).

When speaking about equal consideration of interests, there is also one other interest which we have not, so far, mentioned: the interests of the 'next child in the queue'. One of the more firmly established findings about families with a disabled child is that they are less likely than other families to have a further child (Kew 1975, p. 52). Shouldn't we take the interests of that child into account – the interests of the child who will not be born if the seriously ill or handicapped child survives?

The argument that we should take the 'next child' into account has been well put by R. M. Hare (1976). Discussing the question of whether to abort a foetus known to have a handicap, Hare asks us to suppose that a couple have planned to have two children. During the second pregnancy it is found that the foetus has a serious handicap. If the handicapped foetus lives, the couple will not have any more children. If the foetus is aborted, the couple will seek to have a second child. There is a high probability that this second child will be normal. In this situation, Hare argues, we should consider not only the interests of the child now in the womb, but also the interests of the possible child who is likely to live if, and only if, the foetus dies.

The same sort of reasoning can be applied after a seriously ill or handicapped child is born. Should we exclude the 'next child' from our deliberations on whether to treat a handicapped infant? We think we should not – at least not if we believe that treatment is justified in terms of the interests of the future child or person. There is, of course, another reason as well: the pain and suffering that will sometimes have to be inflicted in our efforts to achieve the survival of a sick or handicapped infant.

Conclusion

We have argued that we should not always try to preserve every infant's life by all available means because quality and kind of life constitute a proper basis for life and death decisions in the practice of medicine. What we have not yet discussed is *how* an infant should die when it has been decided that its life should no longer be sustained.

It is frequently thought that a morally relevant distinction exists between 'doing something' that results in death, and merely 'doing nothing' that also results in death – or between killing a patient and allowing a patient to die. Thus it is often thought that letting die is sometimes permissible in the practice of medicine but killing is not. Depending on this distinction, doctors will frequently not act to preserve the life of a child – as they did, for example, when they decided that Stephanie should not be resuscitated should her heart fail – but not take active steps to end the infant's life. While we can understand that it may sometimes be psychologically easier for doctors to decide not to resuscitate an infant than to administer a lethal dose of a drug, there is no intrinsic moral – and arguably no legal – difference between bringing about an infant's death by an omission or an action. If all other factors, such as intention, motivation, and outcome are the same, then killing an infant and allowing it to die are morally equivalent (Kuhse 1984).

Does this mean that it is morally irrelevant whether an infant's life is ended actively or passively? We do not think so. Once the decision has been made that an infant should be allowed to die, it will often be better to hasten death than to stand by and wait until 'nature' takes her often cruel course. Would it not have been better if Stephanie's life had ended sooner than it did, if those responsible for her care had at least spared her the suffering she endured between the time it had been decided that her life should not be prolonged by resuscitation and the time when her heart finally failed? We believe the answer is a resounding 'Yes'.

REFERENCES

Frohock, Fred M. (1986). *Special Care – Medical Decisions at the Beginning of Life* (Chicago and London: The University of Chicago Press).

Hare, R. M. (1976). 'Survival of the Weakest', in *Moral Problems in Medicine*, ed. S. Gorovitz et al. (Englewood Cliffs: Prentice Hall), pp. 364–9.

Kelly, G. (1958). *Medico-Moral Problems* (St. Louis: The Catholic Hospital Association of the United States).

Kew, S. (1975). *Handicap and Family Crisis* (London: Pitman).

Kuhse, H. (1984). 'A Modern Myth. That Lettting Die is not the Intentional Causation of Death: some reflections on the trial and acquittal of Dr. Leonard Arthur', *Journal of Applied Philosophy 1*, No. 1, 21–38.

(1987). *Sanctity of Life in Medicine* (Oxford: Oxford University Press).

McIntosh, P. (1986). 'Doctors seek pain relief for patients who can't say how much it hurts', *The Age* (Melbourne), September 22.

Pirrie, M. (1986a). 'Pontiff appeals for IVF Morality', *The Age* (Melbourne), November 29.

(1986b). 'Judge: baby should live', *The Age* (Melbourne), July 3.

President's Commission for the Study of Ethical Problems in Medicine and Biomedical and Behavioral Research (1983). *Deciding to Forgo Life-Sustaining Treatment* (Washington: U.S. Government Printing Office).

Ramsey, P. (1976), 'Prolonged Dying: Not Medically Indicated', *Hastings Center Report 6*, 14–7.

(1978). *Ethics at the Edges of Life* (New Haven and London: Yale University Press).

Rovner, S. (1986), 'Surgery Without Anesthesia: Can Preemies Feel Pain?', *Washington Post*, August 13.

Sacred Congregation for the Doctrine of the Faith (1980), *Declaration on Euthanasia* (Vatican City).

Scanlon, J. W. (1985), 'Barbarism', *Prenatal Press 9*, No. 7, 103–4.

Simms, M. (1983), 'Severely Handicapped Infants', *New Humanist 98*, No. 2, 1–8.

Singer, P. (1979), *Practical Ethics* (Cambridge: Cambridge University Press).

Tooley, M. (1983). *Abortion and Infanticide* (Oxford: Oxford University Press).

Weber, L. (1976), *Who Shall Live?* (New York: Paulist Press).

11

Why Child Pornography Is Wrong

TOM REGAN

Paradigmatic Wrongs

Some acts that are wrong are not paradigmatically wrong. By the expression 'paradigmatically wrong' I mean any act that all rational, informed, impartial people of good will agree is wrong. The wanton torture of the innocent is an example of a paradigmatically wrong act. Any adequate moral theory must offer an intelligible account of why those acts that are paradigmatically wrong are wrong.[1]

Some acts involving children that may *be* wrong are not wrong paradigmatically. In some Baby Doe cases, for example, where a defective newborn is killed or allowed to die, it is possible that causing or allowing the child to die *is* wrong but not paradigmatically so. Rational, informed, impartial people of good will, that is, might make conflicting judgements about some of these cases, just as these same people might find themselves in disagreement over the ethics of later-term abortions ('the killing of the unborn child', as some people describe this). There are, one might say, limits to what we can know morally (assuming that we can know some things), despite our best efforts. When we enter the troubled waters of the non-paradigmatically wrong, tolerance may be a virtue greatly to be prized.

In contrast to the cases just mentioned, child pornography *is* an example of a paradigmatic wrong – or so I shall assume. Any adequate moral theory therefore must be able to account for it. As we shall see, few theories are equal to the task.

The Face of the Victims

For my present purposes I shall use the interpretation of child pornography expounded in the 1982 U.S. Supreme Court decision in *New York v. Ferber*. This interpretation limits child pornography to 'works that visually depict sexual conduct by children below a specified age'.[2] What this age is varies from state to state within the United States and from nation to nation. Thus, whereas some states recognise eighteen as the age of sexual consent, others specify sixteen. Among nations, some fix the age of sexual majority at eighteen, while Holland, for example, currently is considering lowering the age to twelve. Whatever the 'specified age' (I shall assume it to be sixteen), the plain fact is that most of the victims are *young*, some as young as one week of age.

The kind of sexual activity filmed or photographed includes bestiality, masturbation, sexual intercourse of all varieties, oral sex, sadistic and masochistic displays, and lewd or lascivious exhibitions of the genitals or pubic area. The number of children involved is unclear. A 1977 estimate for Los Angeles placed the number for that city at approximately 30,000.[3] The national total must be in the hundreds of thousands. Worldwide, the numbers easily could be in the millions.

Runaways and homeless children are likely to be at greatest risk. But children from every class, race, family background, and religion may be and have been exploited. Most enter into this subterranean world because of someone they know – a family member, teacher, friend, or neighbor, for example. As the *Report* of the Meese Commission states, 'many [of these children] are too young to know what has happened; others are powerless to refuse the demand of an authority figure; some seem to engage in the conduct "voluntarily", usually in order to obtain desperately needed adult affection.'[4]

The *Report* indicates that comparatively little detailed research has been done on the immediate and lasting effects on children used in child pornography. The actual photographs or films frequently present the children as if they were enjoying themselves ('having a good time'), but appearances can be deceiving. According to testimony presented before the Supreme Court in *Ferber*, 'the use of children as subjects of pornographic materials is harmful to the psychological, emotional and mental health of the child.'[5] Notwithstanding the paucity of careful research in the field, the *Report* declares that 'the pain suffered by children used in pornography is often devastating, and always significant. In the short term the effects of such involvement include depression, suicidal thoughts, feelings of shame, guilt, alienation from family and peers, and massive acute anxiety.'[6] In the case of those children old enough to understand what has been done to them, there is little reason to challenge the painful accuracy of this assessment.

The Face of the Criminals

Those who sexually abuse children, including those who use them for pornographic purposes, exhibit different psychopathologies and come from every social and economic stratum. The Meese Commission distinguishes between 'situational' and 'preferential' molesters.

The former are people who act out of some serious sexual or psychological need, but choose children as victims only when they are readily and safely accessible. 'Preferential' molesters, on the other hand, are those with a clear sexual preference for children ('pedophiles' in common usage) who can only satisfy the demands of that preference through child victims. 'Preferential' abusers collect child pornography and/or erotica as a matter of course.[7]

The *Report* does not estimate the number of each sort of molester, 'but it does seem apparent,' the Commission states, 'that "preferential" child molesters over the long term victimize far more children than do "situational" abusers.'[8] Certainly the former must be more responsible than the latter for production of and trade in child pornography.

Who are these child exploiters? Sadly, they come in all shapes and sizes, representing every economic, professional, religious, and racial background. There are cases of children being sold by their parents into the eager hands of the producers of child pornography, cases where the parents themselves are the criminals, cases where clergymen and youth group advisers (e.g. a local Boy Scout troop leader) have used their charges for pornographic purposes, and cases where – or so it has been alleged – preschool children, some as young as two years of age, have been sexually molested, abused, and filmed for pornographic purposes. Considered as a group, the victims of child pornography have no safe haven, just as, considered as a group, those who victimise them have no fixed identity: The criminal could be *anyone*.

The Kantian Account

A normative theory's adequacy, I have claimed, depends in part on its ability to account for the wrongness of what is paradigmatically wrong. Whether adult pornography is wrong is a much debated question; even more debated is the question of what if any role the government should play in restricting the availability of material depicting adults in sexually explicit situations. The most commonly offered justification of government regulation of adult pornography concerns the harms done to those who view it. Not so in the case of child pornography. The prevailing, sensible view is that sexual activities among children, coercively arranged for the purpose of child pornography, are wrong independently of any harm done to 'the audience' (which is not to say that harm cannot be done to those who view it). It is the *children* who are wronged.

Everyone agrees, then – or so I shall assume – that child pornography is a paradigm example of a paradigmatic wrong. Any adequate theory of obligation therefore must be able to account for (explain, illuminate) why it is wrong. The most influential normative theories shaping current thought in moral philosophy fail to pass this test. This certainly is true of Kant's normative theory. As is well known, his theory emphasizes the capacity of rational beings to be self-legislative. Consider the first formulation of the categorical imperative (the formula of universal law):

> *Act so that the maxim of your action may be adopted as a universal law.*

According to this formulation, I am to act in such a way that the maxim of my action (the plan or intention that informs what I do) can without contradiction be imposed on every other rational being. Now, in some cases of paradigmatic wrongs (for example, the wanton torture of an innocent person), the formula of universal law seems to offer a plausible account of why the act is wrong. But the situation is markedly different in the case of child pornography.

To begin with, it is unclear how this formulation of the categorical imperative can be applied to the case at hand. One possibility is that child abusers are to ask themselves whether *they* would be willing to be used in the way they are willing to use their young victims. Understood in one way, this question cannot be intelligibly asked. For the adult in this case intends to use the child *for purposes of child pornography*, and *adults* by the very fact of their age cannot be used in *that* way – that is, as *children* – for any purpose. So there certainly is no 'contradiction in the will' of adults who are willing to use children for the purpose of child pornography but who are unwilling to be used this way themselves since, as adults, they *cannot* be used in this way.

In response it may be said that the question to be asked is whether the adult would be willing to be used *for pornographic purposes generally*, not for those of child pornography in particular. But this response weakens the Kantian account even further. The plain fact is, not a few adults are willing to be used for pornographic purposes and only wish that more adults (and possibly children, too) were similarly inclined. These people see no 'contradiction' in willing their maxim universally to include themselves. That acting on this maxim might very well be wrong is not to be denied. What is, is that *willing that this be done* must involve a contradiction in the will of those who are prepared to will it. There simply is no good reason to believe this.

Where a contradiction might arise is if a person were to will that every child except his or her own may be used for these purposes. But any 'contradiction in the will' that might arise in this case can be erased if the person *is* prepared to will that her or his own child may be used for these ends. The plain fact is, we would (or, in any event, should) look with grave disfavour on parents who were prepared to have their own children used for pornographic purposes. No less plain is the fact that those parents who are willing to do this can do so in a logically consistent manner. Thus does the formula of universal law fail to illuminate or explain why child pornography is wrong.

Matters might appear more favourable for Kantians when we consider an alternative formulation of the categorical imperative – the formula of end in itself:

> *Act so that you treat humanity, both in your own person, and in the person of every other, always as an end, never as a means merely.*

Anyone who uses a child for pornographic purposes, it might be claimed, uses the child 'merely as a means' and so violates this formulation of the categorical imperative.

This analysis expresses the spirit of Kant's theory but departs significantly from the letter. A *person* in Kant's theory – and recall that the current formulation prescribes that we are to treat humanity 'in the person' – a person is a morally autonomous individual, the sort of being who is capable of acting in accordance with the first formulation of the categorical imperative. This means that a person must be able to formulate a maxim of his or her own and then ask whether every other person is capable of acting on that maxim. Possibly some children used in child pornography (for example, normal sixteen-year-olds) are capable of formulating their own maxims and asking this question. But not so the two-year-old preschool children mentioned earlier. And certainly not the one-week-old infant cited by the Meese Commission. That these children are *humans* is not to be denied. But that they are *persons* in Kant's sense must be. The result is that the second formulation of the categorical imperative cannot even be directly applied to questions about how young children may be treated. And since that formula cannot be directly applied, whereas the formula of universal law would not prohibit the use of children for pornographic purposes, Kant's theory must be judged to be demonstrably incapable of accounting for this great wrong.

A number of possible defences are available to the Kantian. None carries the rational weight it must bear. One, 'the potentiality defence', invokes considerations about potentiality. Although young children are not persons in the strict sense, they do have the *potential* to become persons in the normal course of their development. To respect 'the person' in their case thus is to respect their potential. By making this slight amendment to Kant's formula of end in itself, it might be claimed, we are able to account for why in his view it is wrong to use children for pornographic purposes.

This is hardly a 'slight amendment' of Kant's views. If potential persons are to be treated on a par with actual persons, then the categorical imperative will entail that the human foetus throughout its development, from the earliest to the latest stages, is to be treated as a person. And that demand will yield a very strong prohibition against abortion, for any reason, from conception onward. There are some who advance this view, but not Kant or his followers, so far as I am aware. It is wildly implausible to interpret Kant after the fashion of this first defence.

But suppose the situation were otherwise and that Kant's position was defended by invoking the potentiality defence. That still would be inadequate, all considered. For there are some children who, because of the extent of their mental incapacities, *lack* the potential to become persons in Kant's sense (that is, they cannot ever become morally autonomous). If having the potential for moral autonomy is the decisive consideration the potentiality defence supposes, then these mentally retarded children would *not* be covered by the formula of end in itself. That being so, one could non-arbitrarily discriminate between these children and those children who have the potential for moral autonomy; in the case of the latter (those who have the requisite potential) one could maintain that it *would* be wrong to use them for pornographic purposes, but not so in the case of the former (those who lack this potential).

Speaking for myself, I must assume that every rational, informed, impartial person of good will would reject this latter possibility. That a child is mentally retarded does not lessen the prohibition against using that child for pornographic ends. Morally, these children, no less than those who are more generously endowed, must be covered by principles that prohibit their sexual exploitation. The potentiality defence is no defence at all.

A second defence ('the indirect duty defence') proceeds along different lines. Kant's theory allows for the distinction between direct and indirect duties. Considering the latter first, we may note that we often have duties involving another person's property (for example, I have duties involving your car and house). But I have no duties *to* your house or car; rather, I have duties to you that involve, include, or make reference to these possessions. My duties regarding your property thus are indirect duties I have to you. Direct duties, by contrast, are not indirectly routed in this way. If I have promised to meet you at a specific time and place, then I have that duty to you directly.

The indirect duty defence attempts to save the Kantian account by using the distinction between direct and indirect duties. We have no duties directly to retarded children who lack the potential to become morally autonomous, given this defence, but we do have indirect duties in which they figure. For if we were to allow child pornographers to exploit the retarded, it is very likely that they would in time begin to exploit normal children too. Thus, since (so this defence runs) we do have a direct duty to protect these latter children against this sort of abuse, we must recognise that we also have a duty, albeit an indirect one, involving these former children.

The *psychological* speculation central to this defense certainly seems tenable. People who sexually abuse retarded children are (or certainly seem to be) more likely than not to extend their attention to include normal children. That much may be conceded. What should be disputed is the *moral* speculation on which this defence rests. One would have thought (at least I myself think) that the retarded condition of a child does not make that child any less deserving of our *direct* moral concern. Granted, in the nature of the case many of these children will not grow up to be morally autonomous adults. But *what they will become* (or *not become*) is morally irrelevant to determing *what we owe them now*. And what we owe these children now, directly, is our steadfast protection from those who would abuse them. This we owe *to them* no less and (let us suppose) no more than the protection we owe to normal children. Any maker of child pornography who uses a retarded or normal child *wrongs that child*. Any adequate account of the wrongness of child pornography must begin with that fact, not attempt to avoid it. Since the indirect duty defence fails to do this, it fails as a defence.

Perhaps there are other ways of attempting to defend the Kantian account. If there are, I do not know what they could be. Whatever the strengths of Kant's moral theory (and they are many and formidable), its inability to account for the wrongness of child pornography must be among its major weaknesses.

The Act-Utilitarian Account

Utilitarian accounts fare no better. Act-utilitarians – those who, roughly speaking, require that we perform that act which will bring about the best balance of desirable over undesirable consequences for everyone affected by the outcome – could make a strong presumptive case against many, perhaps even most, instances of child pornography. Recall the claims endorsed by the Meese Commission: 'The pain suffered by children used in pornography is often devastating, and always significant. In the short term the effects of such involvement include depression, suicidal thoughts, feelings of shame, guilt, alienation from family and peers, and massive acute anxiety'. With such a variety of damaging short-term effects on the children involved, it surely is unlikely that these undesirable consequences will be outweighed by whatever positive results there might be.

But one's confidence in the adequacy of the act-utilitarian's account must be tempered by the recognition that the variety of damaging short-term effects just listed may not always be present. The effects in question (for example, feelings of shame, guilt, alienation from family and peers, and massive acute anxiety) are not within the standard psychological repertoire of very young children (say, those under two years of age). It is just false, I think, to claim that a victimised child of this age experiences these effects in the short term.

As for the long term, the situation is far from clear. We simply do not know what the lasting effects of isolated instances of sexual exploitation are for infants of a few weeks of age, for example. Doubtless the effects are highly detrimental for young children who are *routinely* exploited for pornographic purposes. Everything we know about normal child development points to this tragic conclusion. What is less clear is what the long-term developmental effects are likely to be when a very young child is used for these purposes, not often or routinely, but rarely or on only one occasion. Imagine a child of a week or a year who is filmed during some sexually explicit activity (say, oral sex with another child). Given that the damaging effects listed earlier cannot occur in the short run in such a case, and assuming that the child in question is subjected to such an experience on only one occasion, I think we must confess that we simply do not know whether the long-term effects on the child will be derimental or, if detrimental, how much so.

This cannot be good news for act-utilitarians. According to their account of the wrongness of child pornography, *everything* depends on our ability, in each case, to say *both* what the effects of child pornography are *and* how it is that the bad effects outweigh the good. If I am right and we sometimes simply do not know whether the effects on the very young child who is abused in an isolated case are detrimental (or, if detrimental, how much so) then it follows that the act-utilitarian sometimes will lack the sort of information this theory requires before we can decide what is wrong. Or right. But since (as I am assuming) we do know that child pornography is wrong in such a case, the act-utilitarian's account of why it is wrong cannot be judged successful.

The problems child pornography pose for act-utilitarians actually are more severe than those sketched to this point. For although we sometimes are uncertain about the detrimental effects on young children in isolated cases of child pornography, the pleasures secured by the producers and patrons of child pornography are disturbingly clear. Judged exclusively in terms of pleasure and pain (or satisfaction and dissatisfaction), it is not impossible that the amount of pleasure (or satisfaction) obtained by those with an interest in child pornography might exceed the amount of pain (or dissatisfaction) experienced by a young child who is used in an isolated episode for pornographic purposes. Indeed, the same thing can be true in cases where a child is used *repeatedly* for such purposes. If this possibility should obtain, as well it may, then act-utilitarians would be obliged by their theory to say that the use of young children for pornographic purposes in such cases *is not wrong*. So far, then, is act-utilitarianism from offering an adequate account of why child pornography is wrong, that it actually presents us with a theory that allows that it sometimes may be quite all right – permissible certainly, obligatory perhaps. On this basis, if on no other, we are right to dissociate ourselves from act-utilitarianism.

The Rule-Utilitarian Account

Rule-utilitarianism may seem to fare better than act-utilitarianism. According to this version of utilitarianism we are to act on the basis of valid moral rules, the validity of the rules having been determined by the utility of having everyone abide by them. Why ought we to keep our promises and not kill the innocent? Because the world is a better place in which to live if everybody keeps their promises and does not kill those who have done nothing wrong. Granted, there conceivably may be cases in which better results could be produced by killing an innocent human being (for example, in order to obtain an inheritance which one then puts to praiseworthy civic use – to build a children's hospital, say). Though possible, there is more to be lost than gained by allowing such discretion in observing the rule against homicide, according to the rule-utilitarian.

Rule-utilitarianism thus seems to offer a way around the problems that are act-utilitarianism's undoing. According to the rule-utilitarian, the question we need to ask is whether better consequences will result if everyone always abides by certain rules concerning child pornography (for example, 'Do not produce child pornography or support those who do so') than would result if people did not always abide by these rules. To this question the rule-utilitarian will answer that it would be better if we had such rules and required universal compliance. True, there may be some cases where we do not know the short- or long-term effects on young children who are used for pornographic purposes on only a single occasion; and it is also true that the pain such a child experiences in a single episode might even be outweighed by the pleasures enjoyed by those who produce and seek out pornographic materials. But while either one or both of these truths is sufficient basis for denying any claim to adequacy made on behalf of act-utilitarianism, neither casts any doubt on the adequacy of rule-utilitarianism. Or so it may be claimed. We know enough about the world and the effects of people's behaviour to know that it generally is not conducive to what is good in human life to allow people to decide for themselves whether or not to exploit children. To have anything less than the strictest prohibition against child pornography is to have something less than what rule-utilitarianism justifies and requires.

There are familiar objections to rule-utilitarianism. One asks whether it is a legitimate version of utilitarianism. It seems to demand that we not make exceptions to rules *even if doing so would lead to the best results in a given situation.* It is difficult to understand how someone can possibly be a utilitarian and hold this. Far more important for the present purposes, however, is a second kind of objection. This concerns the method used by rule-utilitarians (and by any utilitarian for that matter) to determine what is right and wrong.

The method prescribed asks that we consider all the consequences of instituting a given rule. Everyone's interests must be taken into account, and equal interests must be counted equally. Whether a person is white or black, a man or a woman, a genius or a retarded child, that individual's interests must be considered. This is the heart of the expansive egalitarianism that utilitarians of every variety take great pride in. This is the utilitarian's fundamental way of being fair to everyone.

This conception of fairness must be operative when the rule-utilitarian is asked to decide whether to have a strict rule against child pornography. If everyone's interests must be taken into account, then the interests of the abused child cannot be ignored. But neither can the interests of the producers and purveyors of child pornography.

After all, these people *enjoy* abusing children for sexual purposes, they rather *like* seeing young bodies engaged in sexually explicit acts, many have a real appetite, a real preference for this sort of thing, which means that they would be terribly frustrated and disappointed if they were prevented from having their sexual desires satisfied. If we are to be fair to everyone involved, not just the children, then we must consider how the interests of the so-called 'pedophile' (a lamentable corruption of what this word means), for example, will be affected if we enforce a strict prohibition against child pornography.

I think this state of affairs, which is created by applying the basic concept of fairness that is partially definitive of utilitarian theory, constitutes a *reductio* of that theory. It is morally grotesque, I think, to suppose that we must (if we are to be fair!) consider whether 'pedophiles' will be disappointed or frustrated before we can fairly decide in favour of a strict prohibition against child pornography. The sexual appetites of these human beings have no role whatever to play in reaching this decision, and it is a symptom of a misguided theory that it should require otherwise. Do we seriously believe that the interests of sadistic torturers must be considered, in the name of being fair, before we can decide to prohibit recreational torture? Do we consult the interests of murderers before we prohibit murder? The questions answer themselves. The situation is no different in the case of the prohibition against child pornography. Some interests, preferences, or appetites do not count, and *must not count* in our deliberations about what is right and wrong. Thus, since the egalitarian aspirations of utilitarianism, including any recognisable form of rule-utilitarianism, demand that everyone's interests, preferences, and the like be taken into account – whatever these interests, preferences, and the like may be – we are on sound theoretical and moral ground when we reject rule-utilitarianism. That we must have a rule that strictly forbids child pornography is true, but that we should validate that rule after the fashion of rule-utilitarianism is false.

Contractarianism

In my view, variations on the theme of contractarianism lack adequacy. Some forms of that theory allow the contractors to know who they are, what they like and want, what their aspirations and plans are. This much allowed, the contractors are then asked to decide what agreements they can strike with other rational agents, with the understanding that each person is to be motivated exclusively out of concern for his or her own self-interest. This (Narvesonian)[9] version of contractarianism does not offer children much by way of protection against their potential abusers. Children, after all, especially those who are very young, do not have the wherewithal to know what is in their self-interest, let alone the capacity to enter into agreements with persons who are able to do this. When it comes to their protection, everything depends on what self-interested adults agree to. And although one may profoundly hope that 'pedophilic' contractors will not meet with success in this quarter, it must be emphasised that what is right and wrong, given this approach to ethics, even including child pornography, is wholly contingent on what people decide is in their self-interest.

Thus, even if it happened to turn out that rational egoists at one time decided to prohibit child pornography, that would be a wholly contingent agreement, one that could be rescinded later on. In other words, if the number of 'pedophiles' grew large or powerful enough so that rational egoists came to have a self-interested reason to allow child pornography, then Narvesonian contractarianism would offer its seal of approval. I must assume that this implication offers more than enough reason to deny the adequacy of this form of contractarianism. Success in getting enough people to accept what is wrong does not make it right.

Other versions of contractarianism (the one favoured by John Rawls in particular)[10] are more subtle and powerful. Rawls asks us to imagine that we are ignorant of the details of our life. We do not know what we want, where we live, when, or even who we are. Am I a man, a woman? An adult, a child? A genius, a moron? An American, a Libyan? Beautiful, ugly? White, black? A university professor or a used-car salesman? On Rawls's approach to morality, I must assume that I do not know the answers to these questions. If I am to be fair, I must ignore the contingent details of my life when I ask what moral principles not only I but everyone should live by.

There is much to be said in support of Rawls's theory, and much, I think, to be said against it. How far the theory is supposed to reach in terms of the rules we are being asked to choose, and whether in particular the theory extends to rules about child pornography, is unclear. If the theory does not extend this far, because, for example, it applies only to the selection of the most basic principles of justice, then it is seriously incomplete: it fails even to offer an account of a great paradigmatic wrong. On the other hand, if the theory is supposed to extend this far, then the situation is even worse. For the Rawlsian theory, if it is applied to child pornography, fails to offer an adequate account of why it is wrong.

Let us recall the challenge. I do not know who I am, where or when I will live, what my sex or race is, or any of the other details of my life (for example, my economic status and my religion). I then select principles on the basis of my self-interest. What principles will I choose? Rawls thinks I will choose conservatively. Thus, for example, Rawls thinks I would not choose principles that would make the poor worse off than they already are, nor would I choose principles that would discriminate against some races or give preference to the members of one sex rather than another. Why not? Because for all I know *I* might be born a member of the group that is hurt or discriminated against. And then it wouldn't be in my self-interest to have rules that harm or discriminate against me.

Now, all of us know that, if we are born into the world at all, we will have a childhood. For this reason it may seem to be very much in our self-interest to choose rules or principles that will protect children, insisting on having a rule against child pornography in particular. I am not sanguine about this theory's adequacy, however, despite its good appearances. One problem concerns *what risks* one is willing to run or what *gambles* one is willing to take. We are asked to choose between having a rule that strictly prohibits child pornography, thereby trying to protect our interests while a child, or not having such a rule, thereby taking our chances while we are a child (just because there is no rule prohibiting this abuse of children, it does not follow that we will be abused) but also permitting the expression of our interests as a 'pedophile' later in life, should we happen to become one. Which choice should we make? I do not understand how Rawlsian contractarianism can give a decisive answer to this question, assuming this is a question we may fairly ask of it. That being so, I do not understand how this version of contractarianism can supply an adequate account of the wrongness of child pornography.

But Rawls's theory is worse than indecisive on this issue (assuming that it even can be applied to it). His theory not only fails to give a determinate answer to the question, 'Should we have a rule prohibiting child pornography?' It fails more fundamentally because it permits us to count, *as being morally relevant*, the interests of the child abuser. After all, for all I know I may be one myself, in which case I will want to weigh my possible 'pedophilic' interests before I decide for or against having the rule. But these interests, whether they are mine or another's, have *nothing* to contribute to the moral assessment of child pornography. In this respect Rawls's theory is just as inadequate, and inadequate for the same kind of reason, as standard versions of utilitarianism.

There are, of course, other familiar moral theories, in addition to those discussed in the preceding pages, competing for our informed assent. Limitations of space prevent a close critical examination on this occasion. Here I must be content to say that those theories that have not been examined will suffer from one or another of the defects found in those that have been. Libertarianism, for example, is open to the objection that it fails to account for the strict prohibition against child pornography because it fails to offer a theory of rights which, if acted upon, *insures or guarantees* that young children, who are not yet morally autonomous, will be protected. And familiar interest theories of rights, which tie the possession of various rights to the presence of various desires, also will come to grief for the same kind of reason. Young children are wronged by their sexual abusers even when these children do not have desires that are frustrated, thwarted, or otherwise denied by their adult exploiters.

I shall sketch part of a different sort of theory below, the one which I believe holds the greatest promise of offering an adequate account of why child pornography is wrong. First, however, we need to take stock of what has been shown in the above.

Criteria of Adequacy

The preceding critique of familiar options in moral theory offers us some guidance regarding what will count as an adequate account of the wrongness of child pornography. From our examination of Kant we understand that the account we seek must (1) recognise and ground *direct* duties in the case of children and in particular must (2) recognise and ground the direct duty not to use children for purposes of pornography. Moreover, this latter duty must (3) apply both to normal and to retarded children. For its part, the examination of utilitarianism reveals that (4) what makes child pornography wrong cannot be that the consequences are always bad, all considered (for they may not be in many cases) and that (5) the interests of those who exploit children for sexual purposes have no role to play in the moral assessment of that exploitation. Finally, the shortcomings of Rawlsian and other forms of contractarianism show that (6) what makes child pornography wrong is not that it conflicts with what is in our own self-interest. The direct duty against child pornography, in short, must be accounted for independently of asking what is in my own interests, what the consequences are or will be for the child, and what the consequences are or will be for others (for example, the public at large). And this is to say that what makes child pornography wrong does not depend on considerations about future consequences. What is wrong with child pornography, what underlies its strict prohibition, must depend on *how the child is treated*, not on the consequences of this treatment.

Now, *how* children are treated in such circumstances (to use Kant's terminology) is as *mere means*. Someone with superior power (the adult exploiter) imposes his or her will on the child for purposes chosen by the exploiter, not the child. Indeed, in those cases where the child is very young the purposes are not even comprehended by the victims and so cannot be chosen by them. Most children, of course, will in time grow into individuals who will understand such things and will be able to make autonomous choices. However, since, as was implied in the preceding, a child's inability to understand sexual activity for what it is (as is true in the case of many retarded children, for example) does not cancel the wrong of coercively using them for pornographic purposes; it follows that the wrong that attaches to using them *as mere means* must depend on considerations about what the victims actually are, not on what the victims might become. So, let us ask what the victims are.

The Species Reply

An obvious response is that the victims of child pornography are human children, and there is no doubt either that this is true or that most people are likely to rest content with this reply. And yet this answer demonstrably does not go far enough. What we want to know is what there is about being a human child that makes it wrong to use the child for pornographic purposes. We are not told what this is merely by being told that the child is human (a member of the species *Homo sapiens*). Although the fact that the child belongs to this species rather than some other does tell us something about the child that distinguishes the child from other individuals, mere species membership does not inform us of anything that is either morally relevant or decisive for judging that it is categorically wrong to use children for pornographic purposes.

A Religious Reply

Some people with deep and abiding religious convictions have an answer to our question. Every human child is made in the image of God – is sacred. That's why using the child for pornographic purposes is the great wrong that it is. I do not think we should dismiss this response cavalierly. Unlike the simple appeal to species membership, religiously grounded responses to the question about what makes human life special have a presumptive cogency that we do well to consider.

It remains true, nonetheless, that religiously grounded conceptions of what human life is face very serious obstacles. First and foremost is the challenge to give reasons for believing in a particular deity since, without such reasons, there is no good reason to accept a particular answer to the question 'What is a human child?' But, second, even if these obstacles could be overcome, the question will still remain 'What is there about being a human being that makes one so special in the eyes of God?' To be told that we *are* special is not to be told *why* we are.

Various possible answers to this question are demonstrably deficient. One cannot urge that humans are special because they are morally autonomous, are capable of entering into a loving relationship with God, or are called upon to represent the deity here on earth. This may be true of most human beings, but it certainly is not true of all (for example, the seriously retarded). And yet religious people *certainly* will not concede that it is therefore all right to use these humans for pornographic purposes.

In the face of these difficulties it is tempting to have recourse to claims about the immortal soul. That, it might be said, is why we humans are so special: we all have immortal souls. But not only is this another declaration of faith which, without the marshalling of considered beliefs in its behalf, stands just as unsupported as the declaration of faith in God; this new declaration fails to offer a credible account of why *it is wrong* to commit the most grievous of sins. Granted, if you murder me, then that will make a difference to what happens to you in the next life. Your terrible sin will be punished, let us assume, and that gives you a strong, self-interested reason for not murdering me. But *that* sort of reason (that it is not in your self-interest to murder me) fails altogether to capture why it is *morally wrong* to do so. What it is wrong to do and what is contrary to one's self-interest are not two sides of the same coin. Declarations of belief in the immortality of the soul thus seem to be logically irrelevant to attempts to account for why such a heinous act as murder is wrong.

The same kind of argument can be given with respect to child pornography. Let us agree that this is a great wrong, a great sin. And let us concede that both the child and the child's exploiter have immortal souls. The question is, 'How does this latter claim help account for why child pornography is wrong?' If the answer is given in terms of what will happen to child abusers in the after-life, then what we have here is an appeal to the abuser's self interest. And that sort of appeal, for reasons offered in the preceding, is not capable of accounting for the wrongness of child pornography.

It would seem, then, that appeals to religious beliefs, including those that involve beliefs about the immortality of the human soul, are unlikely to provide us with the kind of reasoned account we are looking for when we ask why child pornography is wrong. And so it is that we are obliged to reconsider the question 'What *is* the human child, actually?' from a different, less controversial and hopefully more logically relevant vantage point.

The Respect Account

The view I wish to recommend and in part defend is the following: Children of whatever age, the retarded as well as those who are more fortunate, are *subjects-of-a-life*. By subject-of-a-life I do not mean merely an individual who is conscious at one moment or another; rather, I mean an individual who has a psycho-physical identity over time, an individual who has a biography and not merely a biology,[11] one who is an enduring somebody, not an enduring something – one who, to use more familiar terminology, is (or has) a 'self'. You and I are subjects-of-a-life in the sense in which I am using this expression, and so are teenage victims of child abuse. But so, too, are very young children, including both the newly born and the retarded of whatever age. True, some who are subjects-of-a-life have the potential to grow into morally autonomous adults; and some subjects-of-a-life actually are morally autonomous. Others lack this potential. However, even these individuals are biographical beings; considered ontologically, they are the same kind of being as their autonomous 'cousins'. The story of the psycho-physical life of each is the story of a separate, distinct individual, each with a biography, each with an experiential life story of his or her own.

Here, then, are the makings of a different account of why child pornography is wrong. Its wrongness lies in treating a subject-of-a-life as a mere means, as if that individual somebody (the abused child) were merely some thing. To express the same point in different words, the wrongness of child pornography consists in using coercion, deceit, or other reprehensible means to force one biographical being to satisfy the needs, tastes, or preferences of another biographical being. Individuals who are stronger and more knowledgeable use their superior strength or knowledge to make weaker individuals serve as part of their (the stronger individuals') life stories. It is this coercive use of another biographical being that, in my view, underlies the wrongness of child pornography.

The normative position I am recommending can be expressed in other, more familiar terminology. The language of respect is the most obvious (henceforth I shall refer to the account sketched here as 'the respect account'). Using this language we can say that subjects-of-a-life are always to be treated with respect, and this requires that we never treat them as if they exist for us as our resources, as individuals who may be coercively, deceitfully, or in other ways treated merely as means to our ends. Those who traffic in child pornography do this to children, just as those who satisfy their sadistic desires through torture do this to their victims.

The respect account succeeds where the other accounts considered above fail. Recall the positive criteria of adequacy that emerged from the critique of these several options. Any adequate account of the wrongness of child pornography must (1) recognise and ground direct duties in the case of children and in particular it must (2) recognise and ground the direct duty not to use children for pornographic purposes. The respect account satisfies both requirements. According to this account we have a *direct* duty, a duty owed *directly* to children, to treat them with respect, and one implication of this general duty is that we are not to use them for pornographic purposes; to do so would be in violation of the direct duty to always treat them with respect. Moreover, the respect account also satisfies the third criterion of adequacy, namely, (3) it recognises and grounds the duty against using children for pornographic purposes regardless of whether the children are normal or retarded (and, so, regardless of whether they do or do not have the potential to become morally autonomous adults). Retarded children no less (and no more) than normal ones are subjects-of-a-life, are psycho-physical beings with a life story that is underway, and so do not exist as mere resources or mere means to be exploited by stronger, more knowledgeable adults.

The fourth criterion of adequacy, namely, that (4) the wrongness of child pornography must not be made to depend on the future bad consequences of the abuse, including the bad consequences for the victim – this criterion also is satisfied by the respect account. For what is fundamentally wrong with abusing a child for pornographic purposes is *how the child is treated*, not what will happen to the child in the future (which is *not* to say that what happens in the future is never regrettable or even tragic). The respect account insists that the wrong done to the child is to be fixed and described in the way required by this criterion. The child is wronged because the child is not treated with respect. And *that* is wrong *whatever* the future holds.

Some theories of obligation (for example, utilitarian theories) require that we consider the interests of those who exploit children for pornographic purposes before we can fairly decide whether this kind of exploitation is wrong. Any adequate account of why child pornography is wrong must deny the relevance of these interests. The respect account does. The interests of different individuals are morally relevant only if acting on these interests does not conflict with treating subjects-of-a-life with respect. The motivating interests of those who produce and use child pornography fail this test because these interests can be satisfied only at the cost of treating children as mere means, as mere resources, and not with the respect they are due. The respect account categorically denies the moral relevance of these interests, just as it similarly denies, for similar reasons, the moral relevance of the motivating interests of sadistic torturers. It is not 'unfair' to exclude these interests or to refuse to count them 'equally'. What is unfair, and grievously so, is to allow these interests to play any role whatever in the determination of what is right and wrong. The respect account thus satisfies criterion (5).

Lastly, the respect account satisfies criterion (6) that the wrongness of child pornography not be made to depend on considerations about what is in our personal self-interest. The respect account satisfies this requirement because it locates the wrongness of child pornography in what is done to the child, not whether and, if so, how this affects my self-interest. Even if child pornography were in my self-interest, that wouldn't make it morally permissible; and even if it runs counter to my self-interest, that is not what makes it wrong. What makes it wrong has nothing whatever to do with my self-interest or the interests of others, including even the public at large. What makes it wrong is that children, who are subjects-of-a-life, who are somebody, are treated as if they were some thing. The wrongness of child pornography consists in children being treated with a lack of respect.

The respect account, then, meets the relevant criteria of adequacy identified above. However, just because the respect account succeeds in this regard, it does not follow that the more general theory of which it is a part is thereby vindicated or even that its application to the issue of child pornography is complete. That theory's soundness depends on the adequacy of the other principles it recognises and how rationally compelling its supporting arguments are. These are matters that take us well beyond the limited scope of the present essay.[12]

Moreover, the central notion of respect, on which the account favoured here depends, obviously requires more extended analysis. Thus, even the adequacy of the general theory's application to the topic of this essay must remain open to further investigation. These matters remain to be explored. On this occasion we must be content with brief responses to four objections to the respect account and some concluding speculation.

Four Objections

The first objection disputes the respect account on empirical grounds. Young children – especially very young ones, those of a week or a few days – are not subjects-of-a-life, it may be claimed, and so are not protected by the principle of respect. Because this objection is empirical in nature, the reply must be of the same kind. And that reply is straightforward: Given everything we know about early infancy, it is reasonable to view human neonates as conscious creatures, individuals whose biographies are underway by the time they are born. That their story is not yet very complicated may be freely admitted; what is important is that it is *their* story, the story of *their* psycho-physical life, and that their story *is* underway. As such these infants of a few days or weeks of age *are* protected by the principles that inform the repect account.

There are some who will object to the implications of the respect account because of the moral status this view gives to late-term human foetuses. And it is true that the respect account, when coupled with the best information we have about foetal development, does extend the protection of its principles to foetuses in the final trimester (at least). Why? Because from what we know about foetal development we have every reason to believe that a distinct biographical life is underway during that period of development (if not before). Granted, the late-term foetus is not morally autonomous, does not have a conception of itself as existing over time, cannot do calculus, and is in the dark about the ontological argument. But this only shows that the biography is simple at this point of the story, not that there is no story unfolding. The respect account does maintain, then, given the moral principles it upholds and the facts as we know them, that foetuses in the final trimester of their development are not to be treated as mere means. Whenever an abortion involves treating them in this way, therefore, the respect view must oppose it. Whether this counts as a strength of or a weakness in this position obviously depends on a number of very complicated questions which it will not be possible to pursue here. I shall merely repeat a point made earlier, namely, that many cases of abortion, even if wrong, are not paradigmatically wrong – or right. It is therefore unlikely that any theory can be refuted by contesting its implications in contexts where rational, informed, impartial people of good will can and do disagree with one another.

Third, it must be acknowledged that not all human children are subjects-of-a-life. Anencephalic infants, for example, who are born lacking the cerebral hemispheres or the entire brain, are not subjects-of-a-life, given what we know (or must believe) about the connection between human psychology and the brain. Such children have a biology, but no biography. And yet surely it is wrong, a critic of the respect account might claim, to use these children for pornographic purposes. And since it is wrong to do this, what makes child pornography wrong cannot be that biographical beings are treated with a lack of respect.

Part of this objection is correct. It *is* wrong to use grossly defective children for pornographic purposes, just as it is wrong to do this in the case of irreversibly comatose adults or the dead of any age. But the grounds underlying the wrong in these and similar cases do not undermine or conflict with the respect account. The living human body normally is home to a biographical being, and the respect we owe that body is derivative of the respect we owe the subject-of-a-life whose body it is. Were it that biographical beings were never associated with human bodies, then the grounds of respect for the human body would be undermined. Because the human body normally is home to a biographical being, however, the *general* prohibition against disrespectful treatment of the human body can be defended. We are not to treat the bodies of defective children, the irreversibly comatose, or the dead as mere means, out of respect either for what they might have been (as in the case of the defective) or for what they once were (as in the case of the comatose and the dead). And what they might have been or once were is what we now are: subjects-of-a-life.

Fourth, and finally, it should not go unnoticed that the respect account does not limit the scope of respectful treatment to humans only. Religiously based ethics may do this (for example, on the grounds that only human beings have souls), and humanistic ethics certainly have this implication. But not the respect account. That account calls for the respectful treatment of *all* subjects-of-a-life, whether human or not. Given, then, that many non-human animals (mammals and birds, for example) are subjects-of-a-life, the position stated and partially defended here demands that these animals be treated with respect. This we manifestly fail to do when, for example, we treat them as gustatory or scientific 'resources' (when, that is, we raise and kill them for food, or use them as 'tools' or 'models' in research). According to the respect account, our treatment of these animals not only is wrong, it is wrong *for the same reasons* that child pornography is. Some may view this as an objection to this account. I myself regard it as one of its principal virtues. The day may come when we view the use of animals in science and their use as a food source (to mention only two of the more obvious forms of their ruthless exploitation) for the near relatives of child pornography that they are.

Speculation

If the analysis and argument of this essay are sound, then we ought to ask ourselves how it has been possible for most moral philosophers to fail to recognise the fundamental deficiencies of such influential theories as Kant's and Mill's when challenged to account for the great wrong of child pornography. The obvious, chilling answer seems to be: Moral philosophers haven't devoted much attention to ethical questions about the treatment of children. But that answer only succeeds in forcing us to face another question, namely, 'Why have most moral philosophers failed to pay much attention to ethical questions about the treatment of children?' My speculative answer to this question – and it is only speculative – is, 'Because most moral philosophers have been men, whereas the primary caretakers of our children have been women'. Historically, the result of this division of labour has been that we (male) moral philosophers have tended to ignore the moral ties that bind us to our children, a state of affairs which, like the role of women in the home, is changing – and none too soon. Informed attention to ethical questions involving children promises to improve both our homes and our moral philosophy.[13]

NOTES

1 I am well aware that this is not an uncontroversial assumption to make about the assessment of moral theories. I offer a defence of this way of assessing such theories in *The Case for Animal Rights* (Berkeley: University of California Press, and London: Routledge and Kegan Paul, 1983), especially chapter 4.

2 *New York v. Ferber*, 458 U.S. 474, 746 (1982). Cited in *Attorney General's Commission on Pornography: Final Report, July 1986*, Department of Justice, Washington, D.C.: Superintendent of Documents, United States Printing Office, pp. 596–7.

3 Ibid., p. 601.

4 Ibid., p. 611.

5 *New York v. Ferber*, 458 U.S. 474, at 756–57. Op. cit., p. 658.

6 Commission on Pornography, op. cit., p. 613.

7 Ibid., p. 609.

8 Ibid.

9 Jan Narveson on a number of occasions has argued for a contractarian position of this sort. See, for example, 'At Arms' Length: Violence and War', in *Matters of Life and Death: New Introductory Essays in Moral Philosophy* ed. Tom Regan, 2nd. edition (New York: Random House, 1986).

10 See Rawls's seminal work, *A Theory of Justice* (Cambridge, Mass.: Harvard University Press, 1971).

11 I believe James Rachels was the first person to make this point in these words, during a conversation.

12 Some (but certainly not all) of the missing details are supplied in my *The Case for Animal Rights*, especially chapters 7–9.

13 I have benefited from criticisms of an earlier draft of this paper raised by Melinda Vadas, Donald Van De Veer, and the members of the Society for Philosophy and Public Policy of New York. The views expressed and the approach to the issues taken here, however, are mine.

Index

Figures in bold type denote chapter numbers.

216193

Lightning Source UK Ltd.
Milton Keynes UK
16 May 2010

154223UK00002B/31/P

9 780521 369350